MAYHEM

Also by Matthew Thompson

My Colombian Death
Running with the Blood God

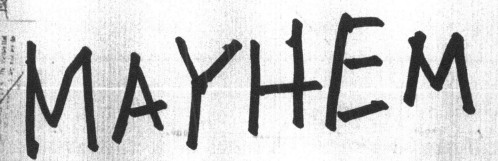

MAYHEM

THE STRANGE + SAVAGE SAGA OF CHRISTOPHER 'BADNE$$' BINSE

MATTHEW THOMPSON

MACMILLAN
Pan Macmillan Australia

From Christopher Dean Pecotic,
AKA Christopher Binse,
AKA BADNE$$, AKA LORD BADNE$$
AKA prisoner 43517
AKA solja 43517:

To Charlize and Runty
&
To my victims
To my mum and brothers
To prisoners left to rot in isolation
To kids in danger of becoming like me

From Matt Thompson:

To Renae, Avalon, Chocolate & Fred
&
To my dad, who dropped dead the morning after
my last book came out.

FOR AFFLICTION DOES NOT COME FROM THE DUST, NOR DOES TROUBLE SPROUT FROM THE GROUND; BUT MAN IS BORN TO TROUBLE AS THE SPARKS FLY UPWARDS.

Book of Job

State Bank ▼ Victoria   BANDIT DESCRIPTION FORM

PERSONAL DESCRIPTION FORM OF BANDIT OR OTHER OFFENDER

Branch/Agency
358 Keilor East

Date 31/5/88   **Time** 2.10 pm

State Nature of Offence, e.g. holdup, forgery, fraud, etc.
Holdup

Notes for Compilation:
Separate form required for each person. To be compiled immediately after incident by each staff member, also customer/s Passer/s by if possible.
Please tick in boxes as applicable.
Do not consult others during compilation.

Names and Nicknames used none

Sex: M ☑ F ☐   **Approx. Age** 25-35
Nationality Caucasian
Approx. weight _____ kilo's _____ /lbs.
Height _____ cms 6 /ft. 2 /ins.

Build Thin ☐ Medium ☐
Stout ☑ Nuggetty ☐

Posture Erect ☑ Stooped ☐
Slouched ☐

Walk Quick ☑ Springy ☐
Slow ☐ Limp ☐
Pigeon-toed ☐

Voice Clear ☑ Loud ☐
Thick ☐ Slang ☐

Accent Aussie
Words Used Fuck Sues the big ones
Demand Verbal ☑ Written ☐

Describe article used for carrying money White Plastic bag + nylon navy blue with orange strip carry all

Colour
Disguise Navy blue full balaclava
Jewellery
Mannerisms Determined + abrupt

Clothing: Including Hat, Tie, Shirt, Coat, Trousers, Dress, Sweater, Shoes etc.
Overalls

Weapon Type Pump action shotgun
Method and Direction of Escape Turned right into Wyong St Vern East

Car/s Used: Make Torana
Model
Colour Orange / white vinyl Roof
Registration Number ICT 849

Method of Operation What did offender/s do? Walked inside door, pointed gun at me + other tellers + demanded "Put the top cash"

Face
Long ☐   Wrinkled ☐
Round ☐   Lean ☐
Thin ☐   Plump ☐

Complexion
Fair ☐   Dark ☐
Pale ☐   Fresh ☐
Ruddy ☐   Tanned ☐
Pimply ☐

Hair Colour
Straight ☐   Wavy ☐
Bald ☐   Curly ☐
Woolly ☐   Long ☐
Crew-cut ☐   Receding ☐

Moustache

Forehead High ☐   Wide ☐
Low ☐   Narrow ☐
Receding ☐

Eyes Colour blue
Wide ☐   Sleepy ☐
Narrow ☐   Starey ☐
Deep Set ☐   Squint ☐
Protruding ☐

Spectacles Colour
Frame
Shape
Thick Glass ☐   Tinted ☐

Ears Size _____ Shape
Nose Size _____ Shape
Lips Size
Tee
Chin
Hand

MAYHEM is a documentary in writing.

It is not a production-line true crime book in which the author serves up a cartoon-level morality of right and wrong, goodies and baddies.

This is a raw blast of a world gone berserk.

MAYHEM is Christopher Pecotic, aka Christopher Binse, aka BADNE$$, aka Lord BADNE$$, speaking directly to you from the grave of long-term solitary confinement in Victoria's so-called 'correctional' facilities: a place where Australia's barbaric zeal for 'supermax' punishment is in full swing, even if largely hidden from public scrutiny. You will also hear from an assorted cast of witnesses and characters.

I am the author of this book in the way that the director of a documentary is the creator of that work.

It came about as an agreement between Chris and me. A smart bloke kept almost around the clock in a small room, Chris wants to tell his crazed but necessary tale. He hopes that by doing so, budding crims – kids like the young him – might change direction, and the public might at last see the naked truth of our often monumentally stupid and destructive prison system – a system that seeks to 'correct' people with serious antisocial tendencies by clustering them in claustrophobic cages of fear, anger, and boredom. If someone within those cages arcs up, acts out or flips out – in other words, has a predictable reaction to being left to rot in society's hopeless, violent dumping ground – then they're 'corrected' further via isolation and solitary confinement.

If and when their deterioration continues, medics offer psych pills to zonk the prisoner into compliance for years of wall-staring and pacing in order to keep a lid on the rage and self-loathing that breed from abject dependency and resentment.

We spring-load people in our jails and then release them.

Of course, there's more to it than that – and there's much more in MAYHEM. This is a wild book but not a simple book.

I told Chris that if I was going to tell his story then he had to be pretty damned honest. 'Don't incriminate others if you don't want to but be truthful about yourself.' He thought about it, agreed, and then asked his mother to open his archives to me and tell me anything and everything.

Chris said that he would give me the tragic ending the book needs to push troubled kids and pig-headed 'correctional' systems alike to change their ways.

'What are you talking about?' I said. 'It's already got a tragic ending – you're doing 14 to 18 in solitary.'

'Fuck that, mate,' he said. 'I'm not sticking around for it.' Chris was not talking about a physical escape.

We were going to shake on our deal, or at least power-knuckle the perspex between us at HM Prison Barwon, in a visit I had booked.

But the night before I was due to fly south, Chris' mum, Annette, rang to say the prison authorities had banned me:

'They told Chris, "We know all about this Thompson,'" she said. So I was scratched from his list of people that he can phone, write to, or who can visit him.

Can't have scumbag authors meeting scumbag crims, can we? But I'm as bull-headed a writer as Chris is a bandit. Tell me I can't do something and I'll tell you ten ways I can. So this slab of madness is built with conversations, diaries, transcripts, reports, documents, telepathy, possession, and jaw-dropping shock at how weird, wild and appalling life can be.

Annette has been shocked in the process not just by Chris' subsequent admissions about his own misdeeds – admissions he even took to the extent of contacting the police about cold case heists he was responsible for – but by her wrecking ball of a son finally facing up to very personal demons, including the legacy of his beloved, rotten, complicated dad.

Chris is MAYHEM's heart and shattered soul. So prepare to jump bank counters, brawl in jail yards, go on the run and go around the twist with this enigmatic, impulsive, exasperating, cruel, caring, cheeky, egotistical, smart, creative, destructive, big-hearted and doom-starred maniac.

Matt Thompson 2016

WITH ME I'VE GOT A KNACK OF INCOM—, I START
ONE SENTENCE, I DON'T FINISH — COMPLETE IT — SO
I'M FOREVER JUMP, JUMPING ALL OVER THE PLACE,
YOU KNOW? THAT'S WHERE MY MIND IS AT THE
MOMENT, YOU KNOW?

Chris reckons he gets a bit hectic sometimes — years
upon years in solitary have set his mind spinning.

REGARDING CHRISTOPHER DEAN PECOTIC, AKA CHRISTOPHER DEAN BINSE, AKA BADNE$$, AKA LORD BADNE$$

Corrections Reference Number (CRN) 43517:

ONE OF THE MOST DANGEROUS MEN IN AUSTRALIA FOR THE LAST 30 YEARS.

John Silvester, co-author of the Underbelly series, rates Chris Binse for listeners of Melbourne's Radio 3AW

WHILE I HAD MY HEAD DOWN I HEARD THE GUN CLICK TWICE. I WAS IN GREAT FEAR THAT HE WAS GOING TO SHOOT SOMEONE.

Female teller, State Savings Bank clerk describing one of Chris Binse's hold-ups

I HAVE ABOUT AS MUCH SYMPATHY FOR HIM AS I DO FOR OSAMA BIN LADEN.

Steve Medcraft, president of People Against Lenient Sentencing, shares his feelings about Chris Binse with readers of the Age newspaper

MOST OF THE ROBBERIES I TRIED TO DO BEFORE LUNCH.

Chris Binse describes an average workday

Voice From The Abyss

EARLY 2016:
CHRIS PECOTIC

Born in Fremantle in 1968. Now buried in long-term solitary confinement, which is against all the guidelines for Australian prisons because it drives people nuts and inmates come out even more angry and antisocial. But the guidelines are routinely ignored because this is an age that seeks absolute and total control: this, the supermax era.

CHRIS:

I feel a strong need and desire to convey a message to those young enough to be my kids.

To those still very much naïve.

To those caught up in a foolish notion: that jail is a badge of honour.

And to those in government, too, to learn from all the terrible mistakes that have been made.

To these ends, I have removed all egotism.

This is just me. I'm not after folklore status.

So here in these pages I lay myself bare in order to reveal the reality of my life and not to glamorise it in any way.

My story must be a deterrent, and thus a tragic end awaits to drive the point home, and to showcase what the system is generating.

If it must be then I will die for this message to be heard. I will die to warn, to deter, to fuel needed change.

I will die if that helps stop all of us from repeating the stupid mistakes that all have made.

I can't warn the young enough of the dangers that others, too, will face if they are to follow the path I foolishly lead.

I was considered a hardcore inmate, too, but look at the result: a miserable end.

It all started off with things so trivial and petty – like shoplifting a bit of chewie – but grew and grew and here I am now: an institutionalised, dysfunctional misfit.

If I could be born again, but not again into this life that has been so traumatising and traumatised, and is so wasted and ruined, then I would want that. Yes, I would.

But every choice, every chance, every curse, everything that ever happened leads here to this terrible madness of isolation.

No roads go back.

So please listen, and keep listening even when the stories I tell make you very glad that you don't know me and never met me and never will.

I'm in Hell.

WELL WORN LINES

Here Christopher 'BADNE$$' Pecotic sits down with a few detectives. The routine they are about to run through makes me think of something Oscar-winning actress Glenda Jackson said: 'The whole essence of learning lines is to forget them.' She reckons that a good drama feels alive and real even though the actors are repeating stuff they've said countless times before. That's pretty much serious crime: utterly repetitive yet forever raw and seething with consequence.

And why is this particular interview happening? Because Chris wants to die purged of his sins. So he has decided to tell the police about a stack of unsolved hold-ups he did in the late 1980s and early 1990s, along with a little drunken gunplay when some nightclub bouncers pissed him off. Chris will not name any living accomplices, nor most dead ones: that's against his code and beside the point. So after he wrote a confession letter to an old nemesis in the Armed Robbery Squad, a few detectives come to see him at Barwon. How many times have they said all this before?

3

Police: What is your full name?

Chris: Christopher Dean Pecotic, aka Binse.

Police: Chris, before continuing I must inform you that you're not obliged to say or do anything, but anything you say or do may be given in evidence. Do you understand that?

Chris: Yes, I do.

Police: I'll also inform you of the following rights. You may communicate with or attempt to communicate with a legal practitioner. You may communicate with or attempt to communicate with a friend or relative. If you're not a citizen or permanent resident of Australia you may communicate with or attempt to communicate with the consular office of the country of which you are a citizen. Do you understand those rights?

Chris: Yes, I do.

Police: Do you wish to exercise any of these rights before we proceed?

Chris: No, it's fine.

Police: Have you had a chance to get some legal advice about this?

Chris: No, I don't need legal advice.

BADNESS IN
ISOLATION

FEBRUARY 2016:
RIP 43517

Acacia Unit, a HIGH RISK section of the maximum-security Barwon Prison in the Victorian town of Lara, where scenes of the original Mad Max were filmed back in 1979.

Inmate 43517 has one last story to tell, but here in this stripped back, no pen, no pencil, no hanging point, no nothing, anti-suicide observation cell, he has zero that he can write with except shit or blood. I mean, come on, what the fuck?

There was a time, actually many times, when 43517 was flying stratospherically high, when he looked in the mirror and grinning back at him was Australia's No. 1 urban guerrilla, when he rampaged through bank jobs as a hardcore 'solja' [soldier] using guns, masks and his berserk will to exact payback from a rotten state, and there was a time when he had his own commando sanctuary deep in the Queensland bush,

Badlands, where he lived with his firecracker of a girlfriend while on the run.

In those brief, snatched-away moments of liberty in a lifetime spent otherwise in the grind-core cages of prison after prison, he scared the living shit out of a stack of regular folk with his banditry and mayhem, and he has pinched cars and motorbikes like other people shoplift chocolate bars.

I AM CARRYING A SLEDGEHAMMER WITH A .45 SEMI-AUTO PISTOL TUCKED INTO THE TOP OF MY OVERALLS. MY COMRADE IS CARRYING A PUMP-ACTION SHOTGUN. PEOPLE ARE SCATTERING. TRAMS PASS BY.

Westpac withdrawal, 1991

Inmate 43517 has raised full-on merry hell, leading swarms of Melbourne pursuit cars and a chopper on an absurd fucking chase in a clapped-out LPG car stuck in second gear; he's leapt to freedom from an old stone bastard of a jail in Sydney under gunfire from a watchtower while his bisexual livewire lover, Roxy, sweats her fanny off with nerves as she sits primed in their getaway car. He's been stabbed and bashed and scarred and slashed, and beaten heads with socks full of heavy cans and had icepick fights and coated his body in shit and run roaring into walls hard enough to knock himself out, and been beaten and tortured by cops as hateful and greedy as himself. When wired tight on ice he once sized up the police parked out front in an armoured car and put a bullet into the window. He also shot their robot. All while dressed in shorts and a ballistic vest.

Prisoner

BINSE, Christopher

43517

I SAW A PUFF OF WHITE SMOKE FROM THE FRONT DRIVER'S SIDE WINDOW AND KNEW THAT THE BULLET HAD STRUCK THE WINDOW OF THE VEHICLE ONLY A METRE OR SO FROM WHERE I WAS SEATED.

... IT WAS DECIDED THAT THE ARMOURED VEHICLE WOULD BE REVERSED OUT OF THE DRIVEWAY.

Siege at East Keilor, 2012

Like what the fuck, ya know.

But time passes, and who would know it better than this wretch whose life has been locked into the literal service of time, a man on the rack of time, strapped to the clock with the click of each second echoing off the walls of his isolation chamber for years and fucking years, the judge who gave him almost two decades for this latest stretch telling him in court that this would drive him insane, or more insane, since this has been such a formative part of his life – no, fuck that, this is his life; he is the wire and the walls and the bells and the bleak house pandemonium of a soul spinning into the void.

Inmate 43517 is now 47 years old, father to a girl, son to a mother, brother to two men.

His name is Chris.

And between writing with blood or shit, he chooses shit.

卌

Chris stands a mattress up against the cell wall. It's his tombstone so it needs his name, dates and an RIP.

He takes a handful of crap and finger-paints these bare facts.

This man, this fool, me, you, what-the-fuck, was born 7 October 1968 in Fremantle. He died today. Died here. Fucking waste of air.

But one more thing – the important part: lower down the tombstone he smears messages to whatever coroner is assigned to today's dead inmate. Listen, he spells out. Get the recordings of me ringing Mum. I tell her; I told her; she knows how it is here. So listen, listen to me tell her how isolation is worse than death and everybody knows and the cunts have done it again and again to me, keeping me in this bullshit for fucking years, man, winding me up, driving me nuts, and I can't take it anymore. It's wrong. It's over. I'm over. I'm dead. See ya.

+++

Sitting ready in the stinking cell. All exits removed, even little points that might carry weight – dying weight, dead weight. No hanging points. Can't get to hell even when you're in it.

They switched his clothes when sticking him in here and Chris can't get the fucking suicide smock off.

Unrippable canvas made to keep us bastards alive when we need to die.

Canvas across the throat: muscle up and clench. Here it comes, here I go, love ya Charlize, love ya more than anything my baby girl, I'll watch over you from the other side, I promise. Yes: comes the blacknessssssssssssssssss.

+++

What the fuck? Awake again. Still here. Canvas across the throat, muscle up and clench. See yaaaaaaaaaaaaaaaaaaaaaaaa.

+++

Awake. What the fuck. Why can't he, I, who, you, keep that cloth tight right through to death? Who wound us so loose in our fucked up misery that we can't even die? Who the fuck is god? Where's your mercy? Cunt of a curse. Curse of the cunts.

-卌-

'Chris!'

-卌-

It's an 'observation cell' and when the officers observe Chris in this abject state, slumped and fouled and unable, they call the medics.

-卌-

Take medication is their advice. Get on prison's mass prescription program. Won't bother you so much then, getting held for years on years in solitary, held in your head, held in all the clipboard flow-chart euphemisms like 'management placement' or 'isolation'. What the fuck, ya know.

For four years now the only people ever standing in the same room as him anywhere in jail are the screws. His captors.

If he's escorted to the phone to make a call then that area is first cleared of prisoners. If he's allowed to use exercise equipment that area is emptied before he gets there.

That's no society at all. He's removed. He's gone. He's erased. He's out of his fucking mind. He's in the space zone.

Chris has done many years prior, for his priors, of this sort of solo space-travel stretch, but never for so long. The judge – whose name was Forrest; last forest he'll ever see – said he'd probably do another fucking decade and a half of this time. What time. No time. All time. No one else here but the screws. Shout into the fucking void.

-卌-

'Take the medication, Chris. It'll make things easier.'
    'Fuck that. I'm not taking that shit.'

✚

So they keep their zombie pills and remove Chris' unrippable smock, leaving him stark fucking naked in this smooth box.

Now there's guards at his door and a camera installed up top of the cell, staring down forever, whatever, wherever he is in this microscope slide, whether sitting or shitting or wanking or lying on the floor pounding his face and crying.

✚

That'll fix him.

Because this is a correctional facility. This is Corrections Victoria and they've got plenty of experience correcting Chris. They've been doing it since he was thirteen.

Chris was an exuberant young lad.

LITTLE GOLDEN BOOK

CIRCA 1972:
IN THE SUPERMARKET

Sitting up late, the house gradually cooling after another baking Melbourne day, Annette passes me a photograph of a cute-looking little brown-eyed munchkin of the 1970s, Chris smiling away under his bowl haircut.

'When did it start?'

'Trouble?' She leans back in her chair. 'Chris was always mischievous, always a daredevil, always playing pranks.' Annette talks about his endless wild feats of climbing and jumping, of go-go-going on bikes and whatever else was at hand to ride or play faster and harder and longer than anyone else; his athletic skills, his

Livewire: the irrepressible young Christopher.

11

irrepressible humour, his pranking her with dead snakes and his Mother's Day present of a dead mouse.

Annette's second son, Barry, was and is very different, she says – thoughtful, considerate, more cautious – and as a result often found it hard living in the wake of his headstrong older brother.

Yet, sometimes he got dragged in. 'There's a photo of them somewhere here,' she says, leafing through the albums. 'They're holding a bag of herbs, making out it's marijuana and I was shocked. I hit the roof and had a go at Chris about that photo, and he told me it was just parsley or something and they were trying to make it look like marijuana. They had me going, the little horrors.'

Funnily enough, Chris has mentioned this very incident to me.

'It was marijuana,' I say.

'No it wasn't,' Annette says. 'It was parsley or something that they made out to look like marijuana for the photo. "Mum," Chris said to me. "It was only herbs; we were only stooging you."'

'That's what they told everybody,' I say. 'Chris said he thought it would be daring to pose with mari –'

'He was just trying to stir me up.'

░░░ ‖‖‖

I ask if she can track Chris' wildness back to any particular time.

She thinks for a while. 'Chris was an early developer: couldn't keep him in a bassinet – any chance he got he'd be out and into everything. He walked at nine months. There was never any containing Chris.'

'What about crime, though? When's the first time you remember him doing something like stealing?'

Her laugh turns into a cough which she bites back.

'When Chris was about four and Barry was still in a pram, I was in the supermarket with them. I turn around and here's Chris, aged four, stuffing a Little Golden Book under his shirt. I smacked him. You wouldn't think a 4-year-old would think like that, would you?'

YOUNG CHRIS' REPORT CARDS

1982–86:
IN THE DOCK

Ever the cheeky young fella, Chris knew how first to keep his mum and then the cops and courts and juvenile detention centres pretty darned busy.

His first stay in the clink was at age thirteen, when he was locked up in the secure Warrawong punishment block of Baltara, the feeder institution for Turana Youth Training Centre which he moved into at fourteen, the age he was declared a ward of the state, a place which, in turn, did what it could to prepare him for adult prisons.

Cheeky: Chris had people pulling their hair out but many couldn't help but like him.

Chris' repeated self checkouts, including wall-leaping shenanigans from Poplar House, Turana's maximum-security section, appear to have accelerated him through the correctional system, for at seventeen he graduated early from juvie, getting shifted from the lads' home at Parkville in central Melbourne to the maximum-security HM Prison Pentridge.

This notoriously brutal funhouse was also known as the 'College of Knowledge'.

Chris will soon tell us himself about the good times he had as a wet-behind-the-ears teeny tossed into Pentridge. First, though, let's have a squizz at his report cards. Given that school and him didn't really take to each other – one expulsion coming after he accepted a dare to flash his willy at a relief teacher – these are Chris' real adolescent report cards.

Aged 13 years

In the dock, 11 May 1982:

–Burglary (4 counts)
–Theft (3 counts)

In the dock, 28 July 1982:

–Burglary (4 counts)
–Theft (5 counts)
–Tamper with motor car
–Handle stolen goods
–Going equipped to steal

In the dock, 3 August 1982:

–Burglary
–Theft
–Going equipped to steal

In the dock, 31 August 1982:

–Theft of motor cycle

In the dock again, 31 August 1982:

–Theft of bicycle
–Unlawful possession

In the dock, 27 September 1982:

–Theft from motor car

Aged 14 years

In the dock, 27 April 1983:

–Theft of motor car (2 counts)
–Unlicensed driver
–Failure to wear seat belt

In the dock, 14 June 1983:

–Theft of motor car (3 counts)
–Going equipped to steal (3 counts)
–Theft from motor car
–Unlicensed driver (3 counts)

In the dock, 12 July 1983:

–Theft from motor car

In the dock, 26 July 1983:

–Unlicensed rider
–Unregistered motor cycle
–Uninsured motor cycle

In the dock, 2 August 1983:

–Theft

Aged 15 years

In the dock, 2 January 1984:

–Burglary

In the dock, 24 January 1984:

–Unregistered motor cycle
–Unlicensed rider
–No helmet
–Carry pillion passenger
–State false name and address

In the dock, 2 April 1984:

–Theft of motor car (2 counts)
–Theft from motor car (6 counts)
–Interfere with motor car
–Smoke drug of dependence
–Possess drug of dependence
–Theft
–Unlicensed driving (2 counts)

In the dock again, 2 April 1984:

–Armed robbery
–Robbery
–Assault occasioning actual bodily
harm (2 counts)
–Unlawful assault (2 counts)
–Assault with intent to rob
–Unlawfully on premises
–Attempted armed robbery
–Theft
–Theft of bicycle
–Escape YTC [Youth Training
Centre]

In the dock, 1 May 1984:

–Attempted theft
–Going equipped to steal
–Unlicensed driving
–Theft from motor car (4 counts)
–Burglary

In the dock, 19 June 1984:

–Burglary
–Theft of motor car
–Unlicensed driving

In the dock, 12 September 1984:

–Escape (2 counts)

–Shorten barrel of a firearm
–Burglary
–Theft
–Theft of motor car
–Possess pistol
–Unlicensed driving

Aged 16 years

In the dock, 29 October 1984:

–Escape

In the dock, 23 November 1984:

–Appealed against convictions and
sentences of 12 September 1984
(appeals dismissed, convictions and
sentences affirmed)

In the dock, 17 May 1985:

–Escape

Aged 17 years

In the dock, 18 November 1985:

–Theft from motor car

In the dock, 12 December 1985:

–Theft of motor car

In the dock, 21 April 1986:

–Unlawfully on premises
–Going equipped to steal
–Receive stolen goods

In the dock, 14 August 1986:

–Burglary
–Theft (2 counts)
–Theft of motor car
–Driving while disqualified

In the dock, 19 August 1986:

–Burglary
–Theft
–Wilful damage
–Escape

Top marks for consistent effort. The standout, however, has got to be April 1983: not only does Chris get done for boosting a car but the safety conscious police officers also sting him for not wearing a seat belt.

Guess it taught him to buckle up because even though he keeps stealing cars right through his adolescence, that charge doesn't reappear.

A bit of caution as a young thief about town in 1980s Melbourne is not a bad thing. These are dangerous days. People are getting maimed and killed.

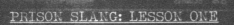

PRISON SLANG: LESSON ONE

Putrid – the lowest insult to another inmate

Dog – informant; if you call someone this there will be violence

Bone yard – the protection yard where inmates who have drama in the main yards are kept separate, where the dogs are, hence the name

CRIME AS GUERRILLA WAR

LATE 1980S: MELBOURNE

In March of 1986, Chris' last year as a minor and apprentice bandit, the ever-tense contest between Melbourne's cops and robbers takes a warlike turn when an armed hold-up crew car-bombs the Russell Street police station.

Constable Angela Taylor dies from the wounds she sustains, while about 21 other people are also injured. The most severely hurt of the survivors are Magistrate Iain West and Constable Carl Donadio.

Over the following two years alone, 1987 and 1988, the Victorian police shoot dead eleven criminals, some in highly questionable circumstances, with many slain by what become Chris' dual foes: the Armed Robbery Squad and the Special Operations Group, or SOG.

To put the killing of eleven people in two years into context, it took the police the previous thirteen years just to kill ten.

If the car-bombing strips away any pretence of old-school respectability from Victoria's cops and robbers circuit, then what happens in October 1988 well and truly spins the game. To its combatants it feels like low intensity guerrilla war.

On the eleventh of October 1988 – just a few days after Chris' twentieth birthday – police shoot dead bank robber Graeme Jensen in what even some former officers later say is an extrajudicial killing. The next morning, a couple hours before dawn, two constables, Steven Tynan and Damian Eyre, respond to reports of a Holden Commodore abandoned across Walsh Street in Melbourne's prestigious suburb of South Yarra.

It's an ambush: they are shot and killed at the scene, Tynan blasted with a shotgun as he sits in the patrol car, while Eyre – who had walked up to the Commodore – is hit but struggles until finished off with his own revolver.

Weirdly, Tynan's blooding in the dicey cops-and-robbers game had come just ten days earlier and only five blocks away. Called to South Yarra's Myrtle Street TAB on the first of October, Tynan finds the manager bailed up and used as a shield by two young men, one armed with a knife and the other a pistol (which turns out to be a replica).

When the TAB manager, Audrey Kirkwood, hits the floor, Tynan shoots Hai Foong Yap, 19, in the spine (leaving him a paraplegic who is found dead within months, bottles of pills and alcohol beside him), and gut-shoots Chee Ming Tsen, 22, who has the imitation pistol.

Tsen, who loses part of his bowel, later tells authorities that he was given no chance to surrender but simply gunned down – also copping a bullet in the knee – while Tynan's account is that he thought Tsen had fired at him. The ill-fated thieves are not underworld identities but rather foreign students with money problems. The bloody encounter at the TAB is not connected to the ambush.

Four suspects in the double slaying in Walsh Street are charged and acquitted (the eventual widow of suspect Victor Pierce later tells reporters that her late husband was in fact guilty), while two other suspects are shot dead by police before the 1991 trial. One of them, Gary Abdullah, was killed in 1989 after he supposedly pulled a replica pistol on two officers, allegedly prompting Detective Cliff Lockwood to empty all six rounds of his service revolver into Abdullah and then grab his partner's handgun and shoot him again for good measure. Lockwood is later acquitted of Abdullah's murder, but eventually jailed for supplying pseudoephedrine to a speed cook. As reported in the *Age*, when Lockwood was arrested on those charges, police found him smeared in excrement in a caravan outside Darwin.

In the build-up to the late eighties hunting season, Chris spends much of his adolescence in juvenile jail, getting accustomed to incarceration and criminal pecking orders, talking shop with other budding entrepreneurs of skulduggery and forming connections.

He also tests the boundaries of the state's discipline regime, absconding without a second thought when opportunity and impulse coincide.

Which, if you listen to his mother, Annette Binse, is exactly how he was as a boy. 'I'd ground him and he'd be out the window,' she says, looking down at a table in her Sunshine North home in Melbourne's western suburbs, piled high with the relentless incoming volumes of Chris' never-ending legal documents, court and police transcripts, evidence photographs, affidavits, appeal paperwork, newspaper clippings and other urgent proof that the man in solitary still has presence.

'There was no keeping him in.' Annette's throaty laugh is resigned, and she shakes her head. 'I could have told them they wouldn't be able to keep him in Turana,' she says. 'He was out straight up. Noticed some workmen had left a plank there so he opens a tap to flood some other area and then, when everyone's distracted by that, he leans the plank up the wall and he's up it and gone.'

'I was friends with one of the officers who looked after Chris in Turana,' says Annette, now in her late sixties. 'Bill was a nice guy, and he offered to drop in a table that Chris had made in the workshop because he knew I came on public transport and couldn't take it.' She swigs a coffee and looks past the felled forest–worth of her son's paperwork and out to the backyard vegetable garden. 'I had a single-fronted house with a long hallway and we're sitting in my kitchen having a cup of coffee when Chris comes running in.' She shakes her head again. 'He's breathless; he'd just escaped.' Annette throws up her hands and shrugs.

'Chris stops dead short; he's looking at the officer and the officer's looking at him. "Oh my god," I said, wondering what's going to happen now. Is he going to notify the police?

'But Bill didn't say anything, and Chris didn't know how to react. So they're facing each other off. Eventually Bill advised Chris to go report to a police station. Chris did his throaty chuckle and took off again. No chance in hell was he going to report to a police station.'

Annette says that she and the guard sat and finished their coffees, not really talking much. 'Bill had a soft spot for Chris. Most of them did. Chris wasn't mean-spirited like some of the boys. He was charming, athletic, always a big smile. He just couldn't be contained.'

Annette flicks through a few old snapshots of Chris at Turana: here he stands, grinning, in the yard, pointing at the wall where he'd scarpered while a long-suffering staffer sits slumped beside him; here's one of Chris hunched over in a workshop, wearing a woollen cap and looking like a kid dressing up as a convict.

Chris has a laugh with staff as he points out his recent escape route over a wall.

'I don't know who that guy is but I know how he feels,' says Annette. 'Bill was a decent guy but he had problems and ended up shooting himself.'

‖‖

Annette goes out for a cigarette while I leaf through the whateverness of it all: a transcript of the police interview with a girlfriend, Silvia, who went through most of the meth-fuelled siege with him; transcripts of interviews with Roxy, the girlfriend who drove getaway for him a decade earlier; ever more affidavits accusing his lawyer of selling him out.

Here's a copy of a search warrant. Let's see what's tucked in with it, in the clear plastic sleeve.

Pages and pages of Property Seizure Records listing the contents of shipping containers rented by Chris.

Out slides page 5 of 13, showing:

```
1 x sawn off single        Round magazine,
   barrel 'Sportco'           magazine clip,
   shotgun                    timber stock +
1 x shotgun cartridge         timber barrel cover
1 x green bag              Assorted firearm
1 x Ruger handgun             parts
1 x Thompson firearm
```

Thompson submachine gun? What else did he have in storage? He likes his bikes – there's ten of them, road and trail:

```
Honda CBR1000 black/       Atomik red
   white                   Apna red
Kawasaki ZX6R black        Harley Davidson black
Yamaha Y2R1 black          Harley Davidson
Megelli white                 black
Yamaha Y2F R1 blue         Buell black
```

Bunch of rego plates, including BAD-013, BADNES, HEKTK-1.

Flicking on, we've got three sets of handcuffs, seventeen or eighteen balaclavas, five Nokia phones, assorted ammunition, a speed loader, gloves, cable ties, and another round-magazine for the Tommy gun, plus ELEY subsonic cartridges for quiet shooting. Here are a couple of bottles of Penfolds, three of Chivas Regal, some Möet & Chandon, and a pair each of blue label and black label Johnnie Walker. Some bags: one holding a stack of masks, gloves, screwdrivers, a bottle of red liquid, a taser, a holster and some plastic strapping. There's a black backpack with ammo in it.

Whoa, starting on page 8 of the seizure record, the cops have listed what they found in a black and orange bag:

Red trigger
1 x stick of explosive
1 x remote
5 x sticks of
    explosives
1 x Ruger .22 sawn
    off single barrel
    firearm with
    silencer
2 x magazines with
    rounds
2 x box of rounds

1 x stick of
    explosives
Yellow and white leg
    wires
1 x mask
Pair of orange gloves
Box white latex
    gloves
Spent rounds
Pair of pliers
1 x scope + black
    'cummerbund' waist
    strap

Christ, it keeps going and going. Here's a suitcase stuffed
with:

2 x wigs
Masks
Disposable hooded
    overalls

1 x ornamental grenade
Assorted ammunition
Assorted paperwork
1 x Motorola radio

A backpack containing:

1 x black ballistic vest + notebook

And then there's a range of loose items, including masks, a
wig, a grey hat, a Dino lock-pick gun, unidentified purple pills,
more rego plates, an Australian passport in the name of Chris
Pecotic, prepaid SIM cards and a camouflage suit. And a pair
of sunglasses.

卌

'Unbelievable, isn't it,' says Annette, back from her ciggie. 'Thinks he's James Bond. It does the head in. He's been doing my head in since he was a child and he's still doing my head in. I would rather have had 24 kids than one Chris.'

'What's all this stuff for?' I ask. 'Explosives?'

'I know,' she says. 'He's even got a grenade – can you believe it?'

'A Thompson submachine gun.'

'I know, I know. The mind boggles.' Again, she shakes her head. 'He's got these fantasies, these delusions, that he's some kind of commando. You'll see it; he signs some of his letters "solja" – that's his word for it. So I think he just collects everything he can that matches the fantasy. Can't help himself.' She mutters about the grenade and then goes to find something.

'He had these printed when he was out once and decided to become a debt collector.' Annette hands me a black business card.

MAYHEM INCORPORATED
0410

Do you need some Mayhem in your life?
Call me 24 hours 7 days a week.
"Lets Get Hectic"

THE ROUTE TO HECTIC

STARTING IN THE 1940S:
FROM CROATIA TO PENTRIDGE

Chris' road trip starts in Yugoslavia during World War II.

CHRIS:

My father, Steve Pecotic, was one year old when he lost his father – a victim of war in Croatia.

My father had nothing to remember about his father. He and his two siblings were brought up in hardship in a small peasant village by their mother.

She had witnessed the murder. It had a profound impact on her. She was later to suffer severe forms of schizophrenia where she not only heard voices, but saw images.

When I have been psychotic from trauma and ice, I too have seen things so this is very haunting and vivid to me. My father's sister was also diagnosed with similar strains of madness. Is this hereditary? Have I now passed this condition onto my daughter?

Chris' parents: Annette and
Steve Pecotic.

When we were living in St Albans in Melbourne my mother and father separated due to domestic violence. I was about four years old and my brother, Barry, about two. I don't recall ever seeing my dad hit my mother, but I was exposed to a lot of yelling-abuse by my dad.

My mother left my dad, taking us with her, and was living in a bungalow at the rear of a house.

I was my dad's boy and loved being with him, even though he was very hard on us. My brother was Mum's boy, but I would look forward to seeing my dad on his access weekends.

He raised me on stories of his exploits as a wayward kid. These were his family stories for me.

From his poor village in Croatia, he'd terrorise the locals with a sawn-off shotgun. He was a kind of bandit and then fled to Australia.

I found his tales to be funny. Criminality was nothing to be frowned upon.

And so I never really gave crime a second thought.

I entered the life with petty thefts of chewing gum from gum racks at supermarkets.

I'd seek out the closed checkouts, empty the gum-racks into a plastic bag, and then exit the store.

My first aspirations towards armed robbery formed when I did banking for my sick grandmother.

The bank was on a corner; sometimes I would see the guards arrive delivering the cash. I studied their routines.

As an 8- or 9-year-old, I'd cock my right hand and tell them to give me the money.

From that time on I dreamt of robbing them.

My mother formed a relationship with a man who became my stepfather. His name was Hans Binse.

But I did not enjoy the presence of my stepfather – it was like my attachment to my dad was supposed to be severed and replaced with a substitute. He tried his best but he could not be my dad ever.

And later they got divorced, too.

My dad at an early age encouraged me into petty theft from work sites. He was a subcontractor carpenter, and would have me keep cocky when he ventured into the garages of those jobs he was at, and lift items.

I wanted my dad to look after me, and when I was allowed to choose who to live with I chose my dad. I wanted to be at home with him, but he got too angry, too violent. His temper was too brutal. Living with him full time was not possible. I couldn't stay for long.

When I returned to my mother's from the weekend visits, I would rebel. I was a delinquent and would run away from home, because I felt I did not fit in at Mum's place either. I would break into cars to sleep in and steal coins from them to buy food to survive, coming to the attention of police who arrested me and returned me to my mother who would complain I was bringing the police to her place and she would talk about what her neighbours would think.

I'd get arrested and returned to my mother's home and then I'd run away again.

My mum could not control me. I was constantly rebellious, and as a result I was abandoned by my mother who took me to court to have me deemed uncontrollable and made a ward of the state.

The courts had sought that I be assessed by psychiatrists, but this was a six to eight week wait, and by the time my file arrived on the desk I had run away again.

Now I was made a ward of the state, and nobody really ever got to find out why I was running away.

At thirteen years of age I got locked up in Baltara, the under-fourteen section of Turana.

At this tender age I was subjected to bashings by staff in the Warrawong punishment block. They told us kids that the bashings were to deter us from coming back to that section.

Yet when I was near release, I would inexplicably run away.

I had a fear of going home, I now feel, because I didn't want to be there at all.

So began my life of crime at thirteen. Bullying was very prevalent at Baltara, and if I wasn't facing that I was spending long periods alone in a cell. No TV or anything.

To this day I refuse to forgive my mother for this abandonment of me, and for all the violence I was subjected to as a minor.

I hated being in custody. It destroyed my spirit. It crushed me.

And from that moment on, figures of authority – the custodial staff – bashed us, bashed me, and so formed the enmity towards the government and guards that would shape my life for so long.

Over the years ahead I would be bashed many times by police, sometimes savagely when they wanted to know where the cash was. Other times they did it thinking they could belt me into giving up others – yet torture made me even stauncher

– or because they wanted to teach me who's boss. Or because I was a cheeky cunt.

Released from Baltara boys' home during the day to go to school, I began using drugs, stealing, and returning to custody.

My life of crime had begun in earnest. Listening to older kids talk about their escapes and exploits appealed to me.

I become a pot smoker at fourteen, and then experimented with all types of drugs including speed and even heroin.

I rebelled. I competed with fate. And when I was in that mindset, I escaped at the first opportunity.

This caused me to accumulate a three-year term as a juvenile: the maximum a kid could get in children's courts at the time.

Due to my frequent escapes, I was housed in the most secure location they had: Poplar House at Turana. A mini-jail for kids: a high-walled fortress with many rolls of barbed wire.

I escaped from this location just to prove I could crack it. And got taken back. And escaped again. And got taken back again.

Bored and restless, I spent a few years there.

When I escaped, it started to become out of sheer boredom with the place – not due to want of liberty. What liberty is there outside as a kid with no family, no home, a mother who went to court to get rid of him?

I was transferred to Malmsbury youth training centre at seventeen, and then, after the death of my beloved grandmother in 1986, I escaped and went on a drug-fuelled crime spree for four weeks until being arrested and sent to Pentridge, a maximum-security adult prison where ugliness and violence were the air and water.

I was seventeen years old.

BORN FROM TROUBLE

1920S–1960S: EUROPE TO AUSTRALIA

Chris is chomping at the bit to tell his story, but before he lets rip let's step back a little further to see the flow of life. No one comes from nowhere. We are all children of something.

A baby girl is born in 1926 to German parents living in Gross-Wender, an old German settlement in what has since become the nation of Ukraine. One day, when Sophia Regina Scheck is a teenager, the Soviet authorities order her family, along with a lot of other ethnic German families, to be deported to remote labour camps in the east. With everybody gathered at a railway station, Sophia frets that they have not packed her father's photographs, so she darts home to grab them. When she returns, the station is empty. The train has come and gone. The dark-haired girl seizes up in shock and grief. She never sees or hears from her family again.

A friendly Russian family with a girl near her age takes in Sophia, who speaks Russian as a native, and they pass off the teen as one of their own. This saves Sophia from the gulags but proves little protection as World War II explodes. History's biggest and most brutal military clash, the Nazi–Soviet confrontation kills tens of millions of civilians and soldiers, leaves as many people homeless, and lays waste to vast regions – including one building that Sophia huddles in

Born into a dark age: Annette's beloved mother, Sophia Regina Scheck.

under bombardment, its walls collapsing around her but leaving the girl unscathed.

For the Ukraine area, the conflict is the latest in a chain of apocalypses, following as it does the death of millions from starvation in a famine that the Soviets caused, the mass killing and deportation of millions seen as resistant to communism, and the preceding civil war that had landed the communists in power. Young Sophia might survive World War II but not without her mind fracturing.

After the Nazi onslaught stalls and breaks, Red Army troops push west, often committing depraved acts in areas they recapture.

And in a forest of this cursed place, a pack of Soviet soldiers brutalise Sophia and her adoptive sister, breaking something in Sophia's mind. The Devil starts talking to her, goading and taunting as he will do for the rest of her life, and she starts seeing things that aren't there.

With the war over but the region pulverised and the Soviets clamping down on much of Central and Eastern Europe,

Annette's mysterious and stern father, Joseph Adamowicz.

Sophia goes west, working as a nurse in occupied Germany. One of her patients is a sternly self-possessed Russian-speaker who has been shot in the gut.

Sophia marries the man, who goes by the name Joseph Adamowicz.

Never will he tell her or the children she will bear to him what happened to him before they met. He never says where he comes from, and for a long time Joseph claims to be three years older than Sophia, yet later it seems that they were both born in 1926.

As Christmas 1946 approaches, Sophia gives birth to their first child. This daughter, Annette, is born in the town of Mölln, which, as folklore has it, is the burial place of legendary medieval trickster and highway robber Till Eulenspiegel.

This cheeky peasant provoked everyone around him with his relentless farting and practical jokes, many of which involved tricking people into handling or even eating shit. As a young fellow out riding with his dad, Till would expose his arse to people behind them. He once pranked a publican by crapping all over the inside of a folding table at the tavern, thereby delivering a foul surprise when lunchtime came and the tables were unfolded for diners. Forever showing up his social betters as hypocrites and fools, this merry chap – who served time for armed robbery – has become a symbol of resistance in parts of Europe, where all manner of people wish others to eat shit.

Sophia, Joseph and Annette live as Displaced Persons in Germany for a few years and then in 1950 set sail to Australia on the SS *Nelly*, arriving that June as part of the huge post-war European migration. They settle in the western Melbourne suburb of St Albans, the cold and stern Joseph working as a builder while Sophia struggles to tend to their growing family as the Devil steps up his torments. A child herself, Annette would sometimes lead her little sisters on middle-of-the-night walks around the local shops: anything to spare her siblings the onslaught of a mother in the grip of madness.

One time Sophia locks the children inside a bungalow and spits on them as Joseph hammers on the door. Neither Joseph nor any doctor explain schizophrenia or anything like it to their kids, not even when Sophia is hospitalised for stretches and pleads with her family to free her. 'Please,' she says, reeling from another round of shock treatment. 'They're trying to kill me.'

Annette assumes more and more responsibility in the household especially when, on her fifteenth birthday, Joseph tells her that he is leaving.

Annette does what she can to care for everybody while trying to have her own teenage years.

Unsettled in Australia: the young Annette.

35

THE POLICE WELCOME A NEW FAMILY TO MELBOURNE

1952:
ST ALBANS

ANNETTE:

The first place we came to after the migrant camp was St Albans. Across the road was a neighbour with a milk bar. My mother used to look after his child while his wife was working.

He had a German shepherd and this dog of his would be barking, barking, barking, all night.

Dad complained about it to him but nothing changed.

Then one morning the dog was found poisoned, so the man called the police and blamed Dad. But there was no evidence Dad was involved, and I don't think he was. There were other neighbours, too, that would have been complaining about the dog.

So a van pulls up with three policeman inside and they drag Dad out of the house, slam him against the van, and start beating him. I run outside and I'm screaming and screaming and screaming, 'Leave my daddy! Daddy, Daddy, Daddy!'

Finally they let him go and left and as he was coming back into the house he sank to his knees and collapsed. He started crying and then we were both crying.

I'll never forget the lumps all over his face, and the blood. From that time on he was deaf in one ear.

I was six. And that was my introduction to the police force.

STEVE

1968:
TO THE WEST AND BACK

ANNETTE:

I was with this guy, Andy, for five and a half years until I walked away. My life had revolved around his friends, dances, and when we split up a lot of my friends moved on. I felt totally alone, and I was on the rebound.

Dance the blues away: Annette at a social event in the 1960s.

I knew Steve's family before Steve came to Australia. I knew his brother and his mother, and that's how I met Steve. He ended up living next to me when I was living with Andy. He didn't speak English then and I could manage to get through in Croatian, which I had picked up.

Then Steve went to Queensland to work on the sugar cane, and I went on a holiday to Sydney to visit some mutual friends of ours and stay with them. One day I walked out the front door only to run into Steve, who walked out the neighbour's front door. We were looking at each other and we couldn't believe it.

So then we started to hang around together in a group and go to different places. And his mother had moved to Spotswood [in Melbourne] and my mother lived at Spotswood. It was amazing – our paths always crossed – and somehow we got together.

Newlyweds Annette and Steve Pecotic. The violence had already begun.

It was my biggest mistake.

Steve was likeable and charming, like Chris is, but the person underneath was totally different.

We got engaged on my 21st and it was after that that I fell pregnant with Chris. That was the reason I got married, you know; it was the old-fashioned way. To be totally honest, I don't think I was in love with Steve.

Even when we were engaged he started to slap me around.

Not so much at first but, for instance, we were driving across the Nullarbor to Fremantle and I was sitting in the back reading the map. We had another Croatian with us – there were three of us – and he was in the front next to Steve. Steve hit a pothole and went off at me, and then he hit a kangaroo that jumped in front of him. The kangaroo hopped away but there was hair and blood. Steve turned around and whacked me. The guy travelling with us asked why and Steve said, 'She should have been watching.' I was in the back seat.

I just took off my engagement ring and threw it on the dashboard. I got hit because he hit a kangaroo. Yeah.

But I had nowhere to go because we were in the middle of the Nullarbor, so I had to continue the trip. We ended up at his cousin's place in Fremantle and I had no one. I didn't know anyone: they were all his relatives, his cousins; I didn't have a job. I was pregnant.

There were a lot of contributing factors to why I married Steve, and it was one of the biggest mistakes of my life.

He was always calling me the Croatian name: *kurva*, prostitute, and bitch, and this, that and the other. There was no respect, no nothing. I had no say, no rights.

When Chris had not long been born Steve brought in two mates who I had to wash for by hand, their clothes, their sheets –

Annette feeds Chris. Almost 50 years later she is still there for him, his well spring of unconditional love.

no washing machine – and I had to make their sandwiches. One day when Chris was about six weeks old I had to go buy sausages and salami so Steve drove me to the delicatessen and gave me a $50 note. The woman didn't have change so she went in the back. Steve was parked right out the front yelling at me, 'Hurry up you bloody bitch!' and tooting the horn and the more he shouted and tooted, the more Chris, as a frightened baby, screamed. 'What's keeping you, you bloody bitch!' I told him I was waiting for change. 'Wait till you get home,' he said, and when we got home I got a severe belting. For waiting for change.

One day Steve brought a dog home. I don't know where he got it but it always went for me. I had no fear of animals, not even snakes, but this thing petrified me. I couldn't go out the door without it going for me. One day it got into the kitchen and I had to get up on the table. I complained to Steve about it but he did nothing.

My sister came over one day and went to the shop for me to get milk. The dog followed her and saw other dogs and took off with them. I got blamed for getting rid of the dog. I hadn't even left the house. I said to Steve, 'The dog took off with other dogs.'

'You didn't like the dog, you bloody bitch,' he said, and he bashed me.

His relative stayed with us and I hated him because he tried to rape me a few times when Steve went to soccer. He was an alcoholic, a real dirty no-hoper type and his family sent him to Australia to get rid of him and he ended up on our doorstep. He was always putting me down to Steve and putting Steve down to me. But when Steve wasn't home he was always coming into my bedroom and trying all sorts of things and Steve didn't take any action. I kept telling Steve, but his kin had more rights than I did.

We'd had problems with him before. He'd had us kicked out of a house in Maribyrnong, and I didn't want him there. But Steve snuck him into the garage. One night I'm at the kitchen washing dishes and I see his relative, carrying a suitcase, and Steve's hiding him in the shed so I wouldn't see him. I hit the roof but I had no say. I had to be quiet. Gradually he moved him into the house.

When Chris was three and Barry about one, I was setting pork chops on the table for dinner and Chris reached out for one so Steve slapped him.

I said, 'What are you doing?'

'They're not my kids. I'm not feeding them.' He was crazy.

And his relative actually stood up for the kids. He said, 'Don't be stupid,' and gave Chris the chop.

Steve took him outside, punched him in the face and threw him out. Because he gave Chris the chop. He defied him.

Trying to rape me was okay, though. There was so much of this stupidity, this insanity. Chris doesn't know all this. I haven't told Chris a lot of what my marriage was.

Barry knows some of it but I don't get too much into it. It upsets me to remember all of this. I don't want to think about it, and I don't see the point in telling the kids all the sordid details. It's like I'm protecting them, and Chris will just think I'm a liar making it up because he wouldn't see his father in the real light. It would be: 'Oh, you're making up stories.' So I just keep a lot of it to myself.

Steve broke my nose once. We were both smokers and he was in one of his funny moods. My mother came over with my sister, who was ten. She came by public transport. I was in the kitchen by the sink and I lit up a cigarette. He just slapped it out of my mouth. Yet we were both smokers; we always smoked. He just decided to hit me, and it started from that.

I got pushed on the ground and then he was choking me and I was trying to release the pressure on my throat because I had been choked into unconsciousness twice before in Fremantle. Nearly died.

So in order to release his grip on my throat I was pinching his face. You should have seen what his face looked like. I didn't realise. All I was trying to do was release the pressure – I was choking.

My mother was screaming hysterically, begging him to stop, my sister was crying, and then finally he let me go and hit me in the face. That's when he broke my nose. Blood was spurting down my face. My mother was hysterical – this is a woman with heart trouble. Then he turned on my mother and was going to hit her and push her out the front door but my sister and I stood between them and I wouldn't let him touch my mother.

She left and I walked to the train station still bleeding. I was covered in blood; people looked at me, but I was past worrying about that and I went to see a girlfriend.

There was no point in calling the police – which I had done in Fremantle – because back then the police weren't that interested. In those days they didn't involve themselves in domestic disputes. They do now and laws have changed, but then they would just turn up and thump them on the chest and say, 'Look at how big you are; look how small she is. If you touch her again we'll deal with you.' It was just empty talk – that was all it ever came to, so Steve had no fear of the police.

I was a mess. I was so thin that I had to go into children's clothing and I was always shaking, my nerves were so bad, and he used to imitate me and say, 'Look at her!' and laugh at me.

But my kids don't know all this, you see. I don't tell them these things. They wouldn't believe me anyway. It would be impossible for them to believe it. They wouldn't want to know about the bashings and his affairs behind my back.

When we were living in Fremantle, Steve got a job in Albany and he got a room with this Croatian idiot, an old man.

I was 21, 22, and this old man had a big testicle hanging down – something went wrong with surgery. Anyway, he rented to Steve one bedroom and we shared the kitchen. In the meantime I had to dispose of everything in Fremantle, pack up everything and get a truck and bring all the furniture over. He left me with the whole caboodle. While I was doing all this in Fremantle, with a baby, Steve is playing around in Albany with this woman, Elizabeth. Finally I get to Albany, I come to this house; the bedroom has dark brown chocolate walls and the bath tub was stained because the guy used it as a toilet. He couldn't be bothered going to the outhouse. I scrubbed it and scrubbed it and scrubbed it and scrubbed it, but anyway.

Steve would go off to work early and I'd be sitting there feeding the baby or eating breakfast and this guy is talking about ejaculation and how good he is with sex and the women and how when he ejaculated he'd spurt it all over the place. I kept saying to him, 'Don't talk of things like that in front of me. I don't like to listen to this.' But he kept on, and every morning we had the sex talk.

There was no lock on our bedroom door so while I'm still in bed he'd come in on some pretext. I complained and complained to Steve but it meant nothing. He was a Croatian; he was his mate. I was his wife, but I was nothing. So Steve didn't take any action, didn't even have a word to him about it. He thought it was funny, actually, and I lived there for nearly six months with this filthy old bastard. I dreaded going into the kitchen knowing he was there but there was no choice.

One night when I was pregnant with Barry my sister came to visit me with about three of her girlfriends. We were in the kitchen and heard crying. Chris was only about one and a half and what this bastard did was slam his head into the brick fireplace. Chris must have touched something. He had an indentation, a dent, on his forehead. And then this bastard took my son and shoved him in the wood cabinet near the stove. And the father? Steve did nothing. He took absolutely no action against his son being assaulted. My sister witnessed all this and said, 'That's it, you're getting out of here.'

'Where am I going to go?'

'You can come in with me.'

That was it: I left. But that was all very well for my sister – she was going back to Fremantle. What about me, afterwards? Some old people on a strawberry farm took me in, parents of a friend. I had no money. When I was pregnant with Chris I did work in a factory making sausages but now I was totally dependent on Steve. When I left him I took the joint bank book and withdrew very small amounts. That's how I survived; I had no pension.

So we ended up on the strawberry farm and one day I was shopping in Albany when Steve came out of the pub and saw me. He said he was thinking of going back to Melbourne and he would take me back with him. I jumped at the chance. But then on the way he decided to dump me on the Nullarbor with Chris. I was so much in fear, so absolutely terrified, that we were going to die there. I did a lot of fast talking, I tell you what.

I was so relieved when we got to Melbourne. I was very vulnerable in Fremantle and Albany – they were all his friends, all his relatives.

I LEFT STEVE THE DAY HIS MOTHER BASHED ME

I left him for good the day his mother bashed me.

She was forever interfering in my marriage, feeding him lies, and she rang me up one day and started to abuse me. I said in Croatian, 'Go to the shit house.' It was the first time I ever fired back. So she came that afternoon with her boyfriend when Steve was there. Steve's relative who tried to rape me was there too because Steve had brought him back again. The relative grabbed my hands in a firm grip and held them behind my back while Steve's mother started slapping me. I couldn't defend myself or even protect my face. The relative was saying, 'Give her what I gave my wife.' Her boyfriend was laughing and my husband was laughing. I was nothing.

And Chris and Barry were there – little kids seeing their mother assaulted by their relatives as their father laughed.

This was the final straw. I contacted a policeman that had been involved in some of the incidents and he organised for a friend with a truck to come down the next day when Steve had gone to the country, and take the TV and the fridge and whatever little else – clothing, the single mattress.

Chris was three and a half when I left Steve. Barry was eighteen months.

I still think Chris doesn't face up to the whole picture – a bit of self-denial. If he reads what I have to say about Steve and what he did I don't think he'll believe it.

I haven't said much to the kids. I think: what's the point of all this? It's past; they don't need to know. It's over. I don't dwell on it; I'm talking about it now but I don't dwell on it. Some people can learn from the past and its lessons but most people don't heed it.

Funny thing, after I left Steve went around telling everybody I was a prostitute, that I stole everything – stories like you wouldn't believe. I left the furniture behind, dinner sets, ornaments: everything but the fridge, the TV, and a single bed. I slept with two kids in that bed. I was often drenched with urine from the kids. It was hard. I left the lounge, the dishes, everything behind. I had no wardrobes, nothing, and ate off suitcases – that was my table.

As soon as I left his mother moved in and she lasted three months with him. Three months she lasted with her son.

It's funny because many years later when I was living with my second husband in Williamstown, out of the blue Steve's mother, Jacqueline, would ring me up begging me to go back to him. She didn't like the other girlfriends and she said, 'You were the best, you did gardening, you were clean and you cooked and you did the garden with two little kids.' She called Steve's other girlfriends benches and prostitutes – the same things she used to call me.

I said, 'Jackie, I'm married and there's no way in hell I'm going back to that household.'

I was with Steve from 1967 until nearly 1972.

He found out where I was living and he kept coming round all the time. I was living with Hans and his [first] wife and my kids. It was a part of the house I was renting – like a bungalow attached to the house – and we were sharing a bathroom. I asked Hans to put a safety chain on the inside of the door and after all the effort Hans went to, Steve just came one day and smashed the whole door in. The frame hit my head. He'd say, 'But you're still my wife. You're still my wife.'

I'm still his wife sometimes and other times I'm a bloody bitch – as he told everybody – a prostitute, a thief who had stolen everything from him. There was one Croatian I ran into, someone who had been told all this crap, and I said, 'Come to my house. Now, look at this. This is my table.' And I showed him the suitcases. I showed him that I had no chairs. I showed him the single bed and said, 'This is where I sleep with two kids. This is all I've got.'

So I moved out of there and moved to Northcote. He didn't know I was there but I felt alienated in a strange area. I'm used to the western suburbs, so I came back to Williamstown.

Hans and his wife divorced and he got in touch and eventually we started dating.

When I married Hans, Steve owed me a lot of money in child maintenance, thousands, and I wanted to change the lounge room into the kitchen and put a window in. So Steve actually did that for me but then Steve kept coming around. He was constantly there and then he started to bring the relative

Christopher (right) and his
brother, Barry, 1973.

around, the one that had tried to rape me. I told him to get out and when Steve started arguing with me I said, 'Get him out now or I'll call the police.' I was remarried and for once Steve told him he'd better go.

After that Steve used the excuse of coming to see the kids, to come around – all the time. He was always hitting on me. He'd grab me all the time and it would end up being a struggle because he wanted to kiss me and I'd end up with bruised wrists.

Steve came around even though we had confrontations. When I was seven months pregnant with my child to Hans, Wayne, Steve tried to kick me in the stomach in front of my mother's neighbour. He said, 'I don't want you having anybody's kids but mine.'

After Hans and I divorced and I was single again he came around all the time, even at seven o'clock in the morning. I'd say, 'What are you doing here so early?'

'I've come to see the kids.'

Chris ran away from home and lived with him for three months. I took it to court, but because Chris was twelve he was allowed to decide who he wanted to live with. And in the court Steve, in front of everybody, approached my solicitor – some young solicitor – and asked if Barry was his [the solicitor's] son. Weird. Steve thought he could see some similarities. The guy freaked out and said, 'No, I've never been to Fremantle.'

And in court, Chris chose his dad because his dad was spoiling him.

That's what hurt me with Chris: he always sided with his father. The father was adventurous and exciting and very much like Chris. The mother was the opposite: strict. That's what hurt me the most when it was me that raised them. I sat up until two or three o'clock working my butt off doing extra embroidery to provide them with Christmas presents and things like that. The father provided nothing and he became the hero and I became the shit. That's what hurt me.

And I could see where Steve's encouragement would land Chris, who was in some ways very much like him – not in the cruel ways – and always wanted his father to like him, wanted his approval. And Steve played up to that, pushing the kids to do stupid things, taking them out on trips to steal and things like that.

I blame Steve a lot.

He rejected Barry because Barry wasn't like him; Barry didn't find all this adventurous. Barry is more conscientious where Chris wasn't, and anything went with Chris in those days. But Barry was conscientious and Chris was Steve's favourite son. He would always say to Barry, 'Ah, Barry, Barry, Barry, you're skinny,' because Barry didn't have the broad shoulders – he took more after me in build. Somehow he failed Steve because he wasn't made all broad shouldered. In those days he was just a normal child and Steve had no idea of genetics or anything like that, how some children take after different parents or relatives.

Steve liked Chris more because Chris was built like him: solid, broad shoulders and more daring, so he favoured Chris. Barry felt that too in his growing up years: Chris got all the presents and Barry got all the promises.

I tried to explain to Steve but we were on two different planets – I just couldn't get through to him. He just didn't grasp it – that this was wrong. That's where we clashed; he always used to say to me, 'You're too smart.' Too smart – more or less that I am trying to be smarter than him. I was just trying to explain, 'Don't do these things,' but I just got abused for it.

Years later, around the time Chris was in St Vincent's from the stabbing, when Steve was so sick from heart failure that he could only take a few steps before turning blue, he'd tell me that he still loved me and he wanted me to come back. When I dropped him home he tried to lure me in to go into the bedroom, wheezing as he said that it would be fun.

'Get out of the car,' I said, and drove off.

He was dying. I ended up doing his washing because his mother was also very sick.

In the end he could barely walk but he was still hitting on me.

Just Too Much

TURANA

Annette Binse on why she went to court to have Chris declared uncontrollable.

ANNETTE:

I was continuously raided. Chris was getting into trouble virtually on a weekly basis.

I also had my mother to look after, and my [much younger] sister, and I'd just lost my home after my [second] marriage had broken up.

I was under so much stress and I was constantly at police stations, sitting up there sometimes for six hours at a time. It was such a regular thing. And then I'd sit for hours in court.

Chris would be quiet in court, just listening. His parole officer was a friend, Jack Wilson, who was a taxation agent. He'd take time off work to be at court and we'd get out and

Chris would laugh – ha ha ha ha – and say, 'We got the coppers,' because he knew Jack wouldn't be very strict.

And it would happen again and again. Chris just wouldn't stop getting into trouble. It was too much.

And as well as the police there were just endless stupid things, like when he changed schools to Williamstown Tech, I went and bought him a whole new school uniform – jumpers and trousers and everything.

At his new school the kids can see he's a bit of a daredevil and they dared him to flash the teacher. So when she has her back to the class he exposes himself.

She can hear them laughing, Chris gets expelled and I give those clothes away. And we didn't have any money.

I just couldn't cope with him, along with everything else going on, so we went to court and I asked the judge to make him a ward of the state.

I just couldn't handle him.

But the raids kept happening mainly because he was on the run or because of the escapes. He escaped from Turana so they put him into Poplar House, the maximum-security section.

He escaped from there twice. When they did maintenance work there some guy left a plank against the wall and Chris scaled it. Simple as that. Took off.

The Royal Park mental hospital where my mother used to be was very close by, so he ran into the grounds, pinched some supervisor's bike, and pedalled all the way from Royal Park to Seddon.

That day I went to one of his female friends, to pick up his clothing because he sometimes stayed there. Chris comes running in, all breathless from pedalling the bike, and here's me in her kitchen.

I'm standing there absolutely dumbfounded, in shock, and I

realised he'd escaped again. Here's me thinking he's in Turana and here he is out of Turana.

Just unbelievable.

So that was my life. I didn't know what to expect from one day to the next.

####

Chris was in court with me when I asked the judge to make him a ward.

He didn't say much of anything. I don't really know what was going through his mind.

But it was just too much. I was in court practically every month, police stations practically every week, and with my mother the way she was it was just too much.

Chris (right), with a friend, was a charming and popular kid but one whose wild streak could not be reigned in.

REVOLVING DOOR MOTHERS

I met a lot of mothers in the same situation at Turana. When you come in regularly you get to know each other especially when it's years and years and years of coming backwards and forwards.

I found out recently that one woman's son is dead of a heroin overdose. Her son was the same as Chris, through the revolving door all the time.

The other mothers were like me – frustrated with their kids. We just didn't know what to do because they were always in trouble, in and out of jail all the time. They came visiting their sons and supporting them but couldn't do anything with them.

The personalities are too set. And there's a genetic factor, too, if you have a look at the father's background. I couldn't change Chris – I tried, but mission impossible. He just didn't listen. Just would not listen.

Barry is a different kettle of fish, a different character altogether, different personality. He wasn't the person that craved attention and notoriety. Barry was more a loner type, whereas Chris was flamboyant, liked to dress up flashy. Barry was just Barry and never one that craved attention and being a big shot.

Different temperaments: Barry and Chris in the mid 1980s.

Freeway Horse Thief

1983:
OUT OF TOWN

BARRY:

Dad was a subcontractor cladding houses with imitation brick and he took us sometimes to help him work, and stuff.

When Chris was about fifteen, we were were out in the country doing a job. I think it was near the town of Stawell, which is a couple of hundred kilometres from Melbourne.

Chris and Dad had a falling out because he thought Dad short-changed him, so Chris got dirty on him and took off to a train station to get back to Melbourne.

But he didn't realise country trains don't come very often. One a day maybe. Two perhaps. Nothing was happening. So he stole a horse and rode for Melbourne.

It was too far, of course, so after a couple of hours he dumped it.

CHRIS:

I do remember that. Ha ha ha ha ha.

I took it from a big paddock where the local horse-riding school put their horses. I just jumped on a horse with no bridle or nothing, just fucking bareback like Tarzan or something, like an Injun. And just rode off.

GOLF COURSE

1984:
SPOTSWOOD

Annette's mother, Sophia, lived a short walk from Spotswood
golf course. Annette and the boys had stayed with Sophia when
they were down on their luck, so Chris knew the area well and
as a boy had turned his entrepreneurial ways to making some
cash at the course.

CHRIS:

We used to sometimes collect golf balls along the creek there.
Some dollars for me as a kid, you know – that's how I used to
get the pocket money.

The creek would be so deep sometimes. And you'd see the
balls buried in the mud. The golfers couldn't be fucked chasing
them, so we'd do all right at times, you know.

Then I come up with a better idea: I thought – get a snorkel.
So I had a snorkel and I had a face mask and I went under the

water and I was cleaning them up, too. Not bad money for a kid but bloody cold and dirty work.

Then I realised, hold on, wait a minute, there's more balls in the golf buggy bags than there are in the creek, and after putting, they all park their golf buggies unattended, just off the car park, and go to the lounge.

So the money picked up and the conditions improved.

Later, when Chris was about sixteen and on release from Turana, he returned to his old haunt. The golf course. On a motorcycle. During play.

CHRIS:

I was doing doughnuts and shit, fucking burning up the grass, just being a hoon, you know, doing burnouts, putting tyre marks in the grass. The golfers were chasing me and teeing off at me.

I knew that creek off by heart and the way it jutted out. I was looking over my shoulder and giving them the thumbs up and the bird, fuck you, and this and that, but by the time I looked in front of me the pace I was going was too quick and I couldn't manoeuvre around it.

Because I was riding along the creek bed, I thought, 'Fuck! If I put the brakes on I'll just slide.' So instead I geared down and gunned it. I thought if I get enough speed maybe I'll make it.

I didn't make it.

I needed a ramp.

I was unconscious.

Having a broken neck was just awkward. I didn't like being fucking held down and restricted to the bed. It was pissing me off. I'm very full of beans, you know. I didn't like just sitting in bed all day and when I had me visitors I'd get them to fucking tie me into a wheelchair. We'd try to escape, like: 'Get me out of here!'

I didn't realise how serious it was. I had a broken vertebrae in my neck and three fractures in my back.

Annette was still very much part of Chris' life, despite having had him declared uncontrollable and admitted to the boys' home a few years earlier. She hasn't forgotten the time he broke his neck and back, and fills in details from when he was knocked out, such as the fact that two of the first golfers chasing him to reach the scene of the crash were a priest and a doctor. Unfortunately, the priest was a nip ahead, grabbing hold of the unconscious teenager and hoisting him up, doing god knows how much more damage to his spinal injuries.

ANNETTE:

I had my 2-year-old, Wayne, with me on my first date with a guy called Bill. It was a warm day and we went for a drive to have a picnic.

We were sitting on an embankment with a blanket and didn't see Wayne climb in the car. We don't know what he did but I was just sitting with my legs straight in front of me and the car rolled over my right leg.

I thought my leg was broken and I kept passing out. This was my first date and I had white slacks on and, being in shock, I wet myself. The most embarrassing thing for a first date.

Poor Bill rushed me off to Ferntree Gully Hospital when I realised my handbag was still on the embankment so he had to turn around and come back and pick up my handbag.

My leg wasn't broken but I had to go on crutches. The next day I was home when Chris' friends came up to me and said that Chris had an accident but that he was fine: that he was in Footscray hospital and fine and it wasn't too serious.

Only to learn that he had a broken neck, and two days later they found three fractures in his back. His chest just came out like this! You've got no idea. The doctors said by rights he should have been dead or quadriplegic.

With an injury like that you're not supposed to move and here is a priest hauling him up on his legs. He just collapsed and they got an ambulance.

The day I went to see Chris in hospital Bill ended up in hospital with appendicitis. So it was one day my leg, next day was Chris' neck, and then Bill's appendicitis. I didn't know which hospital to go to.

That was one hell of a weekend, I tell you what.

When I got in to see Chris, he was lying flat with weight behind his neck. Traction.

I went to see the doctor and he told me he had a broken neck and I completely spun right out. Then Chris was complaining of a sore back. It wasn't until about three or four days later that they x-rayed it and found out he had three fractures as well.

Crushed vertebrae. The sixth vertebrae. Any piece of that crushed vertebrae could have lodged in his spinal cord and caused instant death or paralysis. So it was pretty scary.

Of course Chris, being the active type, couldn't lay there quietly so his mates came to see him and he got them to undo the traction and help him get into a wheelchair.

He was going to leave the hospital with a broken neck – he felt it inconvenienced him.

This is the very next day, mind you. But then he froze; he couldn't move except to push the emergency button.

He got very severely reprimanded.

Then along comes father, of course, visiting his son, bringing him pizzas and junk food.

Because Chris couldn't eat properly laying down the father undoes the traction and helps him get into a sitting position to have his pizza.

I said to Steve, 'You don't do that! This is very dangerous what you're doing.'

'Shut up you bloody bitch.'

This is what I was getting all the time. So I went straight to the doctor. The doctor came in and he really took Steve to task. Steve didn't realise just how serious it was.

Chris had the same attitude, of course. I remember visiting him once and he's rolling up the hallway behind the nurses, going, 'Yeah!!!!!!', trying to run them down – the little horror.

He was in hospital for six weeks, and then came out with a brace which he had to wear for three months.

I didn't know but he was taking it off, hiding it, and going on another motorbike while still recuperating from his broken neck.

So he didn't learn anything.

And meanwhile, there was me, barely able to walk, on crutches, painful.

TEARDROP EXPLODES

1986:
MOURNING BABA

The death of Chris' grandmother.

ANNETTE:

I found my mother dead in her bedroom. On the floor. And I went into shock.

She died of a heart attack. She had heart trouble and she had minor heart attacks but this was a massive one and she died.

Chris and Mum got on well. He'd do little jobs for her: help her with shopping or other things. It never bothered him how she acted with the schizophrenia, because I explained it to the kids, unlike my father who never said a word to us about it. And because even if Chris is sick, even if he is twisted, even if he is deluded, inside him there is a loving heart.

So he'd ride his bike up to the shops for her and do her banking or pick up something she needed. And she'd tell me, 'Chris is a good boy.'

She didn't want to hear about the trouble he got up to. You couldn't say anything like that about my kids. My mother was all love: 'Oh, Chris is a good boy,' she'd say. 'I love him.'

And that was her answer to any ranting and raving I did. I'd say, 'Oh he did this, he did that.'

And it was always, 'Oh Chris is a good boy. I love him.' Which meant, 'Shut up, I don't want to hear it.'

We lived with my mother on and off after I left Hans and our house was seized by the bank. We had no place to go so we moved back into Mum's house.

She had a two-bedroom house where she lived with my little sister and I came with three kids so we were really cramped. It was awkward. Mum, Chris and I shared a double bed, Barry was on a couch, my sister in a single bed and Wayne in a cot.

I did all the cooking, Mum didn't cook because she was too ill. And I had to always watch my mother around the kids.

Because when I was a teenager I lived with Mum because of her needs. I wasn't married then. I had lots of friends and they all came to Mum's place.

And one time there were about five of them over, male and female, and my dear mother's walking out naked in front of them.

She had a picture of the Last Supper on the lounge room wall and she's kneeling down and praying to it.

I was highly embarrassed. I took her firmly by the hand and led her back into the bedroom and then she did it time and time again and I ended up sitting near the glass door from the lounge room to the hallway watching for any movement.

The war caused all this. It was brought on by the trauma of the war. She wasn't born that way.

So when she died Chris had a little teardrop tattooed. I said, 'My god what have you done to your face?'

He said, 'Mum, I couldn't cry so that's the tear I never shed for Baba. It's there now permanently.'

CHRIS:

My grandmother: I was crushed.

When I was a kid I used to ride great distances on a BMX to visit her, to do deliveries. My mum would cook up food and stuff for her and I'd be the delivery boy on a pushbike and do her errands.

When she died I hadn't realised how close she was to me. I couldn't even cry at the grave, at her funeral, so I had a tattoo done when I came to jail – one of my first jail tattoos: a teardrop under my left eye.

I went to jail again because after her death I escaped from Poplar House again and went on a month-long, drug-fuelled crime spree until being arrested and sent to Pentridge. That was when I was seventeen.

Then, when I got released I was at a pedestrian crossing at Footscray Mall and I'm waiting to walk across the road. I see an older lady out doing her shopping and she's looked at me and double-looked at me again, looked at the tattoo on my face and then brought her bag to her chest and clutched it with both hands. I thought, 'What the fuck?'

That teardrop was in memory of my grandmother, the tear I couldn't shed, the tear I put there eternally, but when I was seeing that old lady afraid of me, I thought, 'What the fuck? If that's the reaction I get from other people I don't need that.'

So I went to a tattoo shop and had them remove it. You can still see it a little bit but most of it is gone.

COLLEGE OF KNOWLEDGE INDUCTION

AUGUST 1986:
HM PENTRIDGE PRISON

Chris explains entering Pentridge at seventeen.

CHRIS:

The induction to the Big House from boys' home was a terrifying change in dynamics, thrown in amongst hardened criminals at such a tender age.

Within weeks I was stabbed repeatedly in the yard by an adult.

This was, in part, my fault, as I mailed the seasoned junkie my intentions. Bad move by me.

I remembered this inmate from outside by the distinctive tattoo on his ear lobes.

Living in Footscray at the time, I'd run out of pot. It was the early hours of the morning, too late for my local dealer, so as a last resort I decided to catch a cab to St Kilda. I never used to venture out that way at all.

Approached by a shifty looking bloke asking if I wanted to score, I told him I did and gave him the money to buy an ounce of pot for me. He told me, wait here. So naïve I was, and he lashed me.

Now, spotting him in another yard on remand, I forewarned him of drama. I reminded him that he stole the cash and I called him into my yard to sort it out one on one.

He entered and when I began to throw punches he produced a shiv and stabbed me a number of times.

I never felt it at all. In fact, I got on top of him on the ground, pinned him down and bashed him with both hands, going crazy, adrenalin pumping, raining down blows on his face.

I disarmed him, and my friends then took the weapon from me before I stabbed him with it. The screw in the tower had now caught the scene, so we had to break it up before the screws ran in the yard to do a check.

He left bruised, I might say. I was bleeding, but patched myself up with sticky tape and toilet paper.

In the years to follow, this is something I come to experience time and time again.

PRISON SLANG: LESSON TWO

Hot watering – to throw the contents of a just-boiled kettle over someone

Put on show – to mock or humiliate in front of other inmates or guards

Gronk – an inmate who is less fortunate (has jail shoes not brand shoes), not part of the crew

Lag – to give information to the police or prison authorities: he lagged on other inmates to get favours from the prison governor; she lagged him to the coppers to get off her own charges

Shank, shiv – homemade knife (for stabbing other inmates)

Tool up – to obtain weapons

COLLEGE of KNOWLEDGE 2

1986–88:
PRISON TOUR

Chris turns nineteen. His development continues in this brutal world.

OCTOBER 1986:
B DIVISION

CHRIS:

A couple of months later I am again attacked in the compound [shared] exercise yard of B Division.

Four inmates break my jaw.

It's tied to my history from Poplar House boys' home: the bashing of another inmate is a power–control thing for the running of the place.

Breaking his nose catches up to me.

He is now in the compound with all his mates. And he wants

to show me how he is now in control of the yard, that this is his territory not mine.

The favourite location for most assaults in the compound are the portables that house the table tennis and pool table, as no staff are able to monitor what's unfolding inside.

Lured in, knowing full well what's on their agenda, I am surrounded by the group. One pulls my head whilst another cheap-shots me with a blind side king hit, knocking me out and breaking my jaw.

I refuse to talk to the authorities about this. The Pentridge doctor issues a soft food diet and sick-in-cell chit for a few days.

I have to confront my assailants in the shared compound again, a harrowing ordeal. I am unable to describe the fear it instils in me.

Yet, scared kids in an adult population, surrounded by hardcore violence, we call it even.

‖‖

Frank Waghorn, far bigger at 114 kilograms to my 70-something, older at about 36 years to my eighteen, a veteran prison fighter, bank robber and soon a murderer, attacks me in late December.

I defend myself by 'hot watering' him with a jug of boiled water, but this incident gets me transferred to H Division, aka Hell Division.

After the blue with Waghorn, prison staff are alarmed for my safety and send me to Hell for my own welfare. I refuse to sign any protection requests or safety concerns about this well-known and influential inmate. Waghorn is an old-school crook who has been in the prison system forever, and I am just a young kid.

I'm charged with assault and grievous bodily harm upon him, but after explaining my actions he gets charged with assault, due to my black shiner.

This is heard at Preston Magistrates Court in August the next year, where his charges are withdrawn due to my refusal to lag him. I am warned a number of times by the magistrate.

A contempt charge in the process.

I am extremely afraid.

JANUARY 1987:
HELL DIVISION

The staff are extremely violent. H Division is run as a military camp. It is just brutal. Brutal. Very boot camp. You have to pace, walk, salute. You have to hand your shoes in a certain way to the officers. You have to say 'Sir'. If they feel that you are talking smart to them you get a clip over the head.

You have to roll your bedding just so: you can't be lying on your bed during the day; that's if you are allowed in the cell at all.

You can't be relaxed. If they catch you lying on your bed they'll bash ya. If you didn't do the salute a certain way, they'll bash ya.

No shoes are to be taken into the cell, so you take them off, place them out the front door and salute them. Crazy shit.

They have a cross painted in the centre of the yard. They escort you there and secure you. You have to walk to the cross, turn about face so you're facing back towards the tower, the catwalk, and you have to wait there until the officer in the tower breaks you off.

On hot days they'll leave you there. Twenty minutes, five minutes, one minute: you never know.

But if you break off before that officer gives you the authority he'll radio through and send them in to bash you.

Therapy.

They are brutal, man.

Bastardisation at its worse and most extreme, with no exceptions to the rules, not even for the kids. No TV or anything like that.

We are bashed often and kept in a state of total fear and hate towards the staff. Sometimes they wear Ku Klux Klan hoods, as shown in photographs from Chopper Read's book. It is an extreme world.

When I am not long eighteen and kept in this Hell alongside hardcore inmates, I meet a 19-year-old also named Chris. We get on okay.

Chris can't cope with the fear and hate in H Division. He hangs himself.

So yesterday there was someone struggling in here and now he's a corpse. They take his body out.

When word spreads that a teenager named Chris has hanged himself in H Division, my mum gets a stack of phone calls from people thinking it's me. She panics until she finds her son is alive.

'But my heart really goes out to the mother of Christopher Jergens,' she tells one of the newspapers.

His death causes an uproar about how young he was, yet I am even younger – something my mum points out to the reporters.

'Chris has only committed juvenile crimes, yet he's in a division with mass murderers and armed robbers,' she says.

The bullying and assaults inflicted on me by staff, the extreme atmosphere of threat and fear, foster a condition: me versus the blue uniform; me versus agents of the state.

A solja in revolt.

FEBRUARY 1987:
BEECHWORTH PRISON

I am transferred to Beechworth, a medium-security prison where Ned Kelly and his supporters were held at one time.

But I have anger issues.

And Derek Percy is here: the paedophile child killer. I am disgusted that such a vile creature is walking amongst us in the wing and no one is doing anything about it. They are allowing it to be here – a position not shared by me.

So there is an incident.

It lives on the same bottom landing as I do and five odd cells across. I secure petrol from a lawnmower, a glass jar and rag, and wait for it to return from work.

Light the rag. Throw the Molotov in its cell, close the door, lock it from the outside, and wait for the crispy outcome.

But to my shock and horror some minutes later it bangs on its cell door.

From grand thoughts and images of it alight in its last death throes to disappointment when all the banging draws prison staff to its cell.

Opening up the door, its hand ventures out to pass them the intact Molotov.

It has carpet flooring in its cell; it was washing itself in there, having a bird bath – as it does not feel safe in the communal showers – when the cell door flew open and a balaclava-clad inmate lobbed a Molotov in. It jumped up in alarm, hit by the projectile.

But instead of the Molotov hitting the rear wall and exploding into fire as intended, the glass jar landed without breaking on the carpet, scorching the carpet but it used water from its tub to put it out. So it survives the barbecue and is moved due to this.

卌

Less proudly, I bash an inmate over a petty matter.

Prison staff hear him screaming for help over the console and start a walk of the tier. The cell next to where I am bashing him has a stereo on full bore but it can't drown out the screaming and all the inmates have their heads out looking up to where it's happening.

So the screws literally catch me red-handed, covered in blood, wearing gloves and a balaclava that they have to tear off.

Charged over this, I am sent back to Pentridge, where I stay in D Division until being transferred in early 1988 to Geelong Prison, a maximum-security jail that Barwon will replace.

JANUARY 1988:
GEELONG PRISON

I have never taken Rivotril pills before – zombie sedatives – but during my time at Geelong, I pop them like Tic Tacs.

I am barely able to walk or talk – a bumbling mess – but I still want to fight. An inmate I am provoking sees my state and he tries to avoid fighting, but I keep on until he knocks me down with a big hit to the jaw, and straddles me.

He tries to get me to see reason, but I refuse all attempts and then, as prison staff intervene, he just gets off.

I am now removed from the main body of the prison due to the assault, but when they are distracted I return to the wing to confront the inmate.

I have a Stanley knife concealed down my pants and go for him with it. He takes off and when prison staff try to subdue me I lunge at them and then go to my cell, grabbing a four-by-two bit of wood I have with nails sticking out of one end.

Wielding the nailed club, I call out the inmate's name. Prison staff lock him in the compound yard and then try to approach and disarm me. But I turn on them and they call a jail security squad from Melbourne.

It will take an hour for them to arrive. And they just let me run loose – the jail is mine. But my friends convince me to surrender the weapons just before the squad arrives.

I am transferred from the jail. Not at my request either, I might add (and I would later face Geelong Magistrates Court over the incident with staff).

I arrive at D Division of Pentridge and when the effects of the pills wear off a day later I notice eating is a problem. My jaw is broken, again, so I'm sent to the locked St Augustine's ward of St Vincent's Hospital to get it wired.

RELEASE

9 APRIL 1988:
RAGE AND REVENGE

Chris is nineteen years old.

CHRIS:

I am released full of hate and rage, sourcing weapons and soon involved in acts of violence not seen before. I am involved in a number of serious crimes, targeting elements of the state: financial institutions. Robbing them – not burglaries or thefts now.

When I entered Pentridge as a 17-year-old kid I looked up to the armed robbers of the day. I wanted to be one of them. And I get out and emulate exactly what I heard from them; I put it into practice.

I am very disturbed, very angry. I have been subjected to a lot of violence. And this is the thing: I have resentment towards the Office of Corrections and resentment towards police officers and the authorities because of what I have been subjected to.

I have been tortured. I have been locked in isolation – and the anger when being released from isolation is extreme.

When I get out all I want is for them to pay. That is like compensation. Seriously. My main targets are state banks and government institutions. I didn't want to get out and rob people, battlers or whatever. If I rob houses and stuff like that it will come out of people's pockets and they will suffer a lot more. They aren't the target of my crimes.

So I progress to armed hold-ups. And a number of shootings: true. The armed robberies are done solo. No back-ups for help. I am confident alone. I also purchase a stolen police bulletproof vest to wear during robberies.

I am so angry that I smoke pot to calm myself. But it doesn't hold it in.

ⵜⵜⵜ

While having lunch with my girlfriend at an Asian diner in Footscray, I spot a prison officer from Pentridge. The Red Setter he is known as, a real nasty spiteful individual that works in D Division and had us all terrified: a bad basher he is.

At the diner he is with his wife, but that's no barrier to me at all. The only thoughts running through my head are of the therapy he exacted on so many inmates and how 'It's your turn, fucker. Your dose now.'

At the first sight of him, I unleash a torrent of insults, much to the horror of all those eating in the area, my girlfriend included.

Not content with just a verbal assault, I pursue him and keep unloading an avalanche of profanity, much to the horror of his wife.

I follow him to K-Mart and when I am a few aisles away but drawing near, I select a carpet cutting knife from the shelf, and advance upon him with it clearly visible, while telling him I am going to cut him to shreds.

He takes off with me chasing. But I have no plans at all; I am just head-fucking him as he does to inmates.

As he is leading me towards the checkouts up front, I ditch the weapon, knocking a bunch of other items off a shelf with it, but he doesn't notice, and I make out I still have it, lunging at him at times.

When we arrive at the checkout and are surrounded by security, all of a sudden he pulls out his prison badge – like a *Starsky & Hutch* move – and he tries to make a citizen's arrest with the support of all the security.

He says that I have a concealed knife and tells security to arrest me. So I calmly unbutton my cardigan and open it up for everyone to see that I have no weapon. I just walk past everybody, telling them that I have no idea who he is.

They are lost for words.

The Red Setter decides to retrace our steps and locates the knife. The police are called in and he identifies me and hands the weapon to them.

I am questioned at Footscray police station.

Within days his house is petrol bombed and shot up. Or I guess it was supposed to have been, except whoever did it gets the address wrong, hitting his neighbours instead: it was number 15, not 13.

Needless to say, within a short time the police arrive at my house.

I get charged over the K-Mart matter, landing six months jail for it.

The Red Setter's wife, I'm told, has a nervous breakdown over this, landing in a mental facility for four weeks and popping Valium like crazy. She still has not recovered.

卌

This rage is a constant theme repeated with nasty staff I encounter on the outside. I chase and spit at them on the outside – regrettable at times, I say, if truth be told. I have chased them through red traffic lights, driving them close to getting hit by oncoming vehicles.

Inside I have thrown faeces at them, hot water, eggs; I've pelted rocks at them in their towers for fun: true.

Yet outside if they're decent types I actually shake their hands, offer to buy them a drink and sit down for a coffee to show there are no hard feelings; if they showed no malice to me then there is none given in return.

I have also reached out to decent likeable rogue prison officers. Do unto others as they do unto you, is the motto I practise. No favouritism: I don't see the uniform, just the character of the soul.

The Red Setter has since mellowed out, realising – I feel – that nothing good ever came out of his conduct and that his marriage suffered as a consequence of his attitude to us.

We have shared jokes about how we were fuckwits then, and the things that can happen.

PROLIFIC

Chris confessing his unsolved heists to detectives at Barwon Prison in 2015.

Cop: To say that you were prolific would be an understatement?

Chris: Yeah. Within months of my release I'd be jumping counters. How long's it take me to do an armed robbery? I spot the target, I look at the target, I know the time patterns. Within a week or two. Not fuckin' six months.

LISTEN TO ME, FELLAS

May 1988: TAB Tottenham, Melbourne
Take: between $600 and $700
Chris is nineteen when he does his first armed robbery.

CHRIS:

Here I am, first armed robbery, I've geed meself all up.
I'm peaking. I'm scared.

I put a balaclava on, walk in and say, 'This is a
robbery,' or something like this that I'd seen on the
movies. Know what I mean? I basically use lines from
the movies. 'Everybody on the floor,' I say, 'cos that's a
better position to control them. They're not gonna run;
they're not gonna do this, do that, or try and jump me.
There's more control in that position, you know.

But they aren't interested. It's turned to shit — they
won't stop watching the fucking races. They're fixated.

Three or four times, I'm: 'Everybody down!' But they
are just fixated on the races.

What the fuck? This is not happening. Turning to
shit. 'Listen to me, man! What the fuck? Hey! Listen to
me, fellas, I've only got a short time!'

Some of them are looking over; some of them aren't.
They see the balaclava and they just couldn't be
fucked; they're watching the race. They had bets or

something going on and their horse is running. They're more interested in watching the race than they are listening to me.

I don't have time for them to watch their race! I'm working on three minutes, and it's just become like comedy capers.

'What the fuck! Listen! Hey! Haven't got much time here!' But they're not really tuned in. Maybe they think it's a dodgy gun or some fake. 'What the fuck, hey!'

Boom

Boom

Boom

That gets their attention.

Having discharged a few shots into the wall, I muster 'em. Don't want them behind me, you know, 'cos I have to watch the cunt behind the teller. And I don't have much time. A 100 per cent he will hit the hold-up button. So I hand him the bag, a big sports bag, and ask him to fill it up — just the big notes. I want all the big notes: 50s and 20s.

I have a vehicle parked around the corner, a Holden Kingswood HQ. Very easy to steal. So I run out the back way and onto the side street and I'm looking but no one's following me. I jump in the vehicle and actually drive past home in Braybrook and back onto Sunshine Road and through the train overpass and I leave the car at Footscray Hospital car park.

They've filled the bag but I don't get any big notes — a lot of the money in coins. I get about $600, $700. It isn't that much.

This happens around Mother's Day.

||||

This crime is unsolved until Chris contacts police in 2015 and volunteers his responsibility. He is subsequently charged and in 2016 pleads guilty in Melbourne Magistrates Court.

NiGHTCLUBBiNG

MAY 1988:
HOT GOSSIP

Shortly after the Tottenham TAB stick-up.

CHRIS:

Me and a friend go to a nightclub, Hot Gossip.

He's catching up with someone that owes him money and after he's gone like five minutes I say, 'Where's me mate?' and go and have a look.

As I'm walking into the toilets I see me mate bashing this bloke. You know, kicking him on the ground. It's a bad scene and now there's a pack of bouncers coming in behind me. The fella is affiliated to some of the bouncers while my mate is affiliated to the other bouncers. So there's a stand-off. One group wants to eject me mate. The other group wants to support us.

We get ejected and I am spewing 'cos I've got some sheilas at the bar lined up and I'm supposed to be taking them home.

But now I'm escorted past them, manhandled, and ejected – what the fuck? We're drunk, full of alcohol – what the fuck! – angry, full of hate inside. I run to the car, grab a sawn-off semi-auto .22 rifle with a five-magazine clip, run back a short distance and started shooting at the bouncers.

And then there's a cunt at the hotdog stand nearby, a vendor, and I start fucking shooting at that bloke, too. What the fuck? I'm angry because I got ejected. I had nothing to do with it. Plus the alcohol, too – the alcohol and the bouncers and violence and guns, it gets mixed. Bad combination.

They actually shut the nightclub doors, the front doors, and gather everybody in.

‖‖

This crime is unknown until Chris contacts police in 2015 and volunteers his responsibility. He has not been charged because there is no record of it happening.

Chris still had his charm and humour but the intensifying spiral of crime and punishment was unhinging him.

TOOLING UP BIG TIME

30 May 1988: Ken Kim's Sports Store, Altona, Melbourne
Take: Eight or nine firearms

CHRIS:

There are three people involved in this robbery but
I'm not naming the others. We have a vehicle outside
with the engine running and someone in it, while two
of us go in and jump the counters. I have an imitation
handgun and my comrade has a knife.

We steal between eight and nine shotguns and rifles.

Ken Kim's is a couple of shops down from the Altona
State Bank. I rob that later using firearms from the
sports store.

I'm a busy boy; I'm fucking hectic.

⑪⑪

*This crime is unsolved until Chris contacts police in 2015 and
volunteers his responsibility. He is subsequently charged and in 2016
pleads guilty in Melbourne Magistrates Court.*

HiT THE STATE

31 May 1988: State Savings Bank of Victoria, East Keilor
Take: $21,688
The day after raiding Ken Kim's Sports Store

CHRIS:

I have a legit vehicle parked near the primary school.
That'll be what I drive off in, all mellow and smooth
after dumping the getaway car — a Torana I stole for
the job.

This is a solo operation: I love 'em. It's a big ask
but it's also a blast flying alone, taking all the
responsibility, all the risk, and getting all the earn
— and I don't have to worry about bodgy crew members.

But it's full-on when no one's watching your back.
Get distracted or just look in one direction instead of
the other and you can miss a security guard, a copper,
a bank worker pushing a button, a civilian slipping
out a door: next thing ya know, someone's putting a
bullet through ya.

To have a chance of doing it clean and getting clear
I got two minutes tops — maybe less.

What a challenge; what a rush.

Everything's ready: overcoat on; in the mode; parked
outside; engine idling; grab the pump-action; grab the

bags; balaclava ready; deep breath to fill the chest and fuel my fire; good to go; up and out and in the side door of the bank.

'This is a hold up!'

They freak the way civilians do, get all goosey and confused and indecisive, so I make it easy to know what's happening by cranking the shotgun — God, I love that sound — and point it at the tellers. 'I'm not fuckin' joking!' The handful of customers don't look like trouble and just fucking quiver as I work my way down the row of three tellers, throwing each a shopping bag or two. 'Hurry up! Just the big ones! Just the big ones! Move it — fuck!'

Rampage: Chris' raids left scores of bank staff shaken to the core.

One of the tellers — a sheila about my age — is just gawking at where I missed trying to toss her a bag. 'Stop mucking around!' She starts filling the other bag, though, feeding it from her cash drawer. 'Just the big ones!'

When I hit the end of the row I cover the crowd, control the floor, give the last teller a moment to stuff her bag, then collect it and move back along, collecting the rest of the proceeds.

Out and away to the car swap. Now I ease my foot off the juice and take it easy — on the outside at least, 'cos inside I'm all fingers-in-the-socket; all shocked and charged and coursing with power. I'm on fire.

I'm nineteen and I just made a bit over twenty G's in about 90 seconds.

꘠꘠꘠꘠

This crime is unsolved until Chris contacts police in 2015 and volunteers his responsibility. He is subsequently charged and in 2016 pleads guilty in Melbourne Magistrates Court.

A FEW CREWS LOOSE

17 June 1988: TAB, Moonee Ponds, Melbourne
Take: $5326.58
Approximately 5.50 pm

CHRIS:

The police station is only a few blocks away — a
quick sprint — so my adrenaline is on overload: what
a fucking buzz. The heart's hammering as we pull down
our balaclavas, grab our sawn-offs, walk into the
arcade's rear and enter the TAB via different doors,
taking control in a pincer movement.

My coey (co-offender) tells some quivering old lady
to shut her trap and then trains his weapon on the
manager. I jump the counter and toss the bloke some
sports bags. 'Give us the big notes,' I say, levelling
the business end of my 12 gauge. The cops are gonna be
here fast as fuck and this clown's not exactly rushing.
'Move it! Fill it up!'

As he feeds a bag with cash from the drawers under
the teller windows, my coey gets toey. 'The big ones!'
he yells. But there's not much here. 'There's got to be
more than that!' my mate shouts.

'That's all,' the white-faced manager says. 'No more.'

He passes the bag over the counter and puts his hands in the air.

Time to go. I jump the counter again and then spot the manager opening the safe. No time for it and there's probably a fucking alarm switch inside, but it's worth a squiz before we scarper so I keep the weapon trained on the manager to keep him from pressing the button.

BLAM!

'What the fuck?'

It's raining ceiling.

'What was that for?' But my trigger-happy coey's too geed up to answer, let alone think. Show's over. 'Let's fucking go.' I race for the door and he's right behind me. Down the arcade and out to the car park we run; the engine's on and I fucking fang it, smoking the tyres to rocket us clear.

Ammo from Chris' weapons stash.

When we're good I check the proceeds. Five G's. Fuck all. Loose change.

I feel dudded. I feel really fucking duped.

From now on I'm handing out transparent plastic freezer bags every fucking time so I can see exactly what they're packing.

⫫⫫

This crime is unsolved until Chris contacts police in 2015 and volunteers his responsibility. He is subsequently charged and in 2016 pleads guilty in Melbourne Magistrates Court.

HAPPY EIGHTEENTH, BARRY

JUNE 1988:
DRIVING IN THE SUBURBS

In mid 1988, Chris is on a rampage of armed robberies but he still takes the time to think of others. His brother Barry turns eighteen on 1 July and as the big day nears, Chris finds a way to make it special.

BARRY:

A few weeks before my eighteenth he gave me a car. I

Barry and Chris: brothers always, although life can be hard with an outlaw sibling.

was at my mother's place. My mum had just cooked dinner and we were about to sit down and eat. My brother comes tearing along in this car, an XA Coupe. It was a Fairmont but it had all the good gear in it. It had a 351 top loader, 9 inch diff. It had

12 inch Mickey Thompson racing tyres on the back. It had what they call a shaker. It was all done up as a GT. But the body was quite rusty.

My brother's rocked up in the car and I'm saying to him, 'Fucking nice car.'

He goes, 'Yeah, it's yours.'

'Bullshit.'

'Yeah, it's for your birthday.'

I go, 'Bullshit.' 'Cos I don't trust my brother.

'No, it is.'

'I'll go take some photos of it.'

'No, we'll go for a drive.'

My mum said that dinner was ready, so eat first and then go for a drive. The car was unregistered; it had been unregistered for a while but the bloke it came from used to race it and it had a lot of tricks on it.

After dinner we left the house in Braybrook and went to Footscray, to the service station there that sold AvGas [high octane aviation fuel]. My brother put $20 worth in there which back then was probably half to three-quarters of a tank. Then he took it for a drive. He was thrashing it everywhere and it was all good, didn't worry me, I'm seeing what the car can do.

We went past an area where we used to live and on the corner was a milk bar where we used to hang around – they had a pinball machine – we knew the people in the shop. I seen water leaking across the road: must have been a pipe broken. I just knew, and I said to Chris, 'Whatever you do, take it easy over the water.'

He just looked at me, dropped it back a gear, left his foot on the clutch, revved it, and as soon as we hit the water he let go of the clutch. That car just spun. It done a 180 and we're going down the street backwards at about 150 k's. We cleaned up cars all along my side: hit three cars.

But my brother didn't run away or nothing. He stayed and faced the music. It wasn't a stolen car, just unregistered, and he wasn't licensed. He copped it on the chin with the coppers.

So I never drove it. He gave me a replacement vehicle at a later stage, a ZG Fairlane with a 302 motor, but he drove that sideways around a corner and hit a pole.

ATTACK THE COMMONWEALTH

30 June 1988: Commonwealth Bank, St Albans, Melbourne
Take: zilch

CHRIS:

Warm afternoon for the middle of winter, especially under these heavy dark clothes, and as my carload of soljas, my brothers-in-arms, cruises towards a side street just around from the bank, I'm itching to move — itching to hit the go-switch — but only if everything's fucking just right.

Senses are wired tight: taking everything in — not rubbernecking around like a mad cunt but smooth. I'm absorbing what's here: traffic and pedestrians in normal busy flow as the banking day nears its end, people coming and going from the supermarket across the way; and absorbing what's not here: patrol cars, unmarked vehicles, security guards.

'Get set, fellas,' I tell my crew. The driver pats his balaclava; he'll have it down in a flash when I give the command. The bloke in back takes a deep breath. Shotguns ready. My heart is pounding: not fast but slow — every thud keeping time for the job about to unfold. The bank's closing soon so there's lots of cash to grab. Hands on the tools; the weapon feels beautiful.

We park our stolen car — fucking everything's mine for the taking — in a side street close to the target. Seconds out.

Bloke behind me stiffens. 'Armaguard', he says.

Fucking van across the road from the bank — not directly opposite but parked 30 metres or so away. Picking up from the shopping centre. Still too close. They've got firearms and I don't want them involved. I tell the boys to sit tight. 'We'll wait 'til they fuck off.'

And we wait. And wait. The rhythm is fucking straining. The beat wants action.

Five minutes.

Ten minutes.

The van pulls out. 'We're on', I say and me and me mate in back are up and at it, hot and cold and wired fucking tight as we storm the door, balaclavas down, bags and guns all ready for a king-size take.

Fuck me, they've locked up.

'Open the fucking door, you bastards!' I'm kicking the shit out of the door. 'Open it!' The tellers are down the back — I can see a bunch shitting themselves as I put the fucking boot in and roar, tossing up whether or not to blast the door to pieces with the shotty. A couple teenage fellas stare at us open-mouthed from the ATM right fucking next to us. I kick again but my heartbeat's calling time. This is just comedy capers. 'Abort, abort!'

My coey isn't happy and he walks into the middle of the road and points his gun at a parking inspector who is seeing what all the noise is about. My mate's screaming at him: 'Come on, you motherfucker! Come and get me!'

The bloke's shitting himself.

'Let's go! Let's go!' I'm trying to snap my coey out of it but instead of going for the vehicle he turns and sprints at the bank, roaring and landing such an almighty kick the glass shatters at last. But it's all too late and we bolt for the car which is ready with the doors open and the driver guns it and we're off, empty—handed but alive.

We park near another car that we've pre—positioned, ditch the getaway, and cruise off in an orderly fashion having a laugh and a fucking spew — all at the same time. What a fiasco. Should have called it when the van didn't piss off in time. Can't fucking let greed call the shots in these operations.

卌

This crime is unsolved until Chris contacts police in 2015 and volunteers his – and only his – responsibility. He is subsequently charged and in 2016 pleads guilty in Melbourne Magistrates Court.

FUCK THE MONEY

A few years before, Chris tries to explain his love of heists to the cops (quoted in the Age in 2012):

For the excitement. The rush. Lifestyle: you'd have to know what it feels like. It's like you're on a raid, you're in control, your blood starts rushing, you feel grouse, you're hyped up. Fuck the money. It's more than excitement; it's an addiction. I don't know what it is.

B-ADNE$$ in full flight.

ANYONE SEEN CHRIS?

2 JULY 1988:
MELON STREET, BRAYBROOK

A couple of weeks after Chris gets in early with the hotted up XA Coupe, Barry celebrates his eighteenth.

BARRY:

For my eighteenth I went out to a nightclub with some mates and had a few drinks. Came home pretty pissed.

That morning I was supposed to have the test for my licence but I knew I was too pissed so I slept in instead.

I was asleep and then someone's pulling my doona back and there's a bunch of coppers in the room with their guns trained on me.

They were after Chris.

I don't know where he was or what he was doing but it was me they ended up seeing. Made me wake up pretty quick.

I actually spewed that I didn't go for my licence.

MATCH HEAD THIN

8 JULY 1988:
BRUNSWICK LOCKUP

CHRIS:

I'm arrested for stealing a car that belongs to a police officer from Moonee Ponds. He wants the motor and the identification tags returned, but I don't oblige so all he has is the shell.

They bash me as a result and charge me with drug offences and assaulting police. I'm kept in Brunswick police station's lockup.

I get hold of hacksaw blades, and start feverishly cutting the bars separating the exercise yard from the rear of the watchhouse area. I spend hours on this with only the thickness of a match to go when a bit of bad luck hits. With the changing of the watch, the watchhouse keeper unexpectedly walks past, by pure luck catching a glimpse of what's occurring, yells out to the rest, and they arrive ten deep to find the fresh tailings and the bar cut.

I am moved to another watchhouse as a result, knowing that very soon I'll be landing in D Division's remand wing, where the Red Setter awaits, quite possibly a little dirty about that K-Mart incident from a month or so back.

WELCOME BACK To PRISON

1988–89: PENTRIDGE

CHRIS:

Well, as expected the Red Setter isn't letting it go. His co-workers bash the shit out of me.

A lot of hate in me now. Lot of anger. I'm violent to other prisoners.

One bloke who'd cracked me a good one before is there in the yard so I fill a pillow slip with tins of baked beans, slam him in the fucking head, and then set to work with fists alone. But he's an amateur boxer and a good one and comes back hard, the staff loving the raw value of our war and letting the blood-soaked cage match go the distance.

Twenty-four minutes it takes us to quit from exhaustion, one of my front teeth and plenty of blood gone and our hands hanging like lead. The staff finally enter the yard and we're sent to the doctors for a patch-up and then placed together back out in the yard the next day.

They loathe both of us and no doubt they're anticipating a rematch; no doubt they want one. I am concerned no end, as he has proven such a tough cookie. He gave one of the hardest prison fights I would ever have: the ferocity, the intensity – a brutal bloody clash.

But knowing that we are just spectator sport for the screws offends us both, and denying the screws the satisfaction is the only reason we make peace.

I have the utmost respect for the man. He was the best fight I have ever had in my entire life. Punch for punch, he was a machine.

24 APRIL 1989:
B DIVISION EGGS TO CHOP

What I call not being happy about getting bashed, but they call 'conflict' with the screws that bash me, eventually sees me transferred to B Division, a wing for long-term inmates with behavioural issues – not that I see Red Setter here.

So here in B, I hide in my cell, step into the corridor, lob four eggs in quick succession at the screws' box, and then step back inside.

The target is a particular officer who rides inmates relentlessly and will later get stabbed by a prisoner.

You can hear the eggs hitting: splat, splat, splat, splat. They screws hate it, and a rotting egg smell will linger for days to come.

I have four timed perfectly for the throw and withdraw. That means it's time to go for a PB – personal best – but no, five gets me pinched; I lose privileges and if anything else happens I'm going to Hell.

In the exercise yard, I throw rocks at the towers, smashing the windows in front of screws with bad attitudes.

Off to H.

Where resides that dog, that coward, that copper with a silent 'H'.

Mark 'Chopper' Read.

29 MARCH 1989:
H DIVISION

Hardcore H Division. I'm now a graffiti man expressing the bigness of this world, carving doors and walls with the love that makes H great.

I write: Hate all those who Hate you.

I write: Hate them even more.

They are all hardcore when I arrive. Chopper Read is here, Alex Tsakmakis – the one that Slime – Craig Minogue – kills. There is a group of them, a couple of murders happen, and sometimes they get pinched.

They are all hardcore inmates.

꜔꜔꜔꜔꜔

I am at war with Chopper Read.

I hate the cunt. I don't like him. I have issues with him. He tampers with my food on a number of occasions and fucks around with my washing, 'cos he is the laundry billet, the trusty down here.

I don't put my washing out anymore because I know he will put a cup of piss in the last rinse. That way when you wear it or use your bedding you'll get that piss smell through it.

He fucks around with the food, too.

He's not the sharpest tool in the shed. He thinks by grinding up glass and putting it in the meals it will have the same effect as shards. It doesn't. It's like sand.

He puts it in my jelly. I spot it. I say, 'You fucking imbecile.'

I declare him.

All this started when I verbally confronted him in D Division, where he'd arrived into remand for shooting the Turk at Bojangles.

On my way to parade, I actually open Chopper's cell trap when he's on the bottom landing on protection: 23-hour lockup.

I invite him out to play in the yard. He wants to know who I am so I identify myself and tell him straight that I am not happy with him shooting Chris Liapis at Footscray – a bloke I knew.

He does not take up my offer to enter the yard. But that's what started it.

Then, lo and behold, within six months he's down in H Division and I land soon after. But before I land he establishes himself; he's got all the screws onside: he's worked with them for many years.

He is the laundry wing billet, having easy access to weapons and the tacit support of the Ku Klux Klan screws, who includes 'Maggot', a sadistic prick who actually likes being called that.

He's worked with the coppers, standing over drug dealers at their bidding. At this stage there is a corrupt pocket of coppers in the drug squad. They will stand over you. They will extort you. If you pay them, you won't get pinched – you won't get arrested. If you don't pay, they know you are doing business and they want a piece of the action.

If you don't give them a piece of the action you'll get pinched. A lot of them pay, some of them don't. For the ones that don't, the coppers say, 'Well, fuck youse,' and they send in Chopper.

They can give him all the details – the address, the movements, everything – because they're doing surveillance on these people. They'll supply him a bulletproof vest and guns. He'll run in there, he'll take the drugs, he'll take the cash, and then he'll divide it with the coppers.

That's the truth. That's how he used to operate. Copper with a silent 'H'.

The Turk that he shot at Bojangles [Siam 'Sammy the Turk' Ozerkam, killed with a shotgun blast to the face in 1987 outside a St Kilda nightclub] was a drug dealer that he tried to stand over.

He pleaded self-defence, and guess who gives evidence for Chopper?

The coppers: the corrupt coppers he was working with.

The screws hate a crazy bastard, Richard Mladenich, who Chopper then ambushes, seriously injuring him with a spade to the head. After the attack, Chopper runs to the protection of the staff, the coward.

His yard mate, Craig 'Slime' Minogue, a Russell Street bomber, will kill another multiple murderer, Alex Tsakmakis, in the same spot.

Interesting days here in H Division: anything can happen. Two songs I like are Bon Jovi's 'Wanted Dead or Alive' and Seal's 'Crazy'. Chopper can't stand them, so I play them again and again and again and again and again and again – round and round and round and round until he's losing it. Makes me love those songs even more.

22 AUGUST 1989:
RELEASED FROM CUSTODY

CHRIS:

Outside again. Good times. Smoking a lot of pot but doesn't do shit. What are you looking at, fuckhead? We got issues?

PRISON SLANG: LESSON THREE

The Squad - special emergency response team: feared, not to be messed with

Wing - what cell blocks are called

Safe - anal passage where drugs, syringes and weapons are kept to move around prison

ATTACK THE COMMONWEALTH AGAIN

29 August 1989: Commonwealth Bank, Noble Park, Melbourne
Take: $23,757

CHRIS:

Noble Park is not my area and I don't know it well but I just want to have a go at a different part of town. Why not, ya know?

A week or two before the job I catch the train to this far-flung spot in south-east Melbourne and have a look at it all — do my pre-operation planning: check out the roads, the angles, the other shops around, the cat and foot traffic, the ways in and out.

Not being my area, if I get into a chase with the coppers it's gonna be hard, but the bank's not far from the station so I decide to catch a train after the robbery.

On D-Day I ride to the suburb and steal a couple vehicles to use, positioning the secondary car at the rear of the car park — basically behind the bank.

The primary vehicle carries my work tools: a sawn-off automatic shotgun and a stack of plastic freezer bags. Over a set of regular clothes, I'm wearing an overcoat and trackie pants. I've got plastic gloves on, and the balaclava's ready to pull down.

With only a couple of minutes left before go-time
— high noon — a cop car's parked out the front of the
bank. But this is all about patience. Soon enough they
fuck off — kindly leaving me their prime parking spot.

I leave the car idling while my engine races.

Here we fucking go.

I storm in, a faceless, black-clad guerrilla,
shouting, 'This is a hold-up! Hands in the fucken
air! Now!' Some dickhead customer at the counter's
just staring with an attitude I haven't got time for
so I line up his face with the shotgun. 'You right
just standing there, are ya, ya fucking cunt?' I walk
straight up to the prick and his hands go north. 'Don't
you fucking move.'

Continuously sweeping the room with the business
end of the gun, I move along the line of tellers,
tossing over freezer bags to fill, telling them big
notes first and shouting at them to hurry, hurry,
hurry.

Some bastard's snuck up a set of stairs at the back.
Can't have that shit. 'You! You that's gone upstairs.
Get back here! I can see you hiding.' I'm burning up the
carpet going back and forth to get a view of him, but
in robberies time is the fucking master so I get my
focus back on making the tellers pack faster, faster,
faster. 'Hurry! Hurry! Hurry! Empty your drawers. Move
it!' A white cloth bag sits near a teller: the big stuff.
I've struck it rich — my timing's perfect. 'I'll have
that, too', I say.

While the sheilas scramble some bank bloke's just
sitting on his arse. Can you fucking believe it? 'Get
up, you fuckwit! Get up and help!'

Tick tock: on the job, I never have to look at a watch — me and time are close; I know how it moves; how it can seem to drag or seem to rush but that's just our moods and, actually, each tick of a second is exactly the same distance apart and no matter how crazy shit is I can fill that gap with a thousand things — I can live a thousand times a second on jobs like this where I control the floor, commanding fear and seizing the cash of this rotten state.

The alarm sounds — it's on, man. There's still time — still enough seconds — but the blare puts panic into the punters who are already reeling from shock. And panic is dangerous. Gotta maintain control. Gotta stop everyone, anyone, anything from disrupting my program. I spin and eyeball that fucking prick who gave me attitude on entry, and then point the shotgun at a petrified teller who hasn't produced jack shit. 'Fill the fucking bag! Hurry up or I'll blow your fucking head off!'

She crams more in.

'That wasn't hard, was it?' I take her bags and do the rounds collecting the rest.

Passing the smug prick on the way out, I let the menace in me rise and swell: the gun barrel with it. 'Gonna try anything, cunt?'

'No, no, no — not me', he says.

I growl at him, call out to all 'Have a nice day', and walk into the light, throwing the bags in the vehicle.

At the back of the car park I switch cars, driving just around the corner to where there's an upstairs flat with a parking spot beneath. Tucking the car in there, I pull off the overcoat and trackie pants, and

jam the shotgun and all the money bags — including
the white cloth one which isn't a big-note jackpot
after all but instead holds rolls of two-dollar coins
— inside a fresh sports bag.

The station is less than 100 metres from the bank
and I reach it before the police arrive. I don't see much
of the commotion, however, because I've timed it all so
that a train pulls in very soon after I do.

They won't be looking for the bandit on the train
so I just dump the bag beside me and smile at pretty
girls as we roll on towards Flinders Street Station.

—┼┼┼—

*This crime is unsolved until Chris contacts police in 2015 and
volunteers his responsibility. He is subsequently being charged and in
2016 pleading guilty in Melbourne Magistrates Court.*

AN ABSOLUTELY SHOCKING PIECE OF DRIVING

27 OCTOBER 1989:
ARRESTED IN FOOTSCRAY

Chris turned 21 three weeks ago.

CHRIS:

I have such hatred for uniforms, for police, for authority, for the state, that when I'm driving in my own car I won't even pull over for a routine stop in Williamstown at 1.30 in the afternoon.

I refuse, and what might have been a quick rego check or random breath test becomes an extended pursuit that builds and builds until eighteen cop cars and a helicopter are swarming me.

Lasting 24 minutes – the same length of time as my blood-soaked cage fight in Pentridge last year – it's a crazy car chase.

But not a very fast one.

I'm driving a clapped out ex-taxi with over a million k's on the clock and running on LPG. At one point I reach maybe 120 kilometres per hour but then the four-speed gearbox packs it in, the linkages for third and fourth separating and leaving me with only first and second.

A slow noisy chase is better than no chase at all, I figure, doing 80 in second. The engine absolutely screams, while all around cruise petrol V8 cop cars, with a chopper on top.

We wrangle through a swag of suburbs, but the coppers decide they've had enough as we enter a roundabout by Footscray Hospital and ram me into cyclone fencing.

My cab's a total write off.

And once they make sure I'm all right, they bash the shit out of me. My injuries are said to be from the crash, but since when does a crash leave bruises in boot-print patterns?

When this goes to court the next year, I get twelve to eighteen months for what Magistrate Paul Grant calls 'an absolutely shocking piece of driving'.

Well, it's been hard for me to get sustained practice behind the wheel, although Dad started me early – letting me drive at seven.

The police prosecutor reckons I went above 130 kilometres per hour but I don't believe that. Maybe the coppers did to get in front of me. He also tells the court that three police cars crashed during the pursuit and that I drove through red lights, cut across lanes, didn't obey stop or give-way signs, failed to indicate my intention to turn corners or change lanes, drove on the footpath, and lost control of my own car several times. The coppers who 'crashed' were probably the ones that rammed me.

The *Sun* newspaper writes it all up, quoting my lawyer about how the longest time I've been out of custody in the last seven years has been four months.

ToASTED

CHRIS:

On Halloween they put me in the old Melbourne Remand Centre on Spencer Street but I reckon I can get out with a toaster.

There's a perspex window in the unit outside my cell and getting through that will get me into position to abseil down to the street and get to a motorbike which has kindly been parked around the corner.

A Kawasaki GPZ1100, I'm led to believe it is, and a worked GPZ. I also understand that it's all ready for me with a full tank, sandwiches, a couple litres of drinking water, a radio, and a pistol. The goodies are in a gear sack. Unzip that and the keys should be sitting right on top. Some cunt better not steal it.

So I obtain a commercial toaster and fashion the heating elements to fuse together into a single file burner. When I

113

press this against the window, the perspex melts like butter. It's beautiful.

But when I pull the burner back, plumes of smoke billow up, setting off the supersensitive fire alarms they have here – even when I've got a vacuum cleaner sitting right on it sucking up the plumes. It captured a lot of it but some of the perspex melted onto the elements and that was hard to control.

But that's to be expected. I know to expect the call from control to the officers' station. I work until I hear the phone, then wrap the element in a wet towel and place it in a bin.

The officers call a fire check muster and I stand in front of the window, obstructing the screws' view of the burn. Then back to work, which sets off the alarm again and once more I shield the thermal incision from sight.

I'm that close. The bike's waiting, I have extension cords ready for the abseil, and with just a tiny bit more cutting I'll be able to kick out the window and go.

But the alarm goes off for a third time, and there's no hiding the black, burnt mess of a window.

The screws are having a fit, but nothing directly links it to me. The vacuum cleaner is out on the landing so I'm not in possession of it, nor am I in possession of the bin and the burner in it.

Where things don't look so good is how I'm always standing directly in front of the window.

So, under investigation for an attempted escape, I'm taken to Pentridge's H Division.

IN THE ZONE

1989–91:
PENTRIDGE

CHRIS:

The prison authorities can't prove that I had an active role in the toaster incident – although they bloody act like I am guilty – so I get sent to remand in D Division, and then H for a while before settling into the 'behavioural' zone: B Division.

This period starts in March 1990.

Violence.

Never before in B Division history was such a spike in assaults reported. Ambulances are attending daily at one point to collect those who need to be stretchered out, sometimes twice a day.

The muster in the wing is about 100.

And I am at home in the zone.

I'm in a crew of four, all young, all hectic, and we are feared by many even far-older men. The four of us – Kevin Miles,

Jamie Whelan, Steve Jackson and me – are independent, we're equals yet ready any time to gel together in combat formation.

We make the old guard of hard knockabout crooks nervous. I would suggest that many of them are also on the payroll, led by the likes of supersnitch and killer Keith Faure, who years later would openly implicate anybody, police included. He even lagged his own brother, Noel, over the 2004 shooting of Lewis Moran.

I'm working in Pentridge kitchen. The activities officers in the compound next to the kitchen can't work out why the gym billet uses the vacuum cleaner to 'sweep up' the concrete floor for us.

Truth is, the vacuum cleaner is full of stolen meats and vegies from the kitchen. With the vacuum's wheels squeaking and wobbling under the weight, the billet would transport the food, which I'd already chopped and prepped, safely past the metal detectors of the guard post at B Division's entrance. Too easy.

When he delivers it at the end of exercise time, it's all ready for the pan and then I arrive right on time to cook up a proper decent meal.

The screws can't work out how we eat so well. Security tries their best, but even they concede that once it's in the pan, we earnt and can eat it.

Maybe they are also reluctant to start something when four of the most problematic inmates in the wing are sitting down at the table eating. We would rise to any challenge from them and they know it.

DEEPER INTO THE ZONE

Two of the grubs on the payroll, Nick Levidis and Chris Stone, attack me with an icepick but I take it, stab them with it and then charge into their putrid peer group with a pool cue, cracking everyone within reach until the screws tackle me.

The staff have tried to reason with us. Head Office is putting heat on them about the level of assaults plaguing the wing. But our response has been: 'Go tell someone else what to do, not us.'

The majority of casualties at this time are lesser calibre inmates. They dilute our hardcore gene pool. They weaken the population of B Division. We have to defend our pride.

Worse than gronks, the prison is dropping snitches in B Division, playing us off against each other; pouring petrol on the adversarial madness of 'us versus the system'.

We feel the need to defend our pride and as a result, it's chaos for new arrivals. They have no hope at all.

If they're not vouched for, they bleed.

Even though the staff know that I couldn't have taken the icepick through the metal detectors and they saw me get it off those two clowns and use it in self-defence, they send me and – even though I was acting solo – my whole crew to H Division.

READING THE CHARTS

Prison is a flow chart. Inmate classifications dictate movement up (towards more of what passes for education, work, space and relatively mellow people), movement down (heading past more hardcore and disturbed inmates on the way to solitary) or sideways (same shit, different postcode).

Sentence management panels have a big hole at the top into which justice and prison staff fling such tasty ingredients as the prisoner's offending history, history of escapes or attempts, record of violence inside, drug and alcohol history, mental state, and age.

So that's the past and present down the hole. Now they throw in a bit of risk analysis to spice it up and keep it interesting.

So they ponder what risk the prisoner poses to prison security, the community, himself, herself, any other person or the 'good order' of the correctional facility.

After all that's digested, out plops the fat turd of your prisoner classification.

Anyway, today I wear a zip-up top to my classification review and sit across the table from prison managers Kelvin Anderson and Brendan Money.

After enduring sufficient blah-blah-blah-blah I unzip and bare my t-shirt, which I have duly inscribed with a logo reading, 'Eat Shit & Die'.

Division Staff are ordered to forcibly remove the garment, leading to an argy-bargy very much inconsistent with the 'good order' of the prison.

Both of these gentlemen take a lasting dislike to me, I believe, carrying such sentiments into high places: Anderson rising all the way to the top of the tower as Commissioner of Corrections Victoria, while Money goes on to be Victoria's Director of Sentence Management.

I am 22 years old. When I am more than double that, when I am nearly 50, Mr Money will still be at the top of the flow chart, the grand-fuckin' poo-bah of a system that keeps me in solitary confinement for years on end.

How much shit can I eat?

PRISON SLANG: LESSON FOUR

Classo – where you get your security classification, E: someone who has escaped before

Bronze up – to cover yourself in excrement

BRONZING UP

Chris is turning 22.

CHRIS:

I've entered a radical phase and the staff are now desperate to get out of H Division, clogging the system with transfer requests.

The governor of Pentridge, Clive Williams, has even intervened, telling me that we have reached a truly alarming state of affairs.

No argument from me.

You see, I'm indulging in wayward levels of bronzing up. That on its own would be more than many officers can bear, but it's not all: I'm actively engaging prison staff with human faeces.

Let me explain bronzing up.

I save my shit for a couple of weeks in milk cartons. The older stuff goes to one side. The fresher stuff I piss in, get a bit of a mixture going: make it more or less runny depending on what consistency, what kind of spray pattern, I want.

I get some just right for warpaint, for soldiers putting on the camo. If it's still too hard I water it down a bit more with piss.

My dress code is sunglasses, jocks and a pair of runners.

I open the cartons I need and my body adjusts to it. It takes twenty minutes to acclimatise to the smell.

Now I do this: I put the fucking camouflage, the warpaint, all over me like I'm an Injun.

All over me because then they don't want to come near me: they don't want to grab me; they don't want to bash me – because they'll get covered in shit themselves.

I would never put the fucking old stuff on – that would cause me to gag.

So the old stuff is the ammo: the stuff I use as grenades to throw at the screws.

It has reached the point where if screws catch a slight scent of anything remotely suggestive of shit, they refuse to open my cell.

On one occasion, I'm bronzed up and the whole wing can smell it. When the staff move them past my cell to complete a run out into the yard, some are dry retching.

The officers think they can talk to me and maybe negotiate some way out of this, so they open the trap in my door.

Yeah, right. I slip a hand out so they can't close it, then start flinging shit nuggets in all directions. I also have a cup of shit piss-watered down to the consistency of runny mud, and I give it a mighty flick, sending a brown splash across the wing and collecting anyone in range.

A couple of the officers have to go home.

Some start keeping spare uniforms at work, and they sniff the crack of my door every time I'm to be let out. I have them clamouring to get a transfer out of here and walking on egg shells until they can. One flat out abandons his post, going on extended leave and developing a Serepax habit.

My favourite line to use on the guards was plagiarised from the IRA: 'You gotta be lucky every fucking day; I only gotta be lucky once.'

+++++

In these months, BADNE$$ is born.

Contrary to 'the-wanker-called-himself-BADNE$$'-line pushed by parasitic keyboard jockeys like *Underbelly* author John Silvester, other inmates give me the tag.

The view in the division is that there is Good, there is Bad, there is Badder, and then there is BADNE$$ itself. Me.

+++++

The gates to the community open again. Direct from H Division to you.

+++++

Footnote: each member of our group were released from H Division into the community. Everyone would reoffend.

Kevin Miles jumped counters with me; Jamie Whelan went down for murder; Steve Jackson opened up with an assault rifle on what he thought was a police car.

They are all now dead. I am the last.

If this is life.

BADNE$$ AT LARGE

10 JANUARY 1991:
OUT AND ABOUT
Chris is now aged 22.

CHRIS:

I'm wound as tight as fuck. Fuelled by hate I run amok – me against the state. Within a week of getting out, I'm catching up with Kevin Miles. I decide to pair up and we scout his part of town – the Dandenong region – selecting banks to rob. I have the guns and a bulletproof vest.

Two weeks to the day of release, we raid the Commonwealth Bank at Glen Waverley.

Using a stolen motorbike, I drop Kevin at the rear exit and then ride along the bank and park at the front, leaving the bike idling.

We're at each end of the bank.

We head in, both in helmets and overcoats, my automatic shotgun strapped over my shoulder by a modified holster, allowing me to let go of it and even ride the motorcycle with it dangling by my side.

卌

We strike again within weeks, hitting a Westpac at Keysborough in Melbourne's southeast, this time switching back to a car in order to vary the MO.

卌

A few weeks after that I'm working solo once more, holding up the State Bank at Noble Park.

卌

As Easter approaches I am short of money. I select my local Commonwealth Bank at St Albans, being familiar with the area and the branch – especially after that fruitless attempt a few years ago when they'd already locked up.

It's a busy Friday when Kevin and I pull up out front – hard not to get noticed in balaclavas and overalls.

We park the car on an angle at the corner kerb, still running, and enter the crowded bank. Kevin starts clearing the tellers while I stay at the door to control the floor.

I spot a group of locals, older Slavic men – Croats, Serbs, Macedonians and others – who meet every Friday while their wives shop at the market.

They're crossing the road from the bus stop to our car, trying to be heroes, trying to steal our car and shut us down.

This situation is hard to control. I have to keep an eye on Kevin and watch his back, but I'm also leaving the bank a number of times to shoo them away from the car.

So I yell to Kevin to abandon.

We return to my dad's place in St Albans soon after, and he tells me about the robbery – as he too was caught up with friends there. It's his social meeting spot. Turns out our next door neighbour was also in the group.

Talking about it with my dad, my dad straight away tells me I did it. I have a laugh with my neighbour when I get charged over it later on.

I have only been out of jail for about three months. I'm hectic, to say the least – involved as I am in high speed police pursuit on the Geelong Freeway.

Riding a motorbike, I deliberately overtake six police cars and exit the freeway soon after having lost them.

But Mick Doohan I'm not, smashing head-on at 140 k's into a car parked on the nature strip.

I crawl to the closest house and lie under a carport, my knee wrecked, and can't move when the lady of the house sees me. A crowd is gathering, having heard the smash. She rings an ambulance but the police arrive first. I can't walk at all.

I'm arrested and they ask for ID. They don't believe the fake name I give, and as I'm taken to Footscray Hospital for a knee reconstruction they call in cops from all surrounding police stations in the hope that someone will recognise me.

Eventually someone pegs me for Barry, but then he doesn't have tattoos and I do, so they finally nail me as Chris.

While I'm still in hospital, Kevin drops by to plead for access to some of my weapons.

My arsenal is extensive and expensive, including pistol grip machine guns with silencers.

He tells me he has dramas with people in his area, and asks for something to protect himself with. So I reveal where they were buried in plastic plumbing pipes, telling him to just take one and leave the rest.

Unbeknown to me, outside in Kevin's car is his junkie mate. Kevin knows I hate this mate with a passion. They go to the weapons cache, which is off along a creek and off a dirt track, and they take them all.

Plus, while they're there, they decide to dump the guns used in the last robberies. Kevin was supposed to have destroyed them by now but instead here they are and he's tossing the bag of them less than a metre from the riverbank, leaving them barely submerged.

The guns are found by the next person walking past – a guy giving his dog some exercise. He reports it to the police and they seal off the area.

Matters deteriorate even further when Kevin doesn't even use the weapons for personal protection but gives my precious personal modified and silenced machine gun to his junkie mate to use in a bank robbery. The gun is highly recognisable on camera.

Hungry to score, the robber sloppily leaves his prints all over the car he uses, which, when it's found, will direct the police to him and he will then lag everyone he can, including Kevin and me for the stick-ups that Kevin has told him about.

At the same time, Kevin, who still has my cache, selects an assault rifle for his protection at home, and leaves the rest with a friend.

Kevin has started a relationship with a local gang bang slut from the pub. Soon he wants to show off to her, so he talks her through all our robberies and even tells her about my recent solo job.

This is not how I operate, I should point out. My girlfriends of the past knew nothing of my business. Nothing at all.

Kevin and the gang bang slut have a drunken domestic; she shits herself, takes the assault rifle to the police and reveals everything she knows about both of our activities.

Now I have huge problems. Kevin gets in touch to say that he has a little heat on him and while he can't return the guns he can tell me where they are.

So, on crutches and wearing a knee brace I hobble out and fill my car boot but then find fencing around the creek that I used before, so back home I go to rest my leg and think about what the fuck to do.

I don't get long to think. The next morning, the Armed Robbery Squad raid me, wrench my knee to torture me, beat me in the face and head, and charge me with the solo job at the Noble Park State Bank. They also have my arsenal, including the machine gun that they know was used by the junkie they arrested just days ago.

I'm now facing sentences of several years, with a Major Offender classification. Very shitty territory on the flow chart.

I would like to add that I have nothing against gang bang sluts – the world is a better place with them – but not everyone is for talking business with.

HOLIDAY ON THE APPLE ISLE

MID FEBRUARY 1991:
LAUNCESTON

Early in 1991, Chris was out of jail and raiding banks again. He was also at the tail end of a relationship with 'Lucy', by all accounts, a decent and law-abiding young woman.

Here, Lucy describes taking a Tasmanian holiday with Chris, Kevin, and the woman that Chris calls the 'gang bang slut'.

STATEMENT FROM LUCY:

I am 21 years of age.

I have known Christopher Binse for the past seven years as we went to school together. We have been going out for the last four years.

I was aware that Chris was released from jail on 10 January 1991.

At the time he got out of jail he was hard up, he didn't have any clothes and he borrowed a couple of hundred dollars.

I actually didn't loan him the money but I gave it to him.

With that money he bought a new pair of runners.

For the first two weeks after the 10th of January we saw each other every day. He was staying at my house because my mum was on holidays.

At the end of January or early February, Chris asked me if I wanted to go away for a weekend to Tasmania with a mate of his, Kevin Miles.

I asked him how we were going to pay for this trip because I couldn't afford it and I thought that he wouldn't be able to afford it.

Chris just said, 'Don't worry about it. I'll take care of it.'

At around the end of January 1991 I noticed that Chris had a lot more money than what he had before.

Around that time I remember that we went on a shopping spree where he bought shoes, jeans, tops and other clothes. He probably spent about $1000 on clothes that day.

Chris started taking me out to restaurants and he spent money on flowers and a card on Valentine's Day.

I asked him how he had come to have so much money because I knew he didn't work and he was on the dole.

He would say to me either nothing or, 'You're better off not knowing.'

I had suspicions about where the money had come from. I thought that the money had come from Chris committing some kind of crime or stealing it but Chris never came out and told me directly.

On Friday the 16th of February, 1991, Chris and I left from Chris' house at St Albans and went to Melbourne

Airport. At Melbourne Airport we met Kevin Miles and his girlfriend.

We went to a restaurant and then to a bar at the airport.

Kevin had the tickets for the plane. It was a bit of a rough flight.

We went to a hotel that had a casino in it but we couldn't get into it for some reason.

We eventually booked into the Launceston International Hotel. The hotel was luxurious — something I couldn't afford.

When we booked in Chris asked to be booked in under my name.

We went out to a nightclub and stayed for about two hours and then we all walked back to the hotel.

Kevin and his girlfriend went to their room and Chris and I went to ours. We ended up having an argument over something fairly petty and I just blew up.

I rang my mum at home and asked her to organise me a flight home. I went to the airport but it was closed so I went back to the room and slept on and off until about 7.00 to 7.30 am.

We argued again and he said that I might as well stay and he offered to pay for another room.

I told him to fuck off and I flew home that Saturday morning.

Since the Tasmanian trip I have only seen Chris on two occasions only for a short time and one of those times was when he was in hospital after a motorcycle accident.

ALONG COMES ROXY

1991:
METRO VIP

Amidst interstate jetsetting, bank jobs and associated headaches in 1991, Chris was a man about town. Here he describes meeting Roxy, a woman he would love, who would be his Bonnie to her Clyde, and who would betray him.

CHRIS:

We met at the Metro VIP nightclub in Melbourne in 1991. She was in a group of girls that come from the same area and I was in a group of boys that come from the same area. They all knew each other except Roxy [name changed], who was new to the girls' group, and me, who was new to the boys' group. We left because there were undercover coppers tailing one of the blokes that I was with, Steve Barci, who I later bumped into at St Vincent's 'cos he got shot by the coppers.

At the nightclub they were hounding him; they were sitting off him, and I said to the bloke, 'What the fuck?' 'Cos I picked up that they were coppers. I was there with a mate called Smiles, and I thought, 'Fuck these cunts.'

What drew my attention was one of them was wearing an old cardigan with a younger bloke next to him. They were drinking at the bar and kept looking over, and I said, 'Smiles, what about these cunts?'

The younger bloke picked up a bag that had a little bit of residue of coke in there and he's sniffing it. I said to Smiles, 'Look at 'em.'

He said, 'They're coppers.'

'What?'

'They're coppers, man.'

'I thought they were a bit suss.'

'They're tailing Steve.'

I go, 'What?'

'Yeah, they're fucking tailing Steve for the armoured van.'

That was a job he did before the airport project. He hadn't been charged at that point. I go, 'What the fuck?' and he introduces me to him! And I'm doing jobs myself! 'I'm fucking out of here. Fuck this shit.'

One of the sheilas, Roxy, stood out 'cos she was cheeky, she had attitude, she was cocky, she was cute, she was good lookin'. She goes, 'Oh, my name's Roxy.'

'Oh yeah.'

'I'm a thief!'

Who introduces themself as a thief? The attitude! And she was flying. We were all flying. I had ecstasy. She was on trips.

So what's happened is I'm leaving, and I say, 'They're coppers over there.'

She goes, 'Yeah?'

'I'm fucking going. I don't need to be here. I don't want them to see me. I'm gonna go.'

'I'll come with you, too.'

We end up going to another nightclub and then to a motel.

She was the closest I got to a Bonnie and Clyde thing. She was the driver on a couple of robberies. Roxy was full-on: had a lot of balls. Just an average driver, though, not a rally driver or nothing. She drove because she was female and if they're looking for two males then they're not looking for a couple. So she was just a decoy, really.

Roxy was a professional shoplifter at the time, and she used to make a stack. Three grand a week in cash. She was working with another bloke. They had a lead-lined bag to get the goods past the detectors. He'd carry it while she looked around and bang, she'd slip in the clothes or whatever they were taking. All designer label stuff, all boutique stuff, all brand new and everybody wants it. They'd get a third of the retail price.

I was actually in love with Roxy.

LAGGERS BEWARE

21 MAY 1991:
BACK TO MRC

CHRIS:

My latest spell of custody starts in Pentridge's D Division hospital to treat my torture and bashing injuries, and then I'm off to the Melbourne Remand Centre where it's made clear that they haven't forgotten about the toaster incident.

Here in the MRC, I catch up with the junkie who lagged Kevin and me. He's big-noting himself about 'his weapon', showing everyone the bank security photo.

His body language tells me how nervous he is in my company.

He overdoses twice in a week. One time he turns blue and has to be revived, later telling prison officers that I'm somehow to blame.

Apparently as a result of his drug use, the junkie is moved

to Pentridge, but he can't escape the rumours of his role in my legal matters.

He is severely bashed. The prison officers have inmates line up for him to identify everyone involved in the yard attack. He lags them and then goes into protection, from where I have never heard of him emerging.

HONOUR AMONG THIEVES

CODE AND PRINCIPLES

From a 2012 letter that Chris wrote to Matthew Johnson, the prison gang leader who beat Carl Williams to death with a metal bar from an exercise bike.

CHRIS:

Honour among thieves is something enjoyed by all those who share, respect and practise the Code.

They live by it and they enjoy it.

Those who fail to meet the Code and to abide by it; those who don't respect the values of the Code; those who shun it; those who breach the rules, THOSE WHO LAG, do not live in the world of Honour.

Those who shun the values of the Code and DO NOT live in the world of Honour cannot expect Honour to be given in return.

No double standards; you are either staunch or you're not.

So don't cry foul when people apply their acts in return. Accept it.

Karma, I say, is now done unto you.

Note: sex crimes are no crime of honour and cannot be respected. A sex offender, a sex predator, belongs in the bone yard.

INTERNAL AFFAIRS

1991:
COUSIN MARKO IN QUEENSLAND

It's hard to know what to say about the circumstances surrounding Chris getting bail in September. Without being defamatory.

Interested parties might want to ask Internal Affairs for an off-the-record briefing. Ask them for their honest opinions about the two Armed Robbery Squad detectives that they filmed picking up a stash of cash from the St Albans house of Steve Pecotic, where Chris lived when legally at liberty. This unorthodox pick-up of hitherto unrecovered stick-up proceeds takes place before the police stop well short of 'strenuously opposing bail', as they say.

Chris alleges a number of things about them, including that one of them suggested that they come to a mutually beneficial arrangement concerning hold-ups.

Going to Internal Affairs doesn't exactly endear him to the Armed Robbery Squad – dangerous people for outlaws like Chris to be coming up against at the best of times.

Initially, he settles down into a quiet life with Roxy. Here's how he describes it.

CHRIS:

I am bailed and back on the street. The Armed Robbery Squad is raided, including their homes. They are not happy with me at all. They want me dead.

No way am I going to do any armed robberies now. So me and Roxy start to shoplift professionally to generate easy earnings to live on. It's what she did before and we make a few grand a week. Less risk and we live comfortably.

As part of the Internal Affairs investigation that led to charges against the detectives, a couple of IA cops went up to Queensland for a chat with Chris' cousin, Marko [name changed], nephew of Steve, who is now ailing from heart failure. Internal Affairs were interested in a chat with Marko because he had visited his relatives in Melbourne during some of the time in question and loaned money to Chris to help towards his bail.

The point of printing the following transcript excerpts is not to delve into the corruption allegations, but rather for what they reveal about Steve Pecotic and Chris' broader family, as well as about the enthusiastic and inclusive nature of Chris' approach to romance. And about that wild colonial lass, Roxy.

Internal Affairs: You don't mind if I smoke, do you?
Marko: No, you're right. I'll get an ashtray. I don't smoke, everybody else does. Filthy habit. What happened, like years ago, the old man was bashing the mother and it

was a shit fight and I sort of felt sorry for the kids and I went down there and I started working with Steve and then him and his mate were both gambling real bad and I was fitting aluminium windows with them and I wasn't even getting fuckin' paid. I was nineteen years old – I wanted to go out, you know. Get meself a bit of pussy or something, and I was working my arse out and they'd just piss off, go to the TAB and leave me on the job.

I sort of took a disliking to Chris because I had a Falcon GT and I caught the little bastard jumping up and down on the roof once. He was bad when he was fucking young, and he denied it. I sort of put up with it for a while. I still used to take him out and give him money, tell him that his old man give it to him but Steve never gave him a cent in their fuckin' lives, you know. And then his mother was telling me how he only used to go and see the old man to raid the ashtray in the car and that sort of fuckin' hit me home, you know. Fuck that, you know. That's just a sly little bastard. He's been a sly little bastard all his life.

I never fell out with Steve. Steve's got a good heart, you know, but he just hasn't got a fuckin' brain.

Internal Affairs: He's got a crook heart now, hasn't he?

Marko: You know what I mean. He's a kind-hearted person. He'll do anything for you. But he just hasn't got a fuckin' brain. Like he believes things Chris tells him, and I told Steve time and time again, 'It's an act of terrorism, mate.' I'll be in anything, I don't care, I'm not fuckin' straight, but to go and put a gun in some fuckin' innocent people's head, to me that's as good as an act of terrorism.

Internal Affairs: That's a fairly apt description.

Marko: I don't go for that shit.

I read that statement, you know. Apparently some kid's shit their pants in the fuckin' bank, 14-year-old kid, because a gun was pointing at him. If somebody done that to my kid I'd fuckin' blow him away.

You know I rode in a bike club for years. I've got two mates that fuckin' done an armed robbery. I said to them, 'It doesn't take no fuckin' guts. You want to talk? Fuckin' not women and kids, fuckin' innocent bloody people – hit someone else that's got a bloody gun.' But anyhow so then I sort of just got married. I went to Europe and I got married and I just sort of kept right away from it and then this year, or last Christmas, me mother went down there. Grandma was getting sick so you know, one thing led to another, she went down and then Steve laid the sob story on her how Chris is just in and out of jail and this and that and he's just going to go nowhere you know, he really needs to get away from that company and he's always taking the rap for his mates.

Internal Affairs: So you spent most of the time in the Remand Centre when you went down and took your wife and the kids down?

Marko: Like I said I never took them shopping or anywhere while we were down there. The whole 13 days. Because by the time I got up in the morning, like I used to get up at 7, I'd drive over and pick Steve up, right; by the time he scratches his bum and read the paper and had breakfast and that, then we drove to the Remand Centre. Got processed there, had an hour visit whatever it was. I drove him back, the day was gone. I never took the kids into the city, never took them to the zoo, never took them nowhere. Most of the time I was at the Remand Centre.

Internal Affairs: What car did you bring back?

Marko: The white Fairmont of Chris.

Internal Affairs: Why did you bring that back?

Marko: Because he owed me money. I could not see him getting out for 15 years. That was going through my mind – armed robbery: 15 years. I read the brief and said to his old man, 'Fuck it, right. They were my savings; it's part of the child endowment money. I'm going to go and get that car.' They kept hiding the car and I went around six o'clock one morning.

Internal Affairs: Who's they?

Marko: Oh that Roxy and this other fuckin' hippy looking clown, wears all them fuckin' tigers and shit on his bloody nightgowns. I had to fuckin' drag him out of bed at six o'clock in the morning and took the car.

I don't know what's wrong with his head. [Lucy] stuck by him and he went and gave her a miss for this bloody lezzo, that's what she is, she's a fucken lezzo. Getting all kinky photos taken; that's what we had a big blue over.

Internal Affairs: You and him?

Marko: Well, I showed his mother. He asked me to go and move the photos because he didn't want the cops to get them because he thought they might make fun of her or something. Anyhow I said to Barry, [let's] go and get those photos and as we were pulling them out and havin' a look through 'em, his bloody mother turned up.

'What are you looking at?' she said.

'Bloody look at this shit, you know, have a look at it,' I said to her. So then she couldn't wait to tell him. I said, 'Jesus Christ, the whole family's fucked . . . All you've done is just caused a big stink.'

I had a mobile phone; I went and sold it because Chris kept calling me on it from a remand centre. You don't need that sort of bullshit. You know what I mean? You don't need it.

Internal Affairs: What was he talking to you about?

Marko: He was just abusing me and cursing me out and he said, 'Oh, how would you like it if you had photos of your wife?'

I said, 'If I had photos of my wife? Mate, you're fucken sick.' I said, 'If you respect that woman you wouldn't have fucken photos of her. Not with another sheila anyway. You just don't do that sort of shit, you know what I mean? It's all right when you're 17, 18, [and] you've got some sheila or half a dozen you're fucking. Some bloke! You know what I mean? You go through all that. But she's supposed to be your fucken girlfriend.'

She's having it off on the fucken couch with another sheila in a motel unit and here he is sitting there fucken snapping away.

Internal Affairs: Well, there you go.

Marko: He needs treatment, that fella. He honestly does. He's fucked.

[Chris came up here once] I said I don't want no fucken heat on when you come to my place. I said, 'This is a small town, right.' The first night in town he goes and fucken brings a gin home, black gin, you know what I mean. Bony legged fucken black gin. My mates shouting him drinks, fucken drinks all night out in front of everybody, and I put heaps of young sheilas around the place, and their mothers. You know what I mean. No brains. Just a fucken idiot.

Dickhead threw a stone through a shop window, took an empty till and in the laneway he's using the car tool box to fuckin' get into it. Now has that got a brain or what.

Internal Affairs: Bit ordinary isn't it?

Marko: Like you've got to get real mad. I said to the sergeant, 'Are you for real? No one would do that.' And get caught by two civilians.

Internal Affairs: He's a born loser.

Marko: I hope you're not taping me.

Like I said, I can't sign a statement against him, you know what I mean. All I can do is fuckin' punch his head in when I get into him, when I run into him, if I ever get a chance.

BADLANDS

CHRIS:

After getting bail last month in dubious circumstances, I celebrate turning 23 today by hiring a limousine for a mobile party with a handful of close friends.

I've invited a trio of Italians that I'm mates with: Calibrese blokes from a good family. We call ourselves the amigos.

So they bring their girls and we get on the road, rolling joints to share and stopping first at the local bottle shop to stock up on Crown Lagers and champagne.

The limo driver plays reggae as we cruise the area. When we get the munchies I have him drive us to my local Chinese. The owner is locking the door as we arrive, but on straight away recognising me as a regular, he goes back inside and takes our takeaway orders.

The driver might now live it up with the rest of us, but later he'll lag, giving a statement to the armed hold-up squad – one that omits to mention his own copious consumption of drugs and drink.

卌

But high times never last and the death threats start. The Armed Robbery Squad want me dead; I'm sure it's them. And they do kill people so it seems too dangerous to stay here.

I flee interstate.

Meaning, I've absconded on bail and am now on the run.

While a fugitive, I move back and forth between Sydney and a 388-hectare Queensland property that I buy with cash. It's my base camp: my commando camp where, as a solja at odds with the oppressive state, I train for all possibilities.

I name this domain Badlands.

On a trip to Bundaberg, which is the closest airport, I spot Sir Joh Bjelke-Petersen. I can't follow the news all that closely right now but I know he's on trial for some criminal offence.

So, being a cheeky so and so, I go up and tell him I'm a big supporter and ask to have my photo taken with him. He's okay about it.

卌

The most wanted man in Australia poses with Sir Joh Bjelke-Petersen, while on a supply-run to Bundaberg.

But, as good as it is living up there, I'm a moth to flame.

Roxy and I go down to Sydney and hit the nightlife, spending every day and night in the Cross; we become part of the Cross.

She's bisexual so we have a smoke, coke, eggies, and hang out in the red-light district; we're regulars to all the strip clubs.

Weeks go by and sometimes the life I'm living hits me, how I'm living one day at a time; how I'm just one wrong moment from getting shot by police.

Knowing this has me seeking refuge at St Mary's Cathedral, close to the Cross, just across from Hyde Park. I turn off my mobile phone and enter, seeking solace and time out – peace from city life and peace from life on the run.

I dip my hand into the holy water, make sure no one is looking, and then bless the weapons that I'm carrying. I pray to God that I don't have to use them but if I do then at least they have been blessed.

Then it's from the sacred back to the profane, and the next thing you know it's six weeks later and we say, 'We need to get away from this shit; we need to get away.'

So we go back to Badlands to rest and recover in the wilderness.

Until that need to party builds in us again and then it's back to the Cross.

I'm in touch with the Amigos, but I am red hot and to hang out with them and have a laugh isn't possible in Melbourne. The Armed Robbery Squad is on a mission to catch me.

So from time to time I shout them an all-expenses paid trip to Sydney. First stop is Kings Cross and all the strip joints. I get blind on these fun boys' nights out. Roxy fumes about them.

One night we're all staggering blind back to our motel rooms, and I take them the back street route of the drag queen strip, knowing that in the many office doorways are hidden parties loitering in the shadows for customers.

To liven things up a bit, I pull out a .38 revolver and say, 'Watch this,' then start shooting in the air. Next thing ya know, all these scantily clad drags in fishnets and g-strings appear out of nowhere and run in all directions for cover.

I didn't expect to flush out so many: fucking funny sight.

The Amigos and I were still laughing about it decades later, back when I had the chance to join them for a home-cooked family meal.

I've started doing bank jobs again, by the way. In Victoria.

And because I'm cheeky I worked out how to time a postcard just right so it arrives at the Armed Robbery Squad soon after a job – if it's spot on then the afternoon they're getting back to the office after being called out to one of mine, or maybe the next day.

Either way, they get a cheery hello from BADNE$$ and I'm long gone.

I like playing with them.

Badlands needs a homestead.

I have a builder on the job but he wants his wages in advance. He'll be working hard because I'm keeping the costs down by cutting wood on the land instead of buying it all. But it's still going to cost more than I have.

So I decide to hit another Melbourne bank: the Westpac on Keilor Road in Niddrie.

Leaving an idling stolen motorbike at the rear of the adjacent post office, I walk up to the front and cut a side padlocked gate to allow us access to the front footpath, then turn left and proceed to the ATM area, both of us in overalls and wearing motorbike helmets.

I am carrying a sledgehammer with a .45 semi-auto pistol tucked into the top of my overalls. My comrade is carrying a pump-action shotgun. People are scattering. Trams pass by.

The window refuses to give way as I swing the sledgehammer into it as hard as I can, oblivious to everyone around me, until finally we shoulder it out of its frame.

We've lost the element of surprise, though, and precious time has been lost. The green bag due for pick-up by the Armaguards – who are now only 100 metres away – was visible but now a staff member has hidden it.

My role is to secure the bag, and smash open the inner safe-boxes: 'Nothing,' I yell.

My partner's role is to clear the teller drawers, which he has, now yelling at me to leave. But I refuse to leave without the bag.

Police sirens are getting louder and louder and as my comrade goes through the front door he is shot at by an Armaguard across the road. Lucky to be wearing my ballistic vest, he bolts back inside and yells at me again, saying to forget the bag and leave, and then runs out the front once more only to be forced back in by more shooting. 'Let's go!' he's yelling.

I've ripped open every secure cabinet in a frenzy, hunting that green bag that was out for pick-up – not realising that all a staff member did was drape a jumper over it. I feel I've let the team down.

We run into the field of fire, missed by the hopeless shots of Armaguard, sprint down the side and leave as the police reach the front. The Armaguard has emptied his revolver at us, endangering everybody near us, but we never returned fire.

Now this get the juices flowing, I kid you not. Running into gunfire is traumatic and once the adrenaline wears off, I need a big joint to settle down. Even thinking about this event later causes the jitters.

Given the need to calm the nerves, I catch up with an old mate who has pot. I get a bag of weed, and invite him back to our motel to blow some joints and crash there if he wants. He can see we're flush with cash and accepts.

I've decided to stay on the other side of town, out of my known usual haunts, and we arrive at the Doncaster Motor Inn and book a room for three days.

Helping unload my stuff, my mate can tell I'm agitated. He's never seen me like this before and asks if I am okay.

I've been shot at, I tell him: bullets whizzing past my head. I'm red hot and will be on tonight's news. He thinks I'm joking.

'A bank in Niddrie,' I tell him.

'Bullshit,' he says.

So I hand him the pump-action and say I need a huge joint to unwind. 'Don't play with it, it's loaded,' I tell him.

He places the weapon under the bed, rolls a joint which we smoke outside, and then we head to the bistro.

Watching the evening news of the robbery, I look at him. 'See? I told ya.'

We've placed our orders for dinner, but guests who've arrived some time after us are now being served. This annoys me.

'How are they fed and not us yet?' I ask a waiter. We're not happy with the service. In fact, I'm pissed off. I'm having a bad day being shot at and not getting the green bag and now a fucking argument over dinner. 'We don't want the orders anymore. We're leaving,' I say, and we do, causing a scene.

Unhappy back in the room, I decide to get out of here and we pack up all our stuff in the car, drop off my mate, and then check into another motel.

Going through the bag in the morning, I notice the pump-action's missing. My mate didn't have it when we dropped him off.

Fuck.

Driving back to the Doncaster Motor Inn we wouldn't get there until lunchtime, and room service will have done the room by then.

They'll have called the police, and coppers are going to know who we are from our photo and fingerprints. They'll know it was us at the Westpac and they'll lie in wait for us to return.

I want to go back now but Roxy insists on waiting, so we do.

It's getting dark as Roxy drives the hire car in. I'm in the front seat: machine gun locked and loaded.

A car full of blokes pulls out, passing us as we enter the car park. Roxy stops out front of the motel area, while I grab a pistol and climb the stairs. A metre from the room, I notice the door is ajar and the lights are on.

Opening the door with trepidation, I see the room has been turned upside down and there's fingerprint dust everywhere.

A caretaker putting the rear of the TV back together, spots me instantly and both of us are spooked. He knows who I am and he wasn't expecting me to poke my head in.

I am down the stairs in a flash, jumping into the car. He's rushing out also and running towards the bistro. 'Get the fuck out of here now!' I tell Roxy, and we take off, an incoming car full of men passing us by as we leave.

The Armed Robbery Squad had been waiting all day, saturating the area, with squad members even positioned in trees. The whole area was a trap. But right as we arrived they'd left, having decided to hand over to a replacement crew, but rather than waiting for them they left a two-minute gap in coverage.

That gap saved us from certain death – and maybe some of them, too, given that I had a full clip in my machine gun. God's will.

Due to the heat we leave Victoria the next day. But because I didn't get the green bag I don't have enough money to pay the builder which was the sole fucking reason for the robbery.

So rather than head straight home to Badlands I decide to strike on the way back, selecting a Commonwealth Bank at Sydney's Warringah Mall, which is a big shopping centre.

‡‡‡

During the robbery, I'm in control of the customers and the floor, while a partner clears the tellers.

Still shaken from being shot at the week before, Chris takes an Armaguard officer captive at the Commonwealth Bank.

An Armaguard officer is looking in through the bank's floor-to-ceiling window. Last week's madness flashes through me as I rush out and intercept him. No weapons when I pat him down and then we bring him into the bank. If his colleagues arrive then we're using him as a shield out.

‡‡‡

Poor bastard – I feel sorry for him. Turns out he thought he had flashbacks to 'Nam. He was a security guard, he walked past. But we'd been shot at by a security guard only the week before, you know what I mean? So we were still heightened and still affected by that. But I feel sorry for him.

╫╫

We make it to Badlands but I'm still short for the building work.

Roxy'll stay here this time but I've got to go back to Victoria to cash up or we'll never have a house.

I've chosen a target in advance for a huge haul. I'll fly in and out within a week.

I'm working with different individuals, some that will later on become well-established figures in the underworld wars. They know who; I won't say. I don't lag my coeys [co-offenders], good or bad earn.

But the target turns to shit, and I learn that the Armed Robbery Squad are terrorising all known associates of mine, desperate to get me. No one can breathe it's so hot.

By chance I see a clairvoyant who warns me of a betrayal from a close male friend with blond hair. Too many of them do, either all of their hair or blond tips.

The police are offering huge concessions for my arrest and for many people the heat I'm bringing down is affecting their lifestyles.

Meanwhile, motels and expenses and going to parlours blows my budget, so I decide to hit the State Bank at Noble Park again – the one I was arrested for and then bailed. Given the interest they have in me – and their terrorising of all my friends – this will send the police into an absolute frenzy.

I commit the robbery following the same routine, even wearing the same clothing. Plane tickets are paid for and I'm due to fly out within two hours of the raid.

I notify Roxy that all is good, and I mention to two close associates that I can't catch up later as I'm flying out: Kevin Miles, and Smiles, the bloke who I was with the night I met Roxy.

Rocking up at the airport, I'm wearing a singlet emblazoned with Public Enemy No. 1, I've got a bag full of cash, and the police are waiting for me in the departure lounge.

In the rear of the police car, one of the detectives turns and spits in my face. Later, he will turn Roxy against me.

It's the fourth of February, 1992. I'm 23 years old.

PRiMiNG To BREAK OUT

25 FEBRUARY 1992:
TRANSFER TO MRC

CHRIS:

I'm back in the Melbourne Remand Centre, comfortable in the settings and surrounds, but conscious that I'm under the ever-watchful eye of staff and snitches who'll score big brownie points for spotting any possible escape attempts.

It's five months out from my committal hearing. There's some big time ahead for what I've done and I'm not interested in doing it. I focus on working on my legal case, and such talk becomes a slippery slope to a small but trustworthy group of men who are all looking at big terms and all open to an alternative.

A weakness is identified in the accommodation units. The unit is locked down for two hours a week on Wednesdays, allowing inmates to use the gym.

Those that don't want to go to the gym can stay in their cell or go to the yard compound. There are no staff in the unit during the lockdown.

Being a communal unit, that allowed inmates from others units to visit, it was easy to hide in a cell, and when the staff have locked and secured the unit they leave without locking individual cells.

Then we'd have a good hour to an hour and a half in which to play unchallenged.

This same location was later the exit route for Archie Butterly and Peter Gibb, although they used explosives. My way is quiet and stealthy: no dramas.

Given we have three in the group, one will watch as the other two work in tandem on the holes that have already been burnt into the corners of each window, making it so much easier with serrated blades to cut the perspex and within minutes drop down into the recessed alcove garden off the street.

Timed right, those on the street won't see it. The street cameras are at the wrong angle for it, too. We just need the cutting tools.

We know security is pretty lax in a certain police lockup and we get shoes with blades in the soles to someone there who then does a switch with someone at court who then comes back here and now we have jagged, heavy pruning blades close to 30 centimetres long.

My committal is only a week away. We have timed it so that we will be gone by then or the week after. Vehicles have already been stolen to be left on the street as getaway cars.

The first day of my committal is adjourned to allow my legal team an extension to negotiate a plea in reducing the armed robberies from five down to three. This deal is far better than I could manage if I fight it before a jury, yet to accept this offer is still unpalatable. I cannot bring myself to accept the deal.

Kevin Miles comes into custody and his team led by Andrew Fraser try to negotiate a deal for him in return for him turning Crown witness against me. He is bailed and dead within a week of an overdose, leaving a suicide note, apparently.

Amidst all this, we focus on the escape. It's looking so sweet: we have all the tools. It's going to be quick with no violence – a really, really good escape.

But one inmate gets onto it. He know something's going on. He's watching us. Observing things. He's pretty switched on, too, this cunt, and he wants to try and jump in on it.

We say, 'No, we don't know what you're talking about.'

He starts telling us, 'If I'm not invited I'm going to do it myself.'

What the fuck? We don't trust him. We think maybe he's a spy. He's a threat so we have to remove him.

He lives in my unit – in my pod.

One of the two blokes I'm escaping with lives in the pod, the unit, that we are going from, and the other one lived in my pod.

It was up to me to deal with this bloke. I tried to advise him, to pull him up: 'Listen mate, don't be silly.'

He is persistent so I get some billiard balls, put them in a sock, run in, hit him over the head and really fuck him up, assault him and bang him up, thinking that if he's banged up good enough they'll move him.

But they fucking just move him to another pod in the same unit and so it remains a live issue and the screws know there are dramas.

A group of us go to confront him in a spot with no cameras down towards the gym – near the canteen. There's a group of us armed up with knives and stuff and he shits himself. He jumps the canteen counter and hits the duress button – the alarm.

So he basically lags what's happening, and they arrived thinking what the fuck's going on, why are you behind there? He doesn't say nothing but he is hoping that they'll search us. We are very lucky to get away unchallenged. But after that they must be aware of things. They lock the jail down for fucking three days looking for weapons.

Now the whole prison knows there are dramas. The screws are watching us. We can't move or nothing, you know. You can feel the tension. So I confront him. I say, 'Fuck this shit. We're going to seal a deal.' 'Cos there was a boxing gym in the compound. I used to box. I know the coach, a professional fighter, a really good bloke: Brian Levier. I say, 'Brian, the screws are this-and-that, you know. I want to sort it out in the ring under your guidance. You can ref.'

He goes: 'Yeah, no problem. Fine.'

So we jump in the ring and everybody's watching because all the units face off into the yard. And we go for it. It's a good scrap, too. He can fight; I can fight. I nearly knock him out a couple of times but, fuck, he is a hard cunt. He has a hard head on him and I don't follow it through. I hit him with a couple of combinations, but if I could just kept coming through I would drop him. But I can't.

After that we shake hands, and say that's it. Allowing everybody to see this, to recognise this, will take the heat off us.

But the next day the three of us who are going to escape are shanghaied for the good order of the jail because they find our fucking cache of escape shit.

Now, they don't find weapons because the weapons are in the fucking washing machine. We put the weapons in a bag in the machine on the last rinse so it was in the last spin. Nice clean blades. And when they searched, they didn't look there, but they fucking found the hacksaws and stuff like that secreted in a cell a couple up from me – very close proximity to me – in a little gap for electricity and stuff.

But things happen for a reason. There is a backup. Here we are in investigations because I've been tipped from this jail before for allegations of attempted escape. So they feel that I am a suspect. The three of us get moved but within two weeks we are cleared and so now I start on Plan B.

BREAKOUT

CHRIS:

Within a fortnight we are cleared of links to the seized items. Nevertheless, we're unofficially deemed guilty as sin and sent to Pentridge.

Pentridge is pretty tight but I know that if I get injured badly enough to need a real hospital, they'll send me to the locked ward at St Vincent's, and security there isn't great.

We can bypass things and a gun can be smuggled.

A friend is going to stab me and he's going to do it in the showers to reduce the evidence. 'Just take it easy,' I tell him.

First one's in deep. Winds me. Second is bodgy; superficial.

But he's nearly killed me, the cunt.

The first stab severed the artery at the base of my spine. Went right through.

I nearly bleed out because it takes them fucking two hours to get me to hospital. What the fuck?

They're asking me who did it and I'm saying, 'Dunno. I was washing me hair and someone come in. Felt 'em punch me in the stomach and thought they were mucking around. I rinsed me hair and then see there's fucking blood, you know.'

But I nearly die. They finally get me to St Vincent's and have me on my deathbed. The prison investigators realise that this is serious because my blood pressure is very very low. To me it's all clear as day. I'm not scared of dying. If it's gonna happen it's gonna happen. Not even really thinking about it, to be honest.

They're saying, 'Chris, tell us what happened 'cos you're possibly going to die.'

'Listen, fuck off,' I said. 'If I'm gonna die I'm gonna die. Fuck off.'

And I survive.

My father starts visiting. He wears a chunky belt buckle that sets off the metal detectors every time.

But he's very weak from a disease of the heart. The guards assume it's just his belt again and they don't want to make him undo his daks every time. They're conditioned that way.

So one day he places a .32 calibre semi-automatic pistol under his jeans, positioned behind the zipper and buckle. There's no bulge. Nothing shows.

And he walks it in for me.

My father is dying and knows it and it is basically his last wish for me to get out. He wants me to beat the system; to fuck the system. 'Cos he hates the screws. He hates the coppers. He wants me to get back out, you know.

I am hoping to go to Croatia.

I have it here for three days. It's under me pillow sometimes. Otherwise nearby: always within reach.

You can't smoke cigarettes in here and I've got one bloke smoking in the fucking toilet, which could make 'em search the place. You can smell it. I say to him, 'Mate, listen, I'm going. I've got something in here and if this comes undone because you're smoking cigarettes I'll fucking shoot ya. If you bring this undone I'll fucking shoot ya.'

I asked if he wanted to come but no, he was going for parole. The other bloke in the unit was Steve Barci who the police shot at Tullamarine airport during an Armaguard heist. He was winged and I know people that are visiting him. I say, 'Buddy, if you want I'll take the lead; you jump in the slipstream.'

'Nah.' He is still terrified, still recovering from the SOG arrest. Traumatised. They shot him a few times; nearly killed him. They killed one of his coeys: Norman Leung 'Chops' Lee, the only bloke ever charged over the 1976 Great Bookie Robbery. He got off that but now he's dead. Barci doesn't want to know about my plan. He's not interested.

All right.

I am hoping that when they escort ya they don't search ya, so I'll have it concealed on me and we'll walk out, down the elevator, and onto the street towards the transport. Even if I'm handcuffed, I'll manage to pull it out and say, 'Give us the keys,' disarm them, and that'll be it. Know what I mean? That's my intention. That'll be easy. I didn't want to use it in the ward because I thought if they don't comply I might get trapped with things escalating out of hand.

But there are no beds available in the hospital ward at Pentridge for some time. And here is my father waiting in a vehicle around the corner. He spends three days just fucking sitting there in his car waiting for me.

And there is another car parked nearby with the keys hidden in it. I am going to run to that, and drive it to a second location where my father is. Then we'll go to a safe house.

The escorts are done between nine o'clock and four o'clock, I tell him. So for three fucking days he gets there every morning and sits there all fucking day. I'm trying to get there but there's no fucking beds at Pentridge and no fucking escort happening. So I tell my visitor, 'Listen, fucken this is going to happen tonight. My father's been waiting there three days in a row. I'm going to call it. I'm gonna pull it between such-and-such and such-and-such time.' So he will be there waiting for me.

The officers come in. One officer sits in the ward with us and another three sit in the security box. And there are couple of nurses in the nurses' station.

One of them is in the corner of the room. I have to walk past him to go to the toilet. Sometimes, because he is at a bit of a distance in the corner, he comes and sits amongst us to watch TV. That's what he's doing.

Five minutes before I decide to time it he fucking gets up and goes to the corner so I've got to fucking lure him back. I make out I'm going to the toilet and as I come back I walk up and show him the weapon. My back's to the box so they have no vision. I just pulled it out and say, 'See this, fuckhead? Be smart; listen to what I say. You got a family? Think about your family. You wanna go home? Do what I say.'

He knows me. He knows my history. He knows I am serious. He goes: 'Chris, you don't have to threaten me. Tell me what you want me to do and I'll do it. I won't fuck around.'

'All right. Come back to where you were sitting and I'll explain to you.' And he does, so I say, 'Listen, you're going to get up; you're going to tap up to make out you're going to the toilet or make a coffee and I'll follow not far behind.'

He gets up; he taps up and there's like an airlock. There's one door open into the airlock where there's access to the control room. The control room's very thin perspex, maybe four millimetres. So he's got up there and I've got up there slowly and they're not looking at me.

There is supposed to be two other screws there. Two of them had left their posts, and one of them happens to be Maggot – if he was here, he would try to fucking challenge me.

With one of the guards, someone keeps tampering with his car and making the alarm go off, so he keeps going downstairs. Don't know why Maggot has left his post.

I'm bending over and I've got the dressing gown on, thongs on, and I've got the gun in my hand but I'm holding my stomach because I have a stomach wound. I'm leaning over getting a drink from the tap as the door's opened and all of a sudden, bang, I'm in action.

Within four quick steps I'm up to the first airlock door. It's open and I'm pointing the gun at the first screw's head. He's like, 'What the fuck?'

I say, 'Now open the fucking other door. Don't fuck around.'

He realises. He doesn't even fucking shift. He doesn't take his eyes off the gun. Just his hand moves to open the other door.

Bang, I'm out.

I run down the stairs but because I am in a rush, adrenalin pumping, I lose my bearings and run past the car that has been put aside for me and I think, 'What the fuck?' and run through the Exhibition Building. I know how to steal cars, you know, and there's an XD panel van parked there.

I break the window, steal it, drive through the barrier gates, meet my father and dump the XD. He drives us to another location.

We have drinks and celebrations and a last dinner, and then I say, 'Dad, I've got to go. There's too much heat over this.' He is rapt, you know. He is crook and I'm glad I say my goodbyes. I tell him I love him. Leading up to that there have been arguments between me and him over Roxy, because I was in love with her and he knew she was bad for me. But it doesn't matter how many people warned me about her, I still didn't listen and she destroyed my life.

So I collect the good stock of weapons that have been made available, say my goodbyes, hug him, tell him I love him, and I am on the road within a couple of hours.

I drive all night, reaching Sydney at about eight o'clock in the morning and get picked up by Roxy.

Maggot caused a lot of hate and evil in Pentridge so I suggested later on that he was involved. They thought it was an inside job 'cos two of the screws left their posts! What the fuck? But it just happened to be bad timing; it was just pure arse.

I said that he gave me the gun – a bodgy gun that I paid him ten grand for. And his wife just happened to buy a new vehicle soon after! So they thought there was some credibility in this and he was under suspicion for a long time. There was disciplinary action because he couldn't answer why he wasn't there. It didn't look good. I heard about this later on from the other screws. But I just thought, 'You fucking rat, you bashed us, tortured us, so you know what, mate? I'm gonna fuck you over.' They couldn't prove it but it gave him a lot of grief. And you know I didn't tell the story about Maggot giving me the gun to any investigators – I just said it to other screws, and it got back. So now they're talking amongst themselves and I know he was investigated.

MY AUDACIOUS EIGHT DAYS

8 SEPTEMBER 1992:
OUT OF CUSTODY

CHRIS:

Back in Sydney, catching up with my girlfriend. Holed up at her place which she shared with another couple. That evening her girlfriend answers the phone and the other end asks for 'Erica', Roxy's first name. But she does not use that name, she introduces herself to all as 'Roxy'. Smiles had this number and would send her dollars from time to time to help her out. Her girlfriend denies anyone of that name lives there, and asks, who is this? where did they get this number from? The caller refused to answer and hung up.

Only police call her Erica. This means the place is now compromised. We hastily packed up all that we owned and left that moment, going to a friend of hers named Bill.

The next week, I done an armed hold-up again. This robbery was audacious in any language, committed not even two blocks away from the Major Crime Chatswood North Police Complex, a smaller version of St Kilda Rd, jumping the counter, not out of hospital a week, a major wound still healing, clearing some ten odd tellers. I lost much time inside and I shot out the rear door to make an exit, expecting police to arrive at any moment as they would walk through the mall regularly during the day.

Bold as hell: B-ADNE$$ conducts a solo raid on the Commonwealth Bank, just a stone's throw from Chatswood's major police complex.

Avoiding the arrival of police increased the excitement; that was all part of the challenge. It added fear/danger to this crime done alone by myself in a major shopping centre 180 metres from a police complex. So perverse indeed. It 'excited me'.

(There were far more easy targets around I had ignored.)

Bill was a fencer of stolen goods.

We leave Bill's, all our bags packed up ready to depart the state that day. We're driving to a car lot – we had a car to pick up, had left a deposit on it already days before, and needed to do the robbery to pay the balance off and swap the one we had that was in Roxy's name – when the state protection squad intercept our car.

I had pulled over so Bill could catch up to us across the traffic lights.

Bill was behind us in a two-car convoy to the car yard. He was also picking up a car I paid for, how he was able to drive off in his clapped-out bomb blowing smoke was beyond comprehension. They'd watched us leave his driveway not

50 metres away. Inside the house was a high risk arrest to them.

The State Protection Group knew I was armed to the teeth, all the military weapons loaded ready to go. Their ballistic vests were no match for these weapons at all. So they let us leave the safety of the house, watching what was carried – a small bag placed under the front driver's seat containing the .32 auto pistol used in the escape. Safely out of reach whilst driving observed.

The risk of now making an arrest was dramatically reduced as hands were seen driving, and any attempt to go for the pistol would be noticed, unlike inside the house.

Bill set me up for arrest after I gave him five grand from the armed robbery I done the day before, to buy a car. Great mate he.

He won huge brownie points with police as a result.

I was arrested by the NSW State Protection Group on 16 September 1992.

I was only hours away from leaving the state headed for Queensland and found with assault rifles, including the modified one used in the Warringah Mall robbery nine months before, this unique weapon becoming an issue in my defence at trial.

JUMPIN' OUTTA PARRA

1992:
CATCHING UP

ANNETTE:

I heard he was arrested and taken to Parramatta.

Steve was shattered. After all that, after all the risks, for Chris to be stupid enough to get captured again. It completely crushed Steve.

When Chris escaped from St Vincent's he was the proudest father on the earth. Now he was extremely depressed and withdrawn.

Chris contacted me, asking me to go to Badlands, up in Queensland, to collect the guns he left in a cave and bring them back to Melbourne.

I said, 'Not on your life. You're compromising me. I am not going to be doing that.'

Then he said, 'Well, you can put it on the train.'

'Not on your life.' He just didn't think. I wasn't a member of his gang. I have a smaller child to think of, too, and I'm not a Ma Baker type. I said no, I'm not touching them, not at all.

I was curious to see the property, though, and I could discuss the sale of it with the agent.

The fellow I was seeing at the time, John, came as a relief driver, and Wayne, who was only little, came too. Steve agreed to look after my dog while we were gone.

We visited Chris on the way up. When we pulled up in the car park at Parramatta jail I recognised Chris' voice. He was calling, 'Mum!' from an upstairs window. 'Mum! Hey Mum!'

When I got inside for the visit, do you know the first thing he asked?

Not how are you or how's Dad or anything like that. He said, 'How many doors did you walk through?'

Unbelievable.

I said, 'What? Don't tell me. Not again.'

'Ah, Mum,' he said in his gravelly way. He leaned close: 'I've already got the hacksaw.'

I was stunned. He did my head in. Still does. 'I don't want to know about it, Chris, and I don't go counting doors when I walk into places.'

Badlands was so remote that to get there I had to first see a real estate agent in Bundaberg who knew the way. It was about 100 kilometres west of Bundaberg – the nearest town was Gin Gin – and you had to go up bush tracks and over little creeks. I would never have found it so the agent led the way in his vehicle and we followed him to the property.

There was a little doorless shack on Badlands and that's where he lived with Roxy.

Inside we found a double dildo. I'd never seen anything like it and I wasn't too sure what it was until John told me.

'You're kidding me,' I said. 'I didn't think they made double ones.'

Roxy. It was hers for sure.

John and Wayne played footy with it, kicking it around, sending it flying high in the air.

John was curious about the guns but I said, 'You can go and have a look. I'm not going anywhere near them.' I wanted nothing to do with them.

Badlands had a little creek where there was something like a small cave. Chris said that he had wrapped his guns up in blue tarpaulin and there would be guns in the cave. He didn't think ahead that when it was raining this creek would rise and flood the cave.

The weapons got rusty.

I don't know much about his life at the property or how often he went there because, to tell you the truth, I had nothing much to do with him at that time. I didn't like Roxy. Roxy and I clashed, like I did with most of them.

I could see the writing on the wall with that one: money and adventure, you know, notoriety.

As for John, he later gassed himself in a car.

CHRIS:

As big a headache as life on the run can be, it's never a relief getting captured. The whole point is: I escape to be out of custody. Getting captured crushes you. It depletes you. It takes all the air out of you. It takes the life out of you.

I'm shattered.

And on top of this, on top of fucking everything, I know that it will be affecting my sick father. He's in poor health. I don't want to dwell on it so I don't.

The only way forward is to escape. This is the thought that lifts me out of despair.

Within days I'm scanning the terrain for weak spots. I'm getting out. I know I can.

I meet a few good blokes and say to one of 'em, 'Mate, can we get out of here?'

He points out the reception, which we're overlooking from up here in 5 Wing.

If we can get out through one of the windows here, drop to the roof of the old store that stretches along below us, and jump the gap between that roof and the roof of the reception area, then we're past everything except for the main gate, which is left open.

Problem is there's a watchtower above us.

But in studying the angles, I can tell that if the screw sits in the tower then he has a blind spot: when we're right below him, he can't see us.

It's very audacious – a very audacious plan.

Roxy is bailed and visits, feeling bad that her fucking great mate, Bill, got me arrested.

She can help sort it out, I tell her. We're gonna crack this place pronto. 'Be ready for the move.'

I need hacksaw blades and the price of getting them in is negotiated down to a strip of Serepax and a hypodermic syringe.

Roxy has a nurse girlfriend who takes care of that side. The meds are taped to the blades and we're all good to go.

There's a park next to the jail; Roxy takes some dogs for a walk, strolling by, letting them sniff about like dogs do. When the screws aren't looking, bang: she throws four hacksaw blades and some zombie meds into the oval.

I had considered getting a gun but thought, 'Nah, don't need to do that.' Plus, the people doing the oval pick-up would be shitting themselves.

For this escape, I am going to have to hide in the wing and get access to the top landing's windows and grilled bars overlooking the newly built reception area and gate entry.

A few inmates are vouched for by someone who'd know. 'They're sweet,' he says. 'All on remand, and if there's a chance: all keen to go.'

'I'm good for cutting the bars,' I tell this small group. 'What I need is cover.'

We hang a towel over a rail to strategically block me as I cut the landing bar, and they're watching my back. However, there's a lot of movement in this area and the window is a favourite point for many to wave goodbye to visitors. I'm having to stop all the time.

In order to avoid the constant activity, I decide to hide inside the wing when all the inmates are supposed to be in the compound yard. It's a big risk not having someone to watch my back, but at least I'll get more done.

It's going well now that I'm getting in half hour blocks of cutting. At the end of each session, I patch up the gap with soap and paint.

I'm getting a nice smooth flow happening this time but fuck there's keys rattling; someone's coming up the stairs. I patch the cut and run into the nearest cell, tucking the hacksaw blades into the top pocket of overalls hanging on the door hook.

The screw's boots come to a stop out the front of this cell. Maybe he's seen me – the towel on the rail is only good for certain angles.

My heart's fucking racing; I'm holding my breath.

And he walks in. 'Not your cell, is it?' he says. 'You're the peda thief [prison slang for cell robber],' meaning he thinks I'm the putrid thief that's been active on the top landing.

I think to meself, 'What the fuck?' This offends me, I'm totally against that shit.

He starts searching me. Nothing. 'What are you doing here?'

'The bloke said I could, um.' At last my brain's starting to outpace my heart. 'Said I could lend some of his stick mags. Not a lot of privacy other times, you know.'

'You're here to flog off?'

I'm frogmarched out to the yard with a stern warning that if anything is reported missing from the top landing, I am to blame.

The officer also tells the wing sweepers and the inmates with cleaning jobs to keep a close eye on me because I am the number one suspect for being the peda thief.

Wasting no time, I find the bloke whose cell it is. 'Listen, mate,' I say. 'I'm not a peda thief. I was in there for a reason. I don't really want to tell ya but I will fucking tell ya because I'm up to no good and it's not stealing. Check your overalls. There's something there that belongs to me. I had to hide it, you know. I'm doing something. I had to duck in 'cos the screw was coming. I hear him and ran to the first cell, you know.'

He is rapt. 'Anytime I can help,' he says. 'Don't worry. If you want to use my cell or whatever – fine.'

This bloke will get bail in a week and then die in a car crash a fortnight after.

Now my cellmate has to vouch for me with the wing sweepers and assure them that I'm no peter thief. Last thing I need is them watching me, as they might reveal things to the screws.

I stop work for a few days to let the heat die down. The fellas are now realising just how close this is getting; I've cut completely through one end of the bar and I'm halfway through the other. Another third of the way and we should be able to bend it up.

The big question is, what then? There are some variables and some challenges.

First the tower and catwalk above us. The screw's blind spot only exists when he's sitting.

A second factor to deal with is the roof below us, which is going to serve as our runway. To get airborne we'll have to run down the 45-degree slope of the fucking rickety old slate roof, clear a half metre barrel of razor wire that extends along the gutter, and leap about four metres onto the reception roof, itself steep. Between the two buildings is a six-metre drop onto concrete.

Luckily, the reception roof is lower than the old store roof, so we can afford to lose a bit of height in the leap over. But then there's the razor wire to clear before takeoff. And anything we take with us will weigh us down; for me, that's sheets for the abseiling and a bag of civilian court clothes tied to my back.

There is also a tower further away that has a line of sight which, in turn, means a direct line of fire: tower guards have rifles.

A further headache is that when we've crossed the reception roof, we no longer have to pass through the internal gate – only over the inner perimeter barbed wire fence – but that gate is in constant use by transport vans and visitors and the guards there have handguns.

Audacious, I admit, but doable.

The other blokes, however, seem to be under the impression that we are going to fashion a ladder out of landing rails and use that to bridge the gap.

'It's a jump,' I tell 'em. 'Too much time working it; and too much exposure to the towers when we're on the bridge.' I don't want to waste one more moment than I have to or I'm going to get shot.

The general urgency to get out diminishes. 'Oh no, I'm going to get bail' or 'I'm gonna beat the charge.'

They all pull the pin.

The next step is to practise the jumps, so I go into training in the yard, doing countless leapfrogs and a stack of hop, skip and jumps. There are a lot of funny looks from both inmates and screws wondering what the fuck I am up to. 'Good to stay in shape,' I say, and 'I've always liked athletics.'

The supervisor's office summons me to inform me that Dad has died.

My arrest killed him. He was dying, I know, but that crushed him.

I'm guilty. He's died of a broken heart knowing that he helped his son escape and now I'm pinched on all this other stuff – what the fuck – and in a different state. Would have crushed him. Would have just put him on an absolute downer.

I'm conscious of this. I have regret. I'm responsible for contributing to his condition and now's he just lost the will. What the fuck, you know, it just killed him.

'Dad,' I'm saying to myself. 'I wish you had just held out for two weeks.' I'm lost. 'Dad, don't worry, I'll be out.' But he's dead. He died not knowing this. 'Dad, I'll be out in no time.'

Well, if I don't make it, then I'll be with him. And if I do make the jump and don't catch a bullet, then he'll be watching over me. He'll know.

I don't really care either way.

Now I have to make a rope for lasooing the ventilation pipe on the reception roof and swinging over the inner perimeter razor wire fence in no-man's-land, landing near the entrance of the open gate, hoping that no screws are out at the time.

D-Day: Saturday 24 October 1992. It's two weeks since my 24th birthday and it's 2.10 pm.

I wave to Roxy, who has parked a stolen Ford ute on the nature strip. It's facing me and the gate entrance because I calculated that it would take me ten seconds to reach the gate and if the ute also reaches the gate right at that instant, I'll just jump in the back and then we'll peel away and be gone. That's if I survive the jump and the guards and all goes well.

The car starts rolling and so do I.

Bar's out of the way and I abseil from the window, leaving the knotted sheets behind, basically waving a look-at-me flag to the towers. I land on the old slatted roof, walk the length once to size it up, then run and leap.

I'm on reception, momentum driving me forward instead of teetering back.

Crack. A shot, he's fucking shooting from the oval tower but I surge to the other side of the roof and out of his vision, loop the pipe, and launch out and over the inner fence. Except I don't – the fucking rope snaps and I crash inside no-man's-land. What the fuck? This is not working how it's supposed to. My adrenalin is just going off.

Fuck me, the other tower's got a clear shot from nine metres away and I'm scrambling over the razor wire fence, slicing myself stupid but it's go, go, go before bullets punch through me.

I land hard on the other side, sprint out the front gate and bump into a visitor, but Roxy has crawled the ute to the gate with perfect fucking timing and I vault into the rear, haul canvas over in case the towers are scoping me, and we're the fuck gone.

There's a gun waiting in case I have to return fire but I can't even pick it up, my hand and wrist are so fucked up from the fall; wouldn't be surprised if something's fractured. I have to go left-handed. Luckily on my commando ranch, I practise target shooting left and right-handed, just in case. I'm ambidextrous.

A short distance down the road Edward James 'Jockey' Smith (aka Jimmy Smith) is at the rendezvous point. We dump the ute and jump in with him, Roxy up front and me in the back. It's awkward getting changed with this wrist and some fucking nasty cuts, but all things are possible.

Yes, all things are possible. All fucking things are possible. Anything is. Everything is.

I feel like I've blasted into orbit. Inside I'm racing, heaving, revving, speakers turned to 11, braced for the impending sirens and helicopters, hand on the weapon for a possible last stand, but Jockey's driving really slow and nice – nothing to stand out on this lazy Saturday afternoon in Sydney.

'Daylight savings starts tomorrow,' he says.

BODGY SHOT

Years later the guard who opened fire on me leaves the job in Sydney and comes to work as a prison officer in Victoria. I actually meet him in Banksia [a unit at Barwon prison].

I remember his name 'cos I'd read his police statement. He says to me, 'I've worked in Sydney.'

'Yeah, really? Where?'

'Parramatta.'

'Fuck off! Now I know. Fuck, you made a statement. Were you in Parra when I escaped?'

'Yeah.'

'Were you in 5 Tower?'

'Yeah.'

'You're a fucking bodgy shot.'

'I wasn't a bodgy shot. The rifle was crooked.'

Jockey and I are mates from the kitchen at Pentridge – a prison he was capable enough to escape from without needing to get fucking stabbed. That was in the seventies, 'cos Jockey goes well back. A real old-school crim who abides by the code of honour, is Mr Smith. Interesting work history, too. A previous holder of the title, Public Enemy No. 1, he's had some good earns in his time and even did a little work with Ronald Ryan, the last bloke to be legally murdered by the state back in 1967.

Nevertheless, the stout little old-timer's impressed that I cracked Parramatta, especially so soon after landing. We have a good laugh on the drive north to his place up the coast at Terrigal. We're both Libras, our birthdays only days apart, and we get on really fucking well. He's happy to put us up, too – he knows the life.

'Here ya go, Batman,' says Roxy, dropping an open newspaper in front of me.

'What the fuck?' The photo of me is shit.

BATMAN PRISON ESCAPEE OUT AGAIN

Headline could be worse, though. And so what's everyone got to say: police are searching for a 'dangerous prisoner who escaped for the second time in six weeks.'

That's right, you bastards. I read it again, savour it, and now read it aloud: 'second time in six weeks.'

'Gets better,' Roxy says, squeezing in beside me on the couch.

Okay, let's see. 'Prison guards said the 24-year-old armed robber, Chris Binse, risked a six-metre fall to the ground when

he leapt 4 metres (15 feet) between the roofs of two buildings.'
I give Roxy a kiss. 'You read that bit?'

'Gets better,' she says.

'But it's a six-metre fall onto concrete. It should say concrete!
Why didn't they mention that? Fucking media. Some people
might think it was over the jail's swimming pool or something.'
I read on. 'After being fired at once by a prison guard, he
used rope to shimmy down –.' What the fuck? 'Shimmy?' I
say. 'I fucking abseiled. Who wrote this shit? When fucking
commandos go on ropes down buildings or outta choppers, are
they "shimmying"? What the fuck.'

'Wasn't it more like – falling?' Roxy says. 'Dropping like a
lead weight?'

'Hey, don't be cheeky,' I tell her, lifting my splinted arm and
draping it across her shoulders. 'Shimmying sounds more like
you getting up for a fucking wiggle on the dancefloor with that
fucking sheila in the Cross that night. You two were fucking
shimmying.'

'Keep reading, Batman,' she says, shimmying against me.

Okay, says my escape has sparked an investigation into why
an escape artist like me was in a medium-security prison instead
of a maximum like Long Bay. 'Unfortunately we don't seem to
have been warned about his history,' they quote a source in the
corrections department as saying.

Oh, here we go, the source has a bit more to say. My grin
must give it away to Roxy that I've found what she's been
hinting at because now she's laughing and cuddling in big time.

I read it out loud. 'There was no way we could have prevented
it once he got onto the roof. That 15-foot jump was bloody
monumental. He's got more testosterone than I've got, that's
for sure.'

Roxy nuzzles into my ear. 'Big-balled shimmy.'

'Hang on.' The article goes on about my 'extraordinary' escape just weeks earlier after 'organising a gun to be smuggled to him in hospital inside a cake'. What the fuck? A cake? Can't trust the media. Here we go, a Sydney detective calls me an 'escapologist', and says 'he's done a real Batman this time.' Thank you, officer. Nice to get a little respect where it's warranted. Of course the coppers have to throw in that I'm 'dangerous and unpredictable', warning the public not to approach me. What a load of shit, man. They're just angry 'cos I embarrassed the cunts.

I should clean my guns.

Oh, man, they're breaking protocol. Both Armaguard officers are out of the van at the same time. This is a one in a million, this is fucking gold – this is the jackpot. But we need a car, gotta have a fucking car. Where the fuck's Jockey? Can't see him anywhere. Still fucking around inside Erina Fair. I know we just came to study their movements, their routines, and then make a plan but they're both out of the van right now; I'm tooled up right now; that van's probably fucking creaking on its axles with fucking cash right now. What are they fucking doing? Cigarettes! They're both fucking out for a smoke – for a fucking dart. Fuck it I'll do it meself. He's lighting up right now so that means I got bottom four minutes, top maybe seven to fucking steal and position a vehicle and bail them up. Fuck I'm hotfooting it, but not too obviously, for the car park for any fucking car, for a fucking motorbike. Dad are you watching? I'm alive and at liberty and on the job and if you got any influence up there use it please Dad – there's a car, oh fuck too many people, why didn't I steal a car already, I should steal a car everytime I go fucking shopping just in case I see something, what the fuck man, keep moving, keep moving.

‖‖

What the fuck? The cops are telling everybody I've killed a bloke. The fucking coppers are putting my name to the murder in Sydney of an Armaguard officer picking up car park takings. Scaremongering the public to flush me out and set up a knock: shooting me'll now be justifiable. It's obviously bullshit, too. I've followed all the media. Right after it happened, after three masked bandits hit a van in Darling Harbour and shot a guard, the reports said the bandits were Asian. Do I look fucking Asian?

So now it's all 'Chris Binse the murderer'. I've spoken to a few mates in Victoria and it's all over the news down there, too. My fucking photo in the *Herald Sun* with headlines like, 'Escapee wanted over kill robbery.' They quote some fucking tool called O'Toole from the NSW Major Crime Squad, who calls me 'the most dangerous man in Australia,' and says 'He'll shoot it out if cornered.' Too fucking right, mate: with you. One on one. Yeah, I gotta lot of firepower and I shot out a rear door at Chatswood, but I'm not some desperate maniac escapee hell-bent on carnage to all. The truth doesn't matter, though, does it? Lying fucking dog. And it makes me fucking sick how the fucking media's sucking cop dick and then spitting out fucking copper spoof like 'we're more than 50 per cent confident' that it was me.

Well, fuck youse all. I can even prove it wasn't me. I've got an alibi. That job happened the day I was racing a ciggie around Erina Fair. I can describe everything I saw that day, even the brand of smokes those fellas had.

You know, fuck it. I don't have to put up with this defamatory bullshit. I'm ringing the *Herald Sun*. Time to fucking straighten some shit out.

Ha! Next thing ya know the *Herald Sun's* running a story called 'He's Not a Killer – Escapee's Mum'. And apparently a man 'claiming to be Binse' rang 'em. Fucking oath, I did. And yes indeed, I did 'strenuously deny' having anything to do with that bodgy robbery. Putting the violence aside – and I don't shoot people on jobs – would I stoop to robbing car park takings? Thirty G's split between a crew of three? Get fucked. As for shooting some poor bastard – not my style, as I told the newspaper.

Good to get that straightened out. And thanks, Mum, for sticking up for me.

Jockey's being a real mate but he doesn't need all the attention I'm drawing: his mercury is also rising due to some of his own enterprises. Any hint of me will give the police an excuse to run through his house and run through hard.

'This is fucked, man,' I tell him. 'I'm getting that much heat here I'd rather go back to Melbourne. It's too hot for me here, you know, with my face everywhere.'

He agrees and being the gentleman that he is, even gives me a sawn-off double-barrelled shotgun to take. Since getting shot five times the day after he was released in February, after a fourteen-year term, he well believes in being tooled up and ready. More of a loan than a gift, though, because he's planning to join me in Victoria when I get work lined up.

Melbourne's the last place the Armed Robbery Squad will be expecting me, but it's still a bit warm here so I accept Smiles' offer of the use of a property at Glenlyon, near Daylesford.

It's about an hour to Melbourne, it's on 40 hectares, and it comes with an old Italian fella who's the best cook ever. Suits us just fine.

Whenever I go to the city to scout possible targets I return with a bottle of scotch. The caretaker loves a drink and is great company, always decent to me and Roxy and even her yappy little chihuahua. He's good for a chinwag – although he never asks why I sometimes wear a wig. Keeps his curiosity to the odd quizzical glance.

Yet, to be honest, funds are low. I'm being financially supported by friends and I don't much like that. I feel better when I'm paying me own way.

I have a sawn-off shotgun, two handguns and a stolen car. All I need to earn.

First cab off the rank is the State Savings Bank at Doncaster Shoppingtown, right across from Doncaster Motor Inn with its shitty bistro service.

I've selected this bank after a promising recon. The tellers work behind old-style cages that go about three-quarters of the way to the ceiling, leaving ample clearance to go over the top and drop at the foot of the counting table. I know where the table is because, when I scouted the place, the staff slipped up, failing to fully draw the curtains that shield the table and the bank's stand-up safe from public gaze. It always gives me tingles seeing staff handling bricks and bundles of the good stuff.

Timed right, the safe will be open, and so will the inner drawers – meaning a sledgehammer will not be required. That's good: less to carry and my wrist is still weak.

The distance from the front door to the cages is just over three metres, so I can be up and over before the staff know what's going down, with the operation – including clearing the table and the entire contents of the safe – complete in less than 60 seconds.

Wearing a wig under a baseball cap, a blue plastic glove on my right hand, and a bandana ready to pull over my face, I'm on-site bright and early, loitering a short distance from the bank with a sawn-off shotgun in a shopping bag. There are no customers yet, just staff clearing the night deposit chute and opening and counting the leather deposit bags. The safe will now be open. Roxy is idling out the front; she is today's getaway driver.

Time to strike. An employee arrives, with a young bank staffer inside crouching down to release the floor locking device and admit him. Walk up behind the man, I ride his coat tails as he steps forward to enter. But the young fella inside sees me pulling up the bandana and reaching for the shotgun and the horror shows on his face even as he reacts instantly, shoving the door back at me as hard as he can.

The other man sees the shotgun pointed at them and joins in the struggle to hold the door closed long enough to lock and secure it. Normally in this state I could barge through ten office cunts but my wrist is twinging horribly and just doesn't have the power; I can't meet the pressure.

Everyone in there knows now what's going down – the staffer at the counting table slamming shut the time-delayed cabinet that must have a few hundred G's in it. Every fucking second is slashing my payday and drastically increasing the risk.

All I've fucking got to my name is a two-dollar coin in a stolen car with no fuel so when kicking the piece of motherfucking shit door doesn't work I level the gun, signal to the staffers to get the fuck clear and pull the trigger. Glass sprays everywhere but there's still plenty there and I don't give a fuck what's in the way anymore; I'm running through it and leaping up and over the teller cage to land exactly on point but 40 seconds too late to get all the bricks of cash that were so neatly stacked for me right before that fuckin' hero slammed the door in my face. The inside cabinets, treasury and time delay are all secure. But so be it; we're all just doing our jobs and today he did his better than me, so right now my task is to sweep the deposit satchels into the bag, charge out to Roxy and go go go.

Roxy and I blaze through a couple of fat joints of pot as we kick back with a few close friends and count the earn. A fraction better timing on my part and it would have been $440 G's, but even so I've taken $140 G's and there are worse days in the office than that.

Too hot for me to show my face at present so my mates run an errand for me, heading down to the local newsagency to place a personal ad in tomorrow's *Herald Sun*. Addressed to the Armed Robbery Squad, it simply announces:

BADNE$$ IS BACK

ANNETTE:

Badlands was about 100 kilometres west of Bundaberg and when I got back there I was supposed to call Steve to check on my dog. I was going to be calling Steve at his friend's house on the Friday night. It was a Croatian guy: they had dinner together there every Friday.

But when I rang, his friend said, 'Steve has passed away.' Steve had been found dead on his couch at home.

I tore back down to Melbourne, not knowing what the hell was going on and what's happening with my dog. When I got back I was told that Steve's body was going to be shipped overseas on his brother's authority, Rob's [name changed] authority, so I rang the funeral parlour and said the brother has no right: 'Steve has two sons: they have the final say in what happens to their father's remains.'

But Steve did want to go back to Croatia. So after I thought about it, I told them to go ahead.

They had a memorial service for Steve but I'd missed it because I'd still been heading back down from Bundaberg. And Chris and Barry couldn't go to it either because they were both in jail. Barry not for long – he was no Chris; he was never serious about criminal rubbish.

And then what do I hear all over the media? Chris has escaped. I felt stunned. Disbelief.

He hadn't been kidding when I saw him. He did it again.

The media is all, 'Australia's most wanted, danger man, public enemy number one,' and full of all the sensational headlines they could think of.

He did it again and it just did my head in, again.

I was in shock, again, and petrified, again, that he would get shot. By rights, having this son, I should be in the grave.

Funny thing was the police never bothered me. But they knew me by then – they knew I didn't have much to do with Chris when he was out – and they didn't raid me or come looking for him at my place.

In the end I think they felt that damn sorry for me. They'd raided me many times before when he was a teenager and he'd escaped from Turana. My phone was monitored and I was followed a few times but whenever he was out I hardly heard from

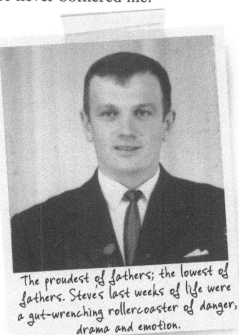

The proudest of fathers; the lowest of fathers. Steve's last weeks of life were a gut-wrenching rollercoaster of danger, drama and emotion.

him at all anyway. He did call me once when he escaped from St Vincent's, and I said, 'Stay away: it's very hot here.'

One day I noticed this car parked a little up the street with two guys sitting there in the usual sunglasses; they just give themselves away. I came out and brought them a cup of coffee each and said, 'I thought you'd be thirsty by now.'

'Oh,' one of them said. 'Thanks.'

'No point hanging around. He's not here.'

One day when Chris was on the run and a huge manhunt was underway – his escape from Parramatta sent them berserk and they were looking for him everywhere – one of my girlfriends was visiting, a German woman.

She was looking out the window and said, 'Someone's walking up your driveway.'

I had a look and here comes this Mexican-looking fellow with a moustache and all this black hair. 'Don't know him,' I said. 'What the hell does he want?'

There's a knock on the door and I open it and this guy lifts his finger to his lips and goes, 'Shhhhhhhhh.' I looked in his eyes: it was Chris.

My girlfriend nearly collapsed. He gave her a kiss and she said, 'I'll never wash that cheek again.'

He was that well disguised I didn't even know him, and I know my son. He just came in and called me outside to talk in case the house was bugged. My girlfriend was reeling with shock. I couldn't believe that he'd do that – he had such audacity.

DUST TO DUST

CHRIS:

'This'll ease you into a whole 'nother world, mate,' says the caretaker's friend, Rob, passing me a fat joint of his highly potent pot. 'And, darl? One for you.'

Roxy is plenty stoned already, but she's never one to turn down another pipe or pill or dance or drink, or anything else that's gonna take her to a higher place. Her eyes don't even seem to open but one hand curls vaguely in Rob's direction, glides by to take between her fingers the expertly rolled joint and plant it between her lips. Her head never moves from where it rests against the back of the couch. I don't think she'll ever move again.

'Migh' washa, washa movie,' she says, slowly floating up and wandering away. I'm not sure what she's talking about because the TV's right here. Tonight we've watched fucking every scrap of news we can: our robbery's all over the media.

There's always something weird, though, about seeing me own jobs on TV. It just isn't how it was, you know. Like the colours or the angles, or I don't know what, are just wrong. They've got to get in there, and not all filmed up from a corner in jerky bloody black and white silent shit. And fuck all that shit with a reporter standing out front of the bank talking all troubled and serious and then lapping up whatever routine shit the coppers serve 'em. I guess I find the bits where scared fucking customers or staff – people who were fucking there – say something about the shock of it, that's the bit I can relate to, you know. 'Cos it is a fucking shock, to me, too, ya know, the stress of it; I'm going through a lot of stress. Maybe not on the same scale as the victims. But the fear, the threat, it does something – seriously – especially if I'm by myself, like today, I've got to be aware of everything, of what the fuck's going on around me. Know what I'm saying? If I don't want to get trapped or shot in the back or whatever, I got to take everything in at every moment.

That's why I draw this joint deep into my lungs. To savour what's inside, savour all that's fucking happened, and then fucking exhale. Release the stress. Release the tension. That's how I step back from that edge.

'Saw a good job done on the telly tonight. You and Roxy, mate. What a team, ay. Bonnie and Clyde,' says Rob, sliding a bag of buds towards me. 'That should tide you over, but you need more just let me know. Don't hold back, all right? You deserve a good smoke after a job like that.'

This friend of the old caretaker's been coming round a lot lately. Unlike the old fella, who's retired for the evening, Rob's not shy of raising the topic of my work. I figure he should be okay, though, if he's allowed here but if there's one thing I miss most about Badlands, it's the isolation.

Sometimes up there it's like there's no one else on the planet – just me and Roxy living like the Garden of Eden: Adam and Eve with bongs, guns and sex toys. Peaceful, ya know. We're content.

Other times it's like, 'What the fuck we doing here? The action's all out there – let's go.'

I've been recreating bits of my Badlands lifestyle here: dressing in boots and camouflage for doing jogs in the bush. Rob's seen a bit of it, of my gear and interests. Sees me shooting left-handed the other day. Worked out all right, though, 'cos I was getting short on ammo and he come up with a bit of resupply.

Shifty cunt seems to have whatever I need.

'Use the Ford today, didja?' asks Rob, referring to the stolen car I've had sitting in the open garage until today. 'Easy to knock off, hey.' Observant fella, he even twigged to the front and back number plates not matching.

He's doing a lot to get on my good side, is Rob, and after another joint or two he mentions he has a mate inside a bank who reckons things could run sweet for a perfect earn. Rob even wants to get in with his hands on the tools, he says. Got a few handguns and knows how to use them – just hasn't had the chance to work and learn with a real pro.

'I'll consider it,' I say.

–‖‖–

I take Rob at his word and start planning the job. Through his friend, we'll know the timing of cash pick-ups, we'll also have keys for all the cabinets and drawers, and everything else an insider player can deliver.

'He's getting cold feet,' Rob says when I'm ready to take things to the next level. 'He's not comfortable.'

So it's sour. Next.

─┼┼┼─

Roxy and I still get out and about some nights. I'd say to meself, 'I'm not going to live as a prisoner in society.' So I'd go out and do what I wanted to do, I would just be a bit more cautious.

Roxy wanted to go nightclubbing, so I'd say, 'All right, but we're not going to go to the venues where we're going to bump into crooks, or off-duty coppers that will recognise me. If we go out, let's have a few eggies with your girlfriends and go somewhere different.' So we'd go to different venues; we'd still bump into people but at least there wouldn't be as many.

We're on the run but I'm enjoying myself. It's life, it's fun.

─┼┼┼─

Christmas isn't far off, and it's the peak of the calendar in terms of the cash movements at banks and in vans. Almost daily I'm in Melbourne researching multiple targets. My thinking is to lay low during this recon phase, then hit hard in a three-day strike period, and after that flee overseas as a very wealthy man. Promised Dad I'd go to the old country and I meant it, but fuck there's a war on in Croatia. Not sure I want to swap one set of armed men hunting me for another, especially when I don't even speak the language. But one day. One day. Maybe if I get a nice Croatian girlfriend who can teach me the native tongue.

─┼┼┼─

Strange things are happening, and I'm getting a bit suss. I've been focusing on two banks and an armoured van. Rob knew about the banks but not the van, and now both bank prospects have soured but no problem with the van.

What's happened is that bank staff noticed us observing them. They couldn't conceal how suspicious they were – in fact they seemed close to panic – no doubt because they'd been hit before in a raid that I'm a suspect in. It was clear that they were troubled by the sight of me. If I get made the police are going to swarm. I told Rob, we're out of here. We were followed by a male bank staffer all the way to Rob's car; the bloke even kept his eyes on us as we drove off, no doubt getting the registration.

I've kept Rob in the dark on the plan to hijack an Armaguard van because I've had to scratch three bank projects in a row now, and counting back three takes me to when Rob got involved.

Jockey's been in contact. He's in for the van project. I've also got a freelancer signed on: a good soldier who impressed me on a previous job. The three of us will make a tight crew. There's no room for error when hitting an armoured van. This is elite level. I've ordered machine guns and ballistic vests.

Given how much Jockey put himself out for a brother, assisting with my escape and then putting me and Roxy up for two weeks, it feels good to be able to put some work his way. Especially now that he's had to flee NSW. It sounds stupid but he got nicked shoplifting minor household appliances from Erina Fair, from Grace Bros department store, I think, pulled a handgun on the store security officer, and then carjacked shoppers to get away.

Makes no sense unless you've been to prison. Spend much time there and you'll completely understand where he's coming from. That kind of reaction – never give a fucking inch – builds up when you've been subjected to all the shit in prison, especially if you've done some big terms like Jockey has. He's spent something like 25 of the last 30 years inside. A man can't survive that if he backs down. That's not how it works in there, and what works in there becomes fused into you forever because it is tied to the survival instinct.

Look at my reactions: if I'm driving I won't stop for the police. It's us and them; that's what jail breeds, man. Everything about it is adversarial, and prisoners who've done it hard and survived are honest people; I'm an upfront, tell-it-like-it-is sort of fella. Instead of putting on a yessir-mask at classification reviews, I tell 'em to eat shit and die. This is how it is; this is the only way you can live in a cage with the hardcore, with killers and thieves. Show any weakness and you're a goner.

Jockey's made it to Melbourne by train but he has no transport. So I do a run in and check a few things, pick him up, and bring him back to the farm. It feels good catching up with someone solid – someone 100 per cent. Rob's still sniffing about, and he's very interested when we get back and I'm giving Jockey a tour of the land and facilities. Guess you don't meet people like Jockey every day. Me old mate and I go for a stroll and I point out a few of the bush tracks where I start commando runs, and some spots where I've been working on left-handed shooting.

There's a spare cabin, but Jockey says he has a property set-up about half an hour, maybe three-quarters of an hour, from here – although he has no transport and is basically dependent on people from Melbourne.

Tomorrow we're having a big barbecue here with lots of crooks coming and catching up and it would be best if Jockey had the use of a car to get himself home and then get back tomorrow for lunch.

'I can give you my vehicle,' I say. Only problem is that it's just a cheap one under a bodgy name and I noticed when picking it up that one of the indicators is hanging out – it's loose and I need to screw it in.

'Listen, I'll give you the car but I need to tidy it up. Or do you want the panel van?' I ask, showing him the Ford XF stolen from over Preston way that I've put aside for the Armaguard robbery. It's the most appropriate vehicle for the task. 'It's nice, neat, clean, full tank of juice; it's not from the area. Even has the keys in it. And it's a couple days old – they're not going to be looking for it.'

'Yeah, I'll take the panel van.'

'There you go – there's a car.' And I give him some clothes, some runners, some magazines, and all that sort of stuff. 'I'll catch up with you tomorrow,' I told him.

'Yeah, no worries,' says Jockey. He wants to get going before it gets dark so we head in and eat a bloody fine Italian dinner from the caretaker and then I see me mate off, watching him trundle carefully away – quite a slow driver, the old Jimmy Smith, as we sometimes call him. Anyway, I'll see him tomorrow.

Rob's rolling some really monumental bloody joints. Roxy's watching something again – she'll probably fall asleep with it on. I know I'm pretty wiped out. Just one of those days.

'See ya, boss,' says Rob, breaking me out of a semi-snooze.

When he's gone I strip off 'cos it's hot, get comfortable on a couch, and let sleep do its thing.

What the fuck? Squeak from the flywire door? Black silhouette, two metres away. In full war-mode I launch at the target, knocking the balaclava man off balance and wrestling for control of his pump-action shotgun: a furious fucking struggle as a mob of gunned-up shadows jam up behind him thrashing about to get through the doorway and join the mayhem and everyone's yelling and roaring as they work to get in at me but I bristle and expand with total driving survival rage, ramming the cunt back through the doorway into all of them and then spin and bolt for the laundry exit but I'm lifted off my feet by an oncoming wave of yet more of them pouring in from that rear door and I'm airborne, flying backwards until getting absolutely fucking slammed into walls and furniture as they swarm me and I'm planted on the floor under a screaming rage of boots and gun butts and grunts that light the world in crystal patterns of pain as they hammer me until I'm blanking out. Now they step off for a handcuffing and the weapon and accomplice questions and then identify themselves as police and rah-rah-rah-rah-rah about this, that and the other, none of which I really respond to beyond mumbling while releasing the build-up of blood in my mouth as I tilt over, trying to slow the cabin's unhinged spin.

Now that the Special Operations Group has its how-do-you-do's out of the way, the coppers start asking the only question that really matters to 'em before any other officers or services get on-site.

'Where's the money?'

'Don't know what you're talking about.'

Roxy. What are they doing to her? That's all I wanna know. Can't hear nothing of her: just police radios and sniggers about putting a few rounds through me. Roxy, baby, what're they doing to you?

'Where's the money?'

Don't ask about Roxy. Play no cards. Show nothing. Give nothing. Prepare for pain. Nothing matters. Prepare for damage. Nothing matters.

'Scum,' says the black mask. 'I'll ask once more.' He kicks me in the face. 'Hey, scum.' He kicks me in the face again. 'I think my colleagues would have a few questions, too.'

The crystals flash again and my heart is heaving and I can't get enough air and I'm bleeding, and it must be from the scalp 'cos there's so much pooling and smearing and splattering, or maybe it's just my nose and mouth, or both, or everything, I don't know, I'm swelling and breaking and twitching, and when have I ever done anything like this in my line of work you fucking cunts; you're just cunts; you're just cunts; you're just cunts; just cunts; just cunts; just cunts; cunts, cunts, cunts, cunts, cunts.

'Where's the money?'

Think you can fucking break me? Think I give a fuck what you do to me, man? Didn't see you in H Division at seventeen, you faggot piece of fuck. All you can do is throw people places you couldn't fucking handle. Or get your army together to torture one captured solja. I'm a fucking solja. I'm a fucking solja. Reveal nothing. Say nothing. Who cares about the fucking money or any fucking things, man. I don't give a fuck about things, about stuff – all I need is my pride and I'll lose it all if I say a fucking word to you. That's why I'm staunch, man. That's why I'm hardcore. That's why –

'Wha –' Have to catch my breath. 'Money. What money?'

A cold circle presses into the back of my head. Can't see what's going on 'cos my eyes are swelling shut and anyway I'm facedown in a red sea. Dad. You helped me fly at Parramatta. Live or die, it doesn't matter. Dad. The gun cocks.

'He was armed and raised the weapon in a threatening manner,' says someone. 'So you're a fucking hero for shooting this criminal scum. Saved an officer. Let's do it. We've got a throwdown to stick in his dead hand.'

'Get it ready because this, this disgusting specimen of criminal filth is going to be removed in a body bag unless he explains in the next fifteen seconds exactly where we'll find the 140 G from Doncaster. Check your watches boys.'

The metal circle grinds into my scalp. Normally I appreciate the smell of a well maintained handgun, a suggestive steely tang with a hint of grease, but all I can smell is blood. 'Fuck off.' He kicks me in the face.

No one shoots me, though.

'Get his hand on the table.'

They haul me across the floor and spread my hand on a tabletop.

'Have a look, scum.' With clear revulsion at touching something so rancid, someone grips my head and twists it towards what they want me to see: a cop who's flipped his pump-action around and is jigging it up and down as if he's preparing for a big downward thrust with the butt.

Oh.

White light. Voices fade, drowned by my own howl along a tunnel of hypercompressed agony. After time I lose altitude and look at the semi-severed end of my finger.

The police are furious. 'You fuckin' fool, Binse! Where's the money!'

Bit of gauze and bandaging and I'm deemed fit for questioning at the St Kilda police complex.

They start quizzing me about the Ford Falcon, the panel van. I'm being cheeky: 'Fuck, I don't know what you're talking about.'

They go, 'Listen, the Ford was seen at the property.'

I'm thinking to myself, 'Yeah?' I goes, 'Seen at the property, was it? You done a search of the property – you find it?'

'Nuh.' Then one of them says it was involved in a police shooting.

I go: 'Police shooting? Really? Well it's got nothing to do with me. It's not on the property. I don't know what you're talking about.' Then they start mentioning his name and I'm going, oh fuck, this doesn't sound good, you know: the vehicle, him. When they said his name I go, 'I don't know him.'

Then they said, 'Do you know Jimmy Smith?'

'No.'

'Do you know James Smith?'

'No.'

'Do you know Jockey Smith?'

'No, I don't know him either. I don't know who you're talking about.'

'Oh, you don't know who we're talking about and you don't know nothing about the car.' They say something to each other and one of them storms out of the interview room, comes back and throws the fucking *Age* newspaper on the desk in front of me. 'You don't know what we're talking about, hey fuckhead? Read that.' The front page is splashed with the photo of a body on the road draped with a blanket. Jockey's last stand, they're calling it.

It's got to be bodgy, right – doctored up or something.

I break down and cry. Lost for words and lost in time.

'So you don't know him, hey?'

I just sat and cried.

We'd been lagged, it turned out. Informants had tipped police off about the Armaguard plot and my location, and on Saturday they were sitting off us all day, sitting off me in particular. They had a forward observation post to keep eyes on the prize and monitor comings and goings.

When I brought Jockey in, they had no idea who they were looking at. So when I gave him the XF van they've seen that vehicle leave and they knew it was stolen but they let it go.

They didn't know who it was and they weren't looking for him. Little did they know, he was just as hot as me if not hotter.

He left at about eight o'clock, just on sunset. He's going through the town of Creswick; he's not really familiar with it; he's doing about twenty k's under the limit – it's a 100 k limit on the freeway there – and it drew the attention of the local copper who was by himself in a marked vehicle. It's Saturday night too, so maybe he's thought, 'Oh, he's had a few drinks; I'll pull the car over.' But first he rung the rego through and it was fucking stolen.

Now the coppers watching me hear this and think, 'Fuck, is he tuned in?' They didn't want to intercept the vehicle just in case he alerted me and it interfered with their arrest. They were worried that I had a scanner, which I did but I wasn't listening to it at the time because I was preoccupied with Rob, who would ultimately be revealed as a fucking police informer. Rob was setting me up, making sure I was stoned, had some pot, had some smoke, this and that. He was the last one to leave the property.

And he baited the dogs. There was no way in the world they would have kept quiet. There was a chihuahua, a little yapper, if leaves rustled he'd start going off his head; there was a fucking German shepherd chained up. I was the only person to let that dog off the chain in its three years. That dog was stupid. It was just a guard dog, and that's what they treated it like – just a guard dog. I don't think they even gave it a name. If anyone come down the drive it would start barking. It was like a warning signal to them. Plus, Roxy had her dog, Meg, and that was with her. They didn't get to Roxy's dog because she left the lounge room and went to the log cabin and Meg went with her.

The police interview me over my last State Bank raid, saying, 'Sign here, fuckhead.'

But they have nothing on me – except, it turns out, Roxy was seen and identified. They also know she's been involved in other robberies and witnesses have even placed her at Parramatta.

I refuse to confess.

They tell me to consider my position over the next 48 hours. If I then cop it sweet, Roxy won't be done for the bank job. If I hold out, then she will be charged with armed robbery and almost certainly spend a few years as a guest of Her Majesty.

The police give Roxy and I some us-time in the interview room. We make a deal: she will walk and I'll keep the funds from the robbery. The rationale being that I expect to be in for a very long time, whereas she has her freedom back and can move on.

I love her but she is a party girl, good for a good time, nothing more nothing less, and I don't expect her to wait ten years for me.

She has been living the high life as shared by me. At my side, she's spent over a 100 G's and owns a nice BMW that I bought her. When I was arrested at the airport about to fly out, she was in control of some twenty G's.

Spending by and on Roxy sent the funds plummeting, which was why I came back here to rob.

But she's fun. Real fun.

I'm not going to give the police my decision now. I'll use the full 48 hours. What's the rush?

BEDSIDE REMAND HEARING

Chris returns to St Augustine's ward at St Vincent's Hospital where he is transferred on 6 December due to his injuries.

Hello.

Where'd I go?

Been three months.

Nearly to the day.
Since I went away.
With a pistol.
And the will to.
Leave.
Now I'm back.
Whack.
What a dud.
Thud.

I kind of wish I was in the same bed as last time; you'll recall that spring-loaded week and a half that started with a stabbing and ended with the Last Supper.

If I was in my old bed, the one that I discharged myself from three months ago, and I was staring at the same dreary patch of ceiling, then for sure what's gone down would have to be some fucked up dream, and tomorrow Dad would come in and tool me up and I could start my run over.

But no.

I'm freshly hospitalised for injuries sustained when 'resisting arrest'. I need microsurgery to remake part of my finger and treatment for multiple head wounds, a broken nose, broken ribs, black eyes and severe bruising to much of my upper body.

Barrels, butts and boots. And another weapon: sound – the click-click-click-click of SOG officers cocking their handguns and pointing them at the back of my head.

Only after a couple of them pulled their triggers and I wasn't dead did I realise they must have unloaded, and this was just an inconsequential mock execution.

My survival was probably the least preferred option for many of the police. After all, they'd named the operation to capture me, Dust to Dust.

Well, fuck them. All their torture and bashing didn't get them what they wanted. Had the opposite effect: sealed me tight with anger.

Now the coppers probably have the farm sealed off under the pretext of searching for suspected explosive charges while they're digging holes like moles on speed in a desperate search for the proceeds. Greedy thievin' bastards.

The next day, a bedside hearing takes place before Magistrate Linda Dessau, who notes the obvious injuries, indeed she refers to them at a later court hearing that she presides over. On 8 December, Chris leaves St Vincent's.

PENTRIDGE HOSPITAL

CHRIS:

At Pentridge Hospital I have the prison staff notify the police that I want to speak to them, and for the love of my girlfriend I take the fall.

Within months the prison governor stops her from entering the jail on security reasons, ending what is left of our relationship. And she'd steal the 50-odd G's left from the robbery – money that I hadn't given up even with the SOG putting guns to my head and savagely bashing me.

So now I'm broke and in prison, while she has her freedom and the money and she's getting tight with my enemies. She even goes to police functions as some kind of trophy for them: BADNE$$' girl.

Talk about rubbing it in my face.

What's next? Her possible NSW charges done away with in return for giving evidence against me?

You got it. She also gets witness protection. Plus, she'll continue to reoffend but be saved on each occasion by agreeing to give evidence against me.

My mum always said Roxy was no good, and it turns out she was right.

I think I knew.

Loved her anyway. Roxy was good company. She was a laugh. She was a good sort. It's sad that she turned on me. It really is sad.

ANNETTE:

When Jockey was shot dead at Creswick and Chris was arrested I wasn't told anything, really. I had to work things out myself, or guess.

I couldn't stand Roxy and Chris knew that, and there was friction because I couldn't stand her.

Roxy was totally different to Chris' other girlfriends – bad in her own way. A very smart-alecky type. She lied a lot, too. They all do.

I went shopping one day and Chris had the key to my front door. I walk in from shopping and I find Chris and Roxy had been there. The lounge room was filled with all these boxes of expensive joggers. I was so angry; I told them I didn't want their lifestyle having anything to do with mine. I am an honest woman, I don't steal.

Another time I went shopping, I get home, go in the back garden and I find all these water pipes. I look at them and there were guns in there. Chris had brought them on the ferry from Tasmania. I contacted him and said, 'Get that bloody shit out of my garden. Now!'

I just didn't know what to expect from day to day. Sometimes I just couldn't cope. It was all too much.

ROXY SAYS

I am 28 years of age.

Chris flew up to Bundaberg with the handgun and money from the armed robbery in Sydney. Chris told me to pick up a BMW which he had put a deposit on some time earlier. He also purchased a Land Rover like a jeep. He purchased the jeep for the property in Bundaberg and put a deposit on the BMW. It was black, a 1977 model and two door.

I picked up the car the next day from the car yard and drove north towards Brisbane. I had only been driving for about 20 minutes when it overheated and I stopped at a service station.

I telephoned Chris and told him what had happened. He started yelling at me so I hung up. I ended up getting to Brisbane with the car by following some police from Brisbane. I saw consumer affairs and as a result ended up in Southport again with the vehicle for the repairs to be completed. After a day or two I decided to join Chris in Bundaberg whilst the car was being repaired.

I joined Chris in Bundaberg on the property that he had purchased, he left a couple of days later. Chris' property was named Badlands. Whilst he was there I saw Chris with lots of different types of firearms. There were big guns and handguns. The big guns he wrapped up in rags which he had oiled and then put into like an army bag. The ammunition was like in a metal toolbox. He hid these guns and ammunition in a cave on the property. I have since shown this location to the Victorian police and those firearms were missing although the tarp and box were still there. The small handguns Chris left in a biscuit container in the shack on the property.

I dropped Chris at Bundaberg airport in the red transit van. On the way back to the property I rolled the van. I rang Chris in Melbourne and he was very angry and threatened to kill me. I was very frightened and decided to get away from him and so I got a lift to Southport where I picked up the BMW. At this time I stayed with 'Mary'.

Whilst I was staying at Mary's place — it would only have been about a week — I found out that Chris had been arrested in Melbourne. During that week Chris spoke to me and apologised and told me to go back to Bundaberg and collect the handguns.

I did what he directed as I knew his temper and he was coming back. I returned to Bundaberg in the BMW, picked up about three or four handguns which had been in the biscuit tin. I put the guns in the tin in a backpack in the car and returned to Mary's place.

I was frightened that the police were after me and also frightened of Chris so I decided to take off to Sydney. Before I left I contacted a guy called 'Ralph' in Melbourne. He was the only person I knew to contact

— he was an associate of Chris. I was scared about having the guns and Ralph flew to Coolangatta and he then accompanied me to Sydney and I gave him the guns. These handguns from the property in Bundaberg are the same guns found at Pittwater Road on the 16th of September 1992 by the police.

I sold the BMW in Sydney couple of days after getting there for $3500. I decided to cut Chris out of my life and start a new life for myself.

I wrote a letter for Chris which I sent via a friend as I didn't want him to know where I was. I got a job in Sydney as a waitress and ended up living in Peakhurst with 'Jane', the girl who ran the business. It was about nine months since I had any contact with Chris.

Out of the blue I received a telephone call at home one morning. It was Chris. I asked him where he was, he told me that he was in Sydney at the central railway station. He just told me that he was out and to come and get me. I didn't think anything at the time.

I took Chris back to Jane's and introduced them. When I picked up Chris he told me that he had escaped. I was very frightened. I decided that I didn't want Jane and her boyfriend to get involved with Chris so I suggested that he stay with a male friend who knew nothing about Chris. I then borrowed Jane's car and drove to Pittwater Road, Gladesville, to 'Bill's'. Chris told me I think on this day that he had arranged for my white Sigma to be transported up from Melbourne. I introduced Chris to Bill but used another name.

I stayed overnight with Chris at Bill's place and the next morning I went with Chris to some truck depot out

Fairfield Way where we picked up my car. We returned Jane's car before returning to Gladesville. Chris left me and Bill's place. Bill didn't have a telephone and we went and used a public phone, came back and he told me he was going out. Chris left me for a few hours, taking my Sigma. This car was unregistered at that time but had been registered in my name in Melbourne. It was a white Sigma station wagon.

When Chris returned Bill wasn't home and he brought into the bedroom we were staying in a number of firearms and ammunition. I recognised the handguns from Bundaberg that I had last seen when I gave them to Ralph. There was also a number of other large guns. He put them in the bedroom that we were using. Some of the larger guns were still in boxes. I asked him where they had come from and he told me he'd brought them up from Melbourne in a car after the escape. I questioned him about the car as he had told me previously that he had caught the train but he didn't elaborate and I assumed he must have had a stolen car hidden somewhere.

The morning of 14 September 1992 — I recall this date as it was the day of the robbery — Chris went for a walk in the morning, returning with the red Laser hatchback. I didn't ask where it came from, it was obviously stolen. It was quite early in the morning, about 8 o'clock, that Chris got the car. I never asked what or why things happened as I was too scared of him. I thought that I had got him out of my life. But he was all controlling and rarely let me alone. I thought of going to the police but knew that I was in trouble myself.

When Chris returned with the Laser he told me to get up and dressed and that we were going for a drive. He ordered me to drive the car to Warringah Mall. I was wearing a white t-shirt and cream pants and Chris was wearing jeans and a t-shirt. I cannot recall if the ignition was pulled out or if I used keys to start the car but I followed Chris' direction and drove to Warringah Mall. I recall that I thought at the time that the car belonged to someone involved with the church as there were tapes in the car which I tested and it was all religious hymns.

After we left the mall he directed me to Chatswood. We drove around and then he told me to park in the Target car park. It was a multi-storey car park and I parked in a secluded spot. Chris said put a carry bag on the backseat. I didn't know what was in the bag but when I saw it there and he directed me to Warringah Mall I thought he was thinking of doing another robbery at some time.

After parking the car Chris told me we were going for a walk. We went to the Chatswood Mall. I waited for him, buying a drink, whilst he wandered off for a while. When he returned after about five minutes he told me to go to the Commonwealth Bank in the mall which was nearby and ask about opening an account. I remember that he also said words to the effect of, 'Go right down the back and check out the back door and see if it's open or shut.' Just like he'd asked me to do at Warringah earlier that morning.

I then went into the bank with Chris. I didn't ask him why. We walked in together and Chris sat down at one of the desks and I went further along the tellers stopping towards the end and enquired about opening an account. I remember being told to go to enquiries. I then walked along a bit further. I think there might have been a partition from getting up to the back door. I remember looking at the door and then I rejoined Chris and we walked out of the bank along a laneway down the side, back to where the car was parked. I told Chris that I thought the door was locked.

I returned to the car and got in and Chris picked up the bag from the back seat. He said, 'I won't be long.' He then left me. There was a pillar behind me and I lost sight of him.

I was pretty frightened as I realised that Chris was going to try and rob the bank. I didn't think he was going to do it straight away. I sat in the driver's seat waiting for him as he told me to wait. He was only gone a very short time, a matter of minutes. When Chris returned running to the car, I saw him at the passenger's door and could see that he was wearing a disguise — he had a black curly wig on and I think a cap on top. He was wearing wraparound ski glasses and a large men's green shirt and was carrying a gun which was cut down with two barrels. He was also carrying the carry bag. You know, one of those shortened firearms. He screamed at me to drive and to head back to Bill's.

Chris had got into the rear passenger's seat and was stripping off. I had to go around to get to the exit and by the time that I got to pay the woman Chris had jumped into the front passenger seat and was wearing the same clothing as before he had left the car.

I was quite panicked and I recall turning left out of the car park and that a four-wheel drive police car came up behind me with the **sirens** going. It reached nearly my car when it **suddenly** turned around the other way. I was quite panicked and I don't recall exactly what happened next. Chris was pretty quiet when the police car was behind us. I presumed the gun was in the back seat as he didn't seem to have it in the front.

On the drive back to Bill's, Chris told me that he had shot out the back door. He also told me that there were a lot of people in the bank and that we hadn't got much. He told me that one of the tellers tried to give him five dollar notes and that he had told the teller that he didn't want that 'shit'. He mentioned something about opening a bottom drawer.

We returned home. I was pretty dazed for Chris having involved me again. Chris went into the bedroom with a carry bag. I was nervy, shaking. I tried to relax, made a coffee and turned on the TV. I think Bill was home and I was just making conversation with him.

Later that afternoon Chris walked up to the local shops in Pittwater Road. I went and did some grocery shopping with Chris. I recall that it had a Liquorland attached to the grocery shop. I remember him buying Jim Beam, the green label one. The first I saw of any money was when Chris pulled out his wallet and paid for the groceries and liquor. I believe that he paid the bill with $20 notes. Chris also went to the post office and newsagent and bought envelopes. We then returned back to Bill's and I recall him giving Bill some money for rent.

I remember watching the 6 o'clock news. Chris turned it on and there was an item on the robbery at Chatswood.

When it came on, he looked at me and grinned. A short time after this Chris and I went into Oxford Street in Sydney. Chris had told me to drive the red Laser and I drove down a side street off Oxford Street. Chris told me to park the car. We walked up Oxford Street to the post office and I rang Jane who was expecting us for dinner. I told her we wouldn't be coming and she was cranky. Then we went and had dinner at an Italian restaurant.

The next day we went into the city and then looking around car yards for another car. Chris suggested to me that I sell the Sigma, as it was in my name. On 16 September 1992 Chris and I left the Pittwater Road address. I was driving the Sigma and we were on our way to St Peters to sell the car. Bill was going to follow us but he forgot his wallet so I pulled over to wait for him. This was only a short distance after leaving Bill's place and that's when we were arrested.

I am very frightened of Chris and I am prepared to assist police as much as possible as long as I am given adequate protection. He has threatened my life on a number of occasions, even holding a gun to me and I know that he is capable of carrying out his threats. I don't want anything more to do with Chris and I am making a life for myself.

ON JULIAN KNIGHT, HODDLE STREET MASS MURDERER

Chris dislikes Julian Knight, an inmate serving time for his 1987 killing of seven people and wounding of nineteen on the August night that he decided to shoot at traffic, bystanders and police around Hoddle Street, Clifton Hill.

Chris has lived alongside Knight, initially in H Division of Pentridge, where Chopper Read had let the mass shooter join his club, the Overcoat Gang.

CHRIS:

He's a fucking rat, a little coward, a fucking rat. He's lucky he's alive, he really is.

I had a few verbals with him down in H Division. He was in Chopper's gang, basically.

After Chopper left there was Slime Minogue [aka Craig Minogue, one of the Russell Street police station car-bombers]; Mr Stinky [rapist and double murderer Raymond Edmunds], Greg Brazel [serial killer, arsonist and former soldier], Olaf Dietrich [aka Hugo Rich, a con man, armed robber, drug mule, and later a murderer], and Dane Sweetman [Neo-Nazi and murderer]. And Julian Knight.

They were the skunks, you know. The Mutley Crew, I used to call them.

What's happened is Julian Knight starts getting smart one day in the yards and I say, 'Hey don't worry mate I'll catch ya.'

Within a couple of days they were doing a movement in the wing and at the bottom of the wing there's a tunnel that used to lead out to the yards. The first, closest yards on the right-hand side were the shower yards and everybody had to use those shower yards. Whoever was in the yard at the time would go there.

They were escorting him out and I spotted him. I jumped over the screw's desk, landed at the top of the stairs that lead down to the tunnel and ran about eight leaps, or bounds, on top of him. I've gone fucking bang with a big right hand to the back of the head – knocked him to the ground.

He's sprawled, he didn't know what the fuck hit him. I'm standing over the top of him and you could see he's dazed, like, 'What the fuck?!?' He didn't see it coming, you know. And I say, 'Hey, won't get fucking smart now, will ya, ya little cunt.' He's lucky I didn't start jumping on his fucking head. 'Got something to say now, fuckhead?' That's when the screws jumped on top of me. After that it's on my file, there's now alerts, and now I can't ever be where he is.

He was in Port Phillip Prison's back units one time and so I couldn't get out of management – they weren't prepared to put me in the back units with him being there. I can't get anywhere near him. He's just a coward, just a weedy little fucking rat. A little coward. Shooting fucking innocent people: women, older people, anyone on the road. And when he come up against the police he shit himself, surrendered himself, handed in the gun and cowed like a fucking little coward rat.

A lot of people hate him.

Well, more so before. Now they tolerate him, accept him. The system's totally different now. Before inmates used to have more morals and principles. The drugs have really fucked things up: eroded the ethics, depleted the gene pool. It's depleted, mate, from all the ice and all the other stuff, the bupe [Buprenorphine]: very similar to methadone but in tablet form. They're all on that, and if they're not on that they're on the ice.

Drugs have fucked everything. Julian Knight wouldn't have lasted before. They've let him out into certain sections of certain jails, controlled areas where he's under supervision, where the screws control that area with a lot of informers, and there's no real threats to him. Anyone that poses a threat to him they remove or they remove him. He's basically a protection prisoner. He's safe.

He's safe and he doesn't give a fuck about the people he shot. He's a fucking rat.

BEER WITH BARRY

One sunbaked afternoon in Sunshine North, I crack a beer with Barry, who can't help but know a thing or two about the underworld and prison life.

Barry shares Chris' assessment of Mr Hoddle Street: 'You're a weak cunt if you gotta hide from a distance and kill people with a gun.'

'But people want him in their club?' I say. Yet what a club. Something that's puzzling me is that within jail's pecking orders, I would have assumed that Knight would rank pretty low.

'How did he get to be in Chopper Read's gang? How does he fit with the others?'

'Well, Chopper Read is dead but the rest are alive. You'd have to ask Fat Minogue or Greg Brazel,' says Barry, who's not really into gossip. 'Both of those despise my brother because my brother absolutely hates them.'

I nod, wondering if, since Chris got dumped in endless solitary with too much time on his hands and no option of face-to-face blueing, these notorious killers have copped onslaughts of what Chris calls – with a chuckle – his 'poison pen' habit. Some very hardcore prisoners have eventually had to shuffle off to management to ask that Chris not be allowed to send them letters anymore, so inflammatory, condescending, and sometimes deranged they can be.

'Like Chopper and Minogue actually worked within criminal networks, right, and they act the part,' I say. 'Just don't see how Knight's like that.'

'He's not,' says Barry. 'But who knows what goes on behind a cell door. Maybe Julian Knight's a closet faggot. I don't know. Maybe he was sucking 'em all off, I don't know. Shit like that happens in there.'

UNCONTROLLABLE

1993:
PLANS TO ESCAPE H DIVISION

CHRIS:

From here to Badlands and back in three months.

What a loop: gained everything at the start; now I'm holding less than nothing. And another brick [ten years jail] will probably get stacked on top of what I was staring at before.

I have some fucking good memories from what's gone down but even they're fucking with me, partly because each one is served up with potent dose of regret and frustration.

I'm putting a brave face on it but I am destroyed. I'm this fucking close to losing it. So I don't want to think too much. Best for now is to zone in and deal with the shit at hand.

||||

'My heart goes out to Christopher Jergens' mother.' That's what Mum said in the newspaper when that other teenage Chris I knew hanged himself. That was, what – 1986? What the fuck? Six fucking years. Maybe H Division really is Hell and there was no other Chris – it was me who hanged himself – or maybe I didn't survive the stabbing; maybe I didn't survive the jump; maybe the SOG killed me. And I'm just going to keep waking up here forever.

I think about the obvious: that we would all leave, right now, never to return, if we weren't squeezed into the centre of locks and bars and guards and dogs and cages and wire and walls and clubs and gas and guns. It takes an army to keep this solja down.

Man, too much shit in my head. It's spinning me out. At night I can't stop thinking about getting woken up in the dark by black shadows rushing at me with shotguns. And then I think about that very fucking thought itself as a kind of black shadow rushing me. And then I think about black shadows rushing at me from everywhere, all hell-bent on my destruction.

Maybe I should give pot a miss when I get out.

But first things first: getting out.

Okay, enough bullshit. Take stock and make plans.

I'm in H Division which is adjacent to A, a section for well-behaved inmates (although more than a little blood gets spilt there too). But its classification means that A isn't screwed down so tight.

The opportunity that they have next door to get their hands on necessaries is, as I've discovered, also an opportunity for me, because if you look closely at the cells up the very end of H Division, the old sand grout between the bluestones is crumbly. With a little careful handiwork to enlarge the gaps and holes in the grout, slim but useful items of contraband could be passed from A to H. Items such as hacksaw blades.

But to what end?

Prisoners are locked in their cells from the afternoon through to morning. Overnight there is a solitary officer stationed in his box, armed with a .38 calibre handgun.

My intention is to cut the lock of my door and then to call the guard to my cell during the night. The bloke in the next cell will have removed one of the big bluestones between our cells and then come through. We'll both have knives and be in position to overpower the guard on his arrival.

We disarm him and get him to call the clinic, ask for the chief, say someone needs Panadol, so he and the doctor and the nurse will have to come to the unit, escorted by another two screws – who are armed. We'll get the jump on them and now we'll have all the keys. All the keys. To the fucking jail. We can get to any cell, any division, and we'll have three .38s.

I've been discussing this in our group, talking about it with those I myself trust and those who are vouched for. So one guy is going to stay behind. He doesn't give a fuck. We're going to leave him a .38. There's a few people we don't like and he's going to clean 'em up. Julian is one. We're going to open the door to people we don't like and people we want to release. You know what I mean. Whatever we want to do.

So first up I need to be in a rear cell.

Every two weeks they're shifting a few of us classed as top security, highest risk, so soon enough we're going to land in those grouse cells adjacent to A Division.

The desirable rotation comes at last and I arrange for hacksaws to arrive in A Division, where a long-time old-school armed robber slips them through to me.

Now that the blades are here and they're full length and not just empty talk, the level of commitment and enthusiasm just gets higher and higher. I feel like I'm commanding a guerrilla unit.

Those of us who are red hot get our cells searched daily. The screws find the hole, which gets them all worked up, and they immediately move both me and the inmate on the other side. But their relentless and thorough searches don't uncover anything else out of the ordinary, and eventually the screws are satisfied that all is okay.

Now my focus is on the task: cutting a cell door lock. I've done my homework, my recon, and found that there is a cell at the bottom of the landing with a different door lock configuration than the others, enabling the tongue of the lock to be cut from inside the cell.

Eventually the fortnightly rotations place me in that cell where a hacksaw blade never looked so beautiful. I could kiss it. Sawing time.

But there's a problem: a security device secreted in the tongue of the lock. The brass cuts like butter but it has a roller – a cylinder – in there so I can't get a grip of it. It keeps on rolling; I can't fucking get past this, although the game's not up straight away because the locking device still operates when it is closed. But that plan's hit a dead end.

Time to activate Plan B.

ANNETTE:

In those days you could bring stuff in, and he asked me for some towels.

'What colour?' I ask.

'Navy blue.

'Oh, okay.' So I brought him navy blue towels and didn't think anything about it. Who would?

CHRIS:

Plan B is now to be activated. This is a totally different approach, a daytime escape from the two labour yards. This will be time-consuming as the four inmates in the two yards will have to cut the steel wire reo [reinforcement] used on top of each yard.

An officer patrols the prison catwalk which runs along the yards but the catwalk tower is actually to our advantage, as it shields us from the outside tower's view, when – as seems to be the preferred option – we climb out of the yard and drop down on the other side of H Division.

That will place us at the rear of prison industries in a no-go sterile zone. However, by now we'll be wearing fake prison officer uniforms and doing a perimeter check. From there we walk to a unmanned padlocked gate separating the rear of prison industries from the oval area; we wave to the tower some 90 metres away, shielding as we do so the tower's view as one of us snaps the lock with an improvised iron bar lever. With the gate open, we walk unchallenged to the maximum-security D Division – another prison itself, basically – and from here the closest towers are a good few hundred metres away.

We then proceed to a lower-security section, G Division, which holds the crazy inmates. The walls here will be much easier to climb. And then we'll be gone.

Everything has come together. We've finally cut through the roof mesh hanging over the yards and we're dressed in uniforms that look passable from distance. Homemade in navy blue, the outfits even sport replica prison insignias.

'The screws have locked down the wing!' an inmate yells to us. 'They've found something wrong with a cell lock.'

What the fuck? Emergency lockdown now? Now? Now? Are you fucking kidding me?

Foiled by sheer tin-ass luck!

As fast as we can, we strip off the uniforms and stash them the best we're able.

The screws go into an absolute frenzy. As they find insignias and bits of fake uniform, they don't know if all that's part of the same plot as the cut cell lock or if two or more plots were underway simultaneously. They don't even know the escape route or routes. They are angry and worried.

When they find counterfeit chief insignias in my cell, I'm charged in a Disciplinary Governor's Hearing with possessing unauthorised items and accused of being the ring leader.

However, it doesn't stick. The paper and colouring pencils I used were authorised items. Dismissed on a technicality.

The screws go crazy over this and do everything they can to make our lives intolerable. Yet it feeds straight into our us-versus-them mentality, fuelling us to bond even tighter into a hardcore unit.

ANNETTE:

I don't normally get the *Age* but for some reason I did and I saw all this news about some massive breakout attempt with a plan for Julian Knight to be held hostage. But you don't know how much is true and how much is media. There was nothing about the towels, just that they made up some uniforms and they got sprung and shoved it down the sewer.

I thought, 'You little bastard. That's why you wanted navy blue towels.' Who would think of towels? But as he explained later on, from a distance it looks like a uniform. Of course, when you bring something you have to sign and I thought, 'Oh shit, I'm going to get in trouble.' But no, nobody questioned me about the towels; they didn't question me at all.

Mothers are sometimes the last people to know and this was the case with me that time.

CHRIS:

Clashes are now regular between us and a hardcore killer group. It is at this time that I jump the screw's desk and punch out Julian Knight.

One of my original hardcore four, the mutual-defence combat unit formed back in 1990, lands back in prison after being pinched on murder. Given his high risk classification, they remand him here in H Division instead of the usual D Division.

We find ourselves reminiscing about the 'good old days' we shared not even eighteen months ago, times that were profoundly disturbing and extremely violent, and from which I was released in a state of fury, almost immediately going on a rampage of bank raids.

We must be more than a little disturbed if we're waxing nostalgic over a time plagued by stabbings and broken jaws and wayward levels of bronzing up and rampant shit-bombing.

But now everything is escalating again and my mate, now charged with murder, and I both go crazy.

‖‖

I'm roaring at the 'PUTRID GRONKS!' outside my cell as I stomp and stride, proud and strong, daubing and smearing ever more onto my full, fresh coat of triple-A rated warpaint. 'HUMAN FAECES!' They have shields and clubs and can get guns and gas but I have a cache of shit-bombs ready and water approaching the boil. I'm the full solja of Hell, locked and loaded and under divine orders not to let any 'PUTRID

SCREWS!' enter this cave unless they drop to their knees and 'BEG ME TO DIE YOUSE FUCKING STOOGES!'

So fierce a barrage and spray defence have I mounted this truly turdacious day that a tactical withdrawal was ordered during the initial assault. Now the screws are licking their wounds and licking my shit. They love it. They gargle with it and then kiss in the streets. And it's all mine. But they're selling it to the police for DNA samples, 'CAN YOU BELIEVE THIS SHIT!' and identity verification: 'HOW WELL DO YOU KNOW THIS PIECE OF SHIT!'

I hear voices. The armies of the beast ready themselves for an assault not just on some run-of-the-mill hill tribe Brown God, but on the very volcanic peak of excremental power: the Lost Command of H Division, the rogue bronze-up elements whose caves are being assaulted one by one in a tactical clearing operation.

'READY TO ENGAGE, YOUSE FUCKING GRONKS?' I enquire of the forces of the Pentridge Cell Extraction Security Unit massing and murmuring outside my cave. 'HUMAN FAECES!'

The shitty kettle clicks off. 'YOUSE READY, CUNTS?' I select a carton of the finest blend: week-old faeces, three-day-old piss, and quite recent spoof. The actions I have been forced to take are against the Geneva Convention but I am a bronzed guerrilla: a solja from the realm of BADNE$$. I baptise you in excrement. 'YOU HAVE NO FUCKING AUTHORITY OVER BRONZE-UPS!'

卌

The Cell Extraction Security Unit proved a clever opponent. Had the raiding party entered the zone 'clean', my ferocious fusillade would have seen them turned tail like the preceding waves of screws.

But respect where it's due: the security officers first cut down my comrades, launching vicious extractions one after the other until BADNE$$ alone remained. At that stage, the officers were well covered in human faeces – a mix and match from all my fallen friends.

Thus they were infused with the strength of many good soljas when they entered my cave, not recoiling and vomiting from all that bronze but giving themselves to it. Those men are worthy opponents.

Later I'm charged in Melbourne Magistrates Court over injuring an officer with boiling water.

HUNGER AND RESENTMENT

1994:
STILL IN H DIVISION

CHRIS:

H Division is unhinged; madness infects everything. The air's thick with rage and hate and the screws are stripping us of what little we have – underwear, sunglasses, crucifixes, anything – and slotting us right, left and centre into solitary, cuffing us even in the showers.

Inmates start refusing food and this gets formalised when five of us start a coordinated hunger strike on Valentine's Day – starvation being our love letter to Hell.

It's now March 1994 and I've been on strict separation since the first of November last year with every indication being that there are still months and months of this to go, even though charges against me have been dismissed.

A letter campaign starts and the media picks up on the HSU-5, or the High Security Unit Five, with mentions here and there in the newspapers of the wretched state of affairs in Pentridge's punishment slot – the lowest place in Victoria's penal system.

 ̶̶+̶+̶+̶

Annette organises a protest on the nature strip outside the front gates of Pentridge in support of the hunger strikers.

Barry comes to support his brother, Chris, as does a bloke they know named Gavin Preston.

Barry gets along okay with Gavin but he's better mates with Gav's brother, Richy, who lives at Barry's place for more than a year – before the heavy drug use that would eventually kill Richy. Barry puts up Gavin on occasion, too, but not for any real length of time.

They're all from the same general area, with the Preston brothers' parents even living just a street or two away from Annette for quite a while.

It's a region that supplies both staff and inmates to the prison system. The governor of Pentridge at the time of the hunger strike is Barry's neighbour.

While Gavin's not as notorious as Barry's big brother, he's had his fair share of scrapes with the law. When he attends the protest he is taking a big risk because at that time he is a wanted man.

Gavin attempts to disguise himself at the protest, but lacking Chris' knack for it, hides behind only sunglasses and a cap.

ANNETTE:

Half of the people who said they'd come didn't show up so there was only about twelve of us. The media sailed past and didn't think it was much of a protest, but the governor was watching from inside. They had their cameras trained on us.

He knew what Gavin looked like because he'd seen him around Barry's place. So when he recognised him from the cameras and knew he was a fugitive, he tells the police and the next thing there's carloads of police pulling up, and everything goes crazy. I was stunned.

BARRY:

There was no getting away. They bundled him up on the boot of a car, and one copper's fumbled and I just seen his gun go flying.

I was about five steps away and I was on crutches [from a motorcycle accident]. I've gone over next to it and I was about two steps away and the copper's looked at me and shit himself.

I had no intentions of getting it. I was just doing it to fuck with them.

ANNETTE:

I yelled, 'Barry!' 'Cos I could see what could happen. If you had the gun in your hand they could have shot you.

BARRY:

Yeah, but like I said I was hoping to get the coppers paranoid. There was two of 'em on Gavin and one focused on me. If one of 'em had left Gavin and come over where I was to get the gun it would have been one copper on Gavin and Gavin could have belted him or something.

They shit themselves, but I seen more cop cars – it wasn't just that one. They were strategically placed.

ANNETTE:

There was about six to eight men just jumping out and running in to get Gavin.

BARRY:

Because he came down there to support me brother and got nicked, he ended up going in for about two and a half years.

To tell you the truth, I don't think he was too happy with that. From then onwards, Gav resented Chris a bit.

And not long after, Gavin and Matty Johnson [who later bludgeoned *Underbelly* kingpin Carl Williams to death] ended up establishing the gang that they've got in jail. It had some other name first – Youth Gone Wild – and then became the POWs.

The HSU-5 hunger strike lasts 30 days, and it becomes part of H Division's (and Pentridge's) endgame. Gradually, H Division's hardcore inmates are transferred to HM Prison Barwon, a maximum-security facility near Geelong that opened only in 1990: a showcase of everything nice and new and humane in corrections – a world away from the Victorian-era horrorshow of Pentridge. H Division is shut in 1996, followed by the whole of Pentridge the year after.

SHACKLED IN BARWON

1995:
ACACIA UNIT 1

CHRIS:

From the rank, rotten, claustrophobic, historical stone hangover that is Pentridge, I land in Barwon Prison's Acacia Unit 1, a modern housing cluster specifically designed to cater for the state's inmates judged as its highest escape risks.

Chris at the gleaming new Barwon Prison (where he obtains a hacksaw blade in short order).

Completely isolated from the rest of the prison population, allowing no contact visits, and run independently with its own staff, Acacia Unit 1 is its own sealed off world. And at full capacity it holds only six inmates.

These unparalleled restrictions are meant to make us feel we may as well be on the moon: no way out, nowhere to go.

But it raises the stakes in the challenge to escape. In fact, it expands our minds.

Soon after arrival I put things in train, and although the security is intense and comprehensive with metal detectors and thorough searching, quickly enough I have a hacksaw blade in my hand. A tool for the free spirit.

I'll need more than one, however, but an attempt for a second blade fails. So be it.

I investigate and test the structure of the cell's window frame, discovering the window is one piece and held into the wall by about twenty screws.

Once cut through, the screws and rubber sealant could be removed from the concrete with the entire window then removed completely intact. I could now gain access to the window bars, cut them and put everything back in place, sealing it all back up with the pliable re-used rubber sealant.

The problem is that one hacksaw is not enough for everybody, hence the development of a tunnel project.

In our new scheme, the hacksaw is of great use in forging other tools from bits of tin, in turn using them to unscrew bolts from the tin roof of the TAFE metal workshops, so we can then peel back the roof to enter and secure the workshops' entire stock of equipment.

The plan is to use the oxy cutter to slice the bars and get us out of high security, but it turns out that the oxy is not portable – the gas bottles are not here and we can't use it.

Given our first goal is to get to the sterile zone on the other side of the metal fence separating our yard from mere maximum security, the only way, it seems, is travelling under the fence's concrete foundation.

Chris in Barwon with his much admired landscaping project which concealed an escape tunnel.

This is no overnight job. It ends up taking about six months to achieve. The grey clay beneath the surface is hard to conceal or to blend in with the topsoil so we use the cover of a landscaping project.

The beautification and improvement task involves raising the perimeters of the yard's corners to form a smooth running track, with garden beds sitting behind the elevated corners.

The veggie patch is strategically positioned in front of our excavation site – our descent point for the journey down under the fence foundations.

The Acacia staff think it's a great idea and they showcase our efforts to visitors as the gainful work of the inmates of Victoria's most secure custodial unit.

Patience and much hard work are the foundation of this; we all have a role to do.

Some get down into the hole and dig, whilst others blend the clay into top soil. Others cut [walk] laps on the sweet track we're making, keeping watch for those down the hole. We rotate through the roles, as tunnelling is bloody hard work, with all that clay and rock to get through and funnel back.

There are some close shaves when the staff enter the unit asking, 'Where is inmate X?' and he's down the hole and unable to surface without being seen: true *Hogan's Heroes* stuff. Another inmate has to pull the staff's attention another way with some bullshit and for long enough to give the tunneller time to safely surface.

The entrances we conceal by slotting in plastic meal trays that are covered with dirt and even have grass sprouting from them. It is perfect.

We all laugh when it rains and the yard turns a pale grey due to the landfill from the tunnel. Mulch, food scraps and newspapers do nothing to restore it back to brown. It's beyond us how the staff never notice.

CLOWN TOWN

The Acacia staff introduce a new uniform policy: clown red.

Make that cheap, ill-fitting clown red.

And in their endless quest to not only dress us up as fools but also remove our identities, they strip us of our private white t-shirts, shorts and thermals. The only non-red items we are now allowed to own are socks and jocks.

I refuse to be dressed as a clown in red synthetics and instead wear a couple of prison towels on my exercise periods, even in the rain and the bitter cold of winter.

One towel draped over my shoulders covering my upper torso, and the other wrapped around my waist is my uniform, not theirs.

For weeks another inmate and I brace the cold and wet in towels, refusing to wear their cheap, crappy clown outfits.

We ask if we can source reds that fit the new colour code but are higher quality and fit better – as we had been allowed to do with the white t-shirts they've seized. Denied.

I complain of having an allergic reaction to synthetic material, which is what the cheap new reds are made from. I'll break out in a rash if I don't wear natural fibres, I tell them –

adding that only natural fabrics agree with me: leather, cotton and silk.

To break our resistance, the Acacia Unit staff tell us that if we do not comply and wear their nasty clown gear, then we will be charged for disobeying a direct order and face a governor's disciplinary hearing.

The only way out is through a medical certificate.

The Senior Prison Officer, a certain Mr Norman, says he doesn't believe me about the allergy and that he wants to see the rash for himself.

'If I wear your reds tomorrow and go for a jog,' I tell him, 'my pores will open up and I'll be covered in a rash.'

'Rubbish.'

'All right, I'll show ya, then.'

I have just the thing: a tube of clear, odour-free, extra strength deep-heat balm.

The following day I apply a good coating to the inside of the clown shirt, and then when the exercise period starts, I walk out in my white towels, carrying the red t-shirt.

I call out to Mr Norman, who is watching me from behind the mirrored perspex, and ask him to look for any visible rash on my body before I put on the red top and go for a ten-minute run. He confirms no skin irritation is evident.

Donning the shirt, I start running and within minutes I can feel the heat being generated by the balm. The longer I run the hotter it gets. When ten minutes is up, I pull up, walk to the mirror, call to Mr Norman to witness this and then pull off the t-shirt. I'm as red as a lobster.

'Look,' I say. 'Are you fucking blind or what? Do you see it now?' It's obvious to all of them and they can't argue. So I tell Mr Norman that I want my skin sensitivity confirmed and reported.

Leaving the red t-shirt on the ground, I finish my yard time and return to my cell, still covered in a red rash. 'It worked,' I tell the other inmate who's holding out, and I give him a good dollop of balm to spread inside all his reds.

The next day he refuses to wear their synthetics, is told he'll be charged if he refuses the order, and now tells Mr Norman he has the same sensitive skin condition as me.

'Bullshit,' says Mr Norman. 'The chances of both of you having the same things are one in a million.'

So the inmate goes back to his cell, dons the red top, and then runs the yard, all the time being watched like a hawk by Mr Norman.

'Get over here,' says Mr Norman after the run. 'Remove the shirt.'

The inmate is covered in a huge red rash.

Mr Norman is fuming: he's carrying on about not believing for a minute that we both have the same allergy to the inmate uniform. But he can't work it out and reluctantly reports this inmate as also excused from general issue reds.

Due to this they have to get in new stock for us and we're both issued with decent cotton tops, t-shirts and shorts – not the Warwick Capper up-the-arse type that the others are made to wear.

Strutting about in the yard, I show off to the others watching from neighbouring yards. 'Gee, these feel heaps better,' I say. 'They're not up my crack.' I want to rub it in their faces for not holding out with us. If they had, they could be dressed better, too.

Some of them start complaining to the staff that we have better shorts; that it's not fair that ours don't give us wedgies. So to shut them up, new shorts are handed out but they still have to wear the rest of the clown set.

卌

A bigger problem develops in Unit 1, however, due to tension between me and inmate Peter Gibb who, with fellow prisoner Archie Butterly and a female screw Gibb was screwing, used a small explosive charge to blow a hole in the same Melbourne Remand Centre window that I previously burnt, and abscond.

The issue I have with Gibb is that when the police eventually closed in on them, Archie was shot dead with a police revolver that the two had earlier stolen and I don't think Archie shot himself.

Gibb knows I don't like him, and although we've set our differences aside for the escape the animosity is close to the surface.

One day in the yard Gibb makes some smart remark and in a flash I'm landing a flurry of punches. He grabs a pitchfork and confronts me with it but I don't run and there we stand when staff separate us. Gibb leaves the yard with two black eyes, the 'hardcore' crook then refusing to return into my company. The progress of the tunnel now slows, as we're on half-day run-outs [permitted time out of cells]: Gibb out in the yard while I'm locked in and vice versa.

Mere days out from the escape, the staff make a snap demand for us to change cells. Work on my window had been the most advanced of the group's, some of whom had only begun cutting out the screws holding in their window frames, and the cell I land in has had the least work done so now I'm behind everyone and cutting feverishly to make up ground.

As the day nears and I'm finishing my window, the others ransack the TAFE workshop for the tools we need. I manage to take the window out but I'm having trouble getting it back in as the sealant is tough and not budging at all. When one of the marauding inmates is out in the sterile zone behind the cells, I ask him to help push my window back in.

The sterile zone here is fenced off and out of sight except through a triangle opening about ten centimetres wide that's been cut out at the gate for accessing the padlock.

Unbeknown to us, a guard is having a smoke at the other side of the gate and spotted the roving inmate. He realises this isn't right and hits the alarm. Sirens blare: the inmate shits himself and scurries back down the tunnel but in his haste he fails to put the lid back in place. The prisoner makes it back to his cell before they enter the unit and conduct a lockdown head count.

The officers can't work it out – nobody's missing in the entire jail and doubt builds over the smoker's claims. Guards go up on the roof: still nothing, so they start dispersing, one officer walking the line of the fence until he falls down a hole, and, startled, is suddenly looking up instead of down.

We're all at the windows watching with bated breath. He screams that he's found something and officers pile back in. The tunnel is found and they storm the unit. A search of the laundry and day room uncovers a stack of equipment taken in the raid on the TAFE workshop. Due to being locked in over the Peter Gibb incident, I'm the only one to have an alibi.

Head Office goes berserk, turning Acacia upside down and spending a stack updating the unit which was already high security.

Time for Plan B.

Now, I like to plan for emergencies like this, so a little while back I staged a skirmish with staff and, given my confrontational past, they tipped me straight to Punishment Block Unit 4 where I secreted a third of a hacksaw blade.

And when the shakedown hits, the officers neglect the punishment block.

Plan B is for a smaller escape team of two at the most. And my Plan B running mate, Johnny Lindrea, also manages to secure a third of the blade through the upheaval. So now, for the two of us, it's all systems go.

The plan was that I would arrive in the punishment block and he'll follow weeks later so as not to draw suspicion. It works perfectly – he lands in the adjacent cell, allowing us to talk after emptying out the water in the toilet bowl, as they were on the same pipeline.

First we had to run tests by placing empty butter satchel wrappers over the area we wanted to cut. If the guards paid no heed and the satchels stayed there we assumed we could start cutting the door locks, just covering them with wrappers at the end of a session so the staff wouldn't notice when they opened and locked the doors each day. They left the wrappers alone. Yes!

Within days we start cutting the steel covers of the door locks, and then into the locking device that is housed inside the gap in the frame, covering our work with empty butter wrappers.

It's time.

We hip, shoulder and kick out the rear cell doors, the metal cut out around the locking device bends out easily, offering no resistance at all. So now we're out in the yard with four hours to cut a padlock and the rear mesh and be on the jail rooftop.

There we'll have the high ground to observe the hourly security patrols that start at 8 pm when the rest of the jail is locked down after the last muster of the day.

All we have to do is cut the padlock off the inner rear gate of the yard, then reach the next outside gate, and this time cut the security mesh so as not to alert guards to a damaged lock, because they rattle them there by hand on roving hourly patrols.

Both of us are out of our cells, but when I try to cut my gate's padlock, it won't cut. It is security-hardened steel. 'I'm stuck,' I tell him. 'I can't cut it.'

Johnny says that his is cutting easy, and that he is going to push on without taking the risk of waiting for me.

I begin to cut the steel tubing frame of the gate above the hinge, as once this is removed I'll be able to drop the gate off the top hinge and detach it.

When Johnny cuts through the padlock easy, I tell him to target the security mesh at ground level so that they'll be less likely to see it. I say to peel it back, crawl through out of the yard, and then bend it back into place.

I get through the tubing, unhinge the gate, put it back in place and work on mesh, I cut through in no time, and my mate is now behind me.

But I wait for him, unlike he was going to do for me.

He fucking cuts out the mesh section at the padlock level; I can't believe it. The damage is fully exposed: right in their line of sight. To make things worse, when he tries to squeeze through the gap he gets stuck and I have to then use the steel tubing frame to bash out the hole. It's still a tight fit and he's cut to pieces, now leaving a blood trail that even the blind couldn't miss.

His desperation to get out is going bring us down. I think of something that might survive a few patrols – but definitely not a change of shift – and run back into my cell for some A4 paper and a black Texta.

'YARD DAMAGED – NOT IN USE', I write, signing it off as the area chief of Acacia Unit and positioning it over the damage. This actually fooled them for the first three patrols.

We now head off to the prison industry area, climb the roof and crawl along until reaching the fenced-off industry yard where we drop down. Aware that the industry roller door can be lifted with force, we gain entry to the loading dock where a six-metre stepladder and a nine-metre extension ladder are padlocked and chained to the wall.

As I lift the roller door to allow him to crawl under, he spots a box in the corner over the door with a red light visible beneath it. Thinking it's a motion detector, he halts to avoid setting it off. We decide to damage it and set it off, then hide and wait for the staff to attend, think it's a false alarm, turn it off and leave.

The problem now is to create a hiding position out of material lying around the yard, but this is taking up precious time that we can't afford.

We cut a fire hose to tie at one end of the nine-metre extension ladder, which we're going to use to slide down the the far side of the wall instead of jumping, and then prop a ladder up by the alarmed inner fence. We'll throw the other ladder over that fence into the sterile zone, jump after it – also without touching it and triggering the alarm – and then stand it against the last wall and breach for freedom.

When everything is in place, we return to the roller door. Johnny slides underneath whilst I hold it up, wedges it open with a container, and now I slide under, too.

Only to find out that our motion detector was nothing but a 'fire exit sign box' positioned over the exit door.

We cut the ladders free and secure the fire hose to the end of the extension ladder. It's no more than 100 metres across the oval to the first inner alarmed fence, which we'll clear in a jump from the extension ladder.

I'm up the ladder, my head over the industry fence when I spot the change of shift. They're starting their patrol for the night from the front gatehouse. I expect the yard damage to be discovered and say, 'Let's go.'

'No,' he says. 'Let's wait til they do the patrol. Then we'll have an hour head start before the next patrol finds the ladders and hits the alarms.'

Johnny's reasoning is that because the jail is in a semi-rural location, we need the head start to get out of the area.

But we have car theft implements and Corio is less than six kilometres away so I say we should go for it. Waiting is a bad idea. I'm adamant than even if they set off the alarms we can cross over the outside wall and clear the area.

'But it's your call,' I tell him. 'You have longer time than me.'

His call doesn't change, and I reluctantly climb down from the extension ladder and start concealing that and the stepladder in the industry yard.

In my gut, I know I have made the wrong choice. I think of that solo flight at Parramatta: that solo run in a hospital gown in Melbourne. My solo leaps over the walls at Poplar House. But today I'm in a team and Johnny's the one with the deadening term ahead.

They find the damage to his yard and call it in, launching a search of Acacia that reveals we're missing. Saturating the exterior of the jail with security, search teams work from the outside in, as they guess we haven't yet breached the perimeter.

We're pinned down inside the industries fence by a roving vehicle and foot patrols. A helicopter hovers above, its spotlights trying to work over the jail but more so they set the fog ablaze with white light. Huge contingents of security crews with dogs pour in through the gatehouse.

Johnny doesn't want to get bitten by the approaching, barking German shepherds, but I refuse to declare our position and I hold out until the very last moment – three hours after the search began. I'm not comfortable at all in surrendering.

They're also fuming. After all, it's only some weeks since the previous escape attempt was exposed and they're still reeling from the media attention.

The head office of Corrections Victoria hits the roof yet again, and as a consequence Johnny and I are placed in leg-irons and handcuffed to body belts during our one-hour exercise periods.

Johnny's restraints are removed after fourteen days. He has vowed to abide by the rules and regulations.

Johnny Lindrea would get out eighteen years later, walking free this time out the front gates not over the wall. I'd see him that day and give him a bundle of cash to help him out and get on his feet – our paths going separate ways once more.

I launch legal action and the governor, Clive Williams, an old foe from Pentridge, tells me to drop it. I tell them to fuck off. 'Leg-irons? Shackles? I'll see you in court.'

Williams claims I've said I'll escape again and so I remain chained for three months, even on box visits. It's totally absurd but my challenge fails in the Supreme Court of Victoria.

In the exercise yard I hobble about in prison-made shackles with about half a metre length from one end to the other. Their hinged clasps are secured with big padlocks and I look like some medieval dungeon rat. They wear away the skin inside my ankles.

With my hands cuffed to a body belt, I grip hold of the exercise bike and, inch by inch, force it across the yard until it squarely faces the staff sitting hidden behind the mirrored perspex.

Now I climb aboard and pedal like mad, staring dead at where they sit, feeling nothing at all as the chains strip my skin to blood.

My ankles still carry the scars of this today.

Escape maestro Chris loses his court challenge against being kept in leg irons and shackles. A chain can be seen connecting his ankles.

A LETTER TO BARWON PRISON

1995:
ACACIA UNIT

Shackled, Chris writes a letter to the prison.

CHRIS:

You tell me who I have injured, maimed, raped, molested or killed to justify being treated in this manner.

Yes, it is true I have used a gun in obtaining a financial advantage in the commission of a crime in the past. This may be due to lacking ability in seeking a financial benefit with the ease of a stroke of a pen, like so many others, or the gift or the qualities that amount to becoming a politician.

Yes, some may have suffered during bouts of terror associated during the act of armed robbery by verbal threats, for which I apologise, yet does anyone shed a tear for the suffering, trauma and torment inflicted upon me by a number of aggressive, abusive staff assigned to cater and handle my care. No.

I do not seek forgiveness or sympathy by any but only to remind others that I too am human.

I shall enter back into the community one day as a member of society and hopefully a productive member in the workforce. I have done wrong and have paid the ultimate price with the loss of my liberty, amongst other things, but surely I don't need to suffer to this extent at the hands of my keepers and to be treated far worse than an animal, being trussed up and placed in chains in this day and age.

THE BANALITY OF SUPERMAX

1995: Barwon Prison diary

CHRIS:
DAY 1

8:40 AM.

Strip search. Refuse to turn sox inside out when requested. Stated if so much desired to do it themselves! SPO F, PO B, PO H present. Alleged incident occurring as a result of my response to their attitude and conduct. Officers leave cell, leaving me locked in cell and informed me no exercise.

8:45 AM.

SPO F and Gov M arrive; open cell conduct another strip search, SPO F orders me to visualise and keep my sight focused on outstretched hands while engaging in strip search. I voiced my protest as no such regulations or rules exist of that nature. He threatened to have me charged as a result of my refusal to comply with his 'visual' instructions.

8:50 AM.

Strip search completed. Advised to go out in exercise yard while cell searched. In doing so advised SPO G I

had requests to be processed and recorded. His reply:
'I'll get back to you very shortly.'

9:10 AM.

Let out to use phone. Not able to get in contact with solicitor.

9:15 AM.

Let out to go back to exercise. Notice SPO F in possession of legal folders removed from my cell, in company of PO H. I confronted F on why he had removed items.

He replied, 'They're John Lindrea's and not yours.'

I said that he lent them to me to hold the vast volumes of paperwork I hold.

He said, 'Bad luck, you can't have them.'

I said, 'You're kidding.' He had also removed 1 pkt of gum and quantity of rice — opened bag.

I had not been informed of this.

9:20 AM.

Notified officer whilst in yard I desperately needed to go to the toilet and informed him I had weak bladder!

9:45 AM.

Again asked what the delay was. No reply from officer so I relieved myself on the spot. To my surprise SPO F was present during whole episode and informed me I was to be charged as a result of my actions of relieving myself. I stated I had given adequate

warning and could no longer suppress nature's demands
and he was a party to such outcomes.

10:20 AM.
Notify need to use phone at 10.30. Important call
required at this time by expecting party at receiving
end.

10:30 AM.
Again informed SPO G I had requests to be submitted.
Reply 'Soon.'

10:40 AM.
Finally given access to phone room.

10:50 AM.
Finish phone and informed to go directly back into
cell, that my exercise period had been reduced by Gov
M. F instructed me of this, yet it was not the case, but
done so he could avoid coming back ten minutes later to
let me out of exercise yard to cell: 'avoid unnecessary
movements to him'.

11:00 AM.
Requested to G per requests which we had done and
registered in senior's request book — done from my
cell doorway.

11:50 AM.
Meals arrive in unit [not the cell, but a small section
around which a number of solitary cells are clustered,
Chris' being one].

12:04 PM.
Meals issued cold.

12:05 PM.
Notified and advised staff via intercom of the state
of meals. Response: 'Bad luck.'

I suggested there was a microwave available to
reheat meals.

Reply 'No: that's the way they arrived; that's the way
you get 'em.'

I then stated via intercom that the microwave was
present for just such occasions.

Female officer then buzzed off from intercom.

12:30 PM.
Via intercom enquired as to when I would receive
access to typewriter. Female officer replied, 'When
staff become available.'

I stressed it was an urgent and important matter
to complete and forward on, and why do I have to face
working my case at the staff's convenience?

Buzzed off once again no reply.

1:20 PM.
Via intercom asked once again for typewriter.

1:40 PM.
Cell door opens and handed typewriter.

1:41 PM.
Via intercom notified staff the ribbon had been removed
and not able to use it as a reult. Informed SPO G of

such. 'Highly unusual ribbon removed as was okay the
other day', was his reply. Yeah, right. Funny that, isn't
it, give me it finally — in the end rendered useless.

1:50 PM.
Notified Gov M of the act of missing ribbon from
typewriter. Suggested would have arrangements for a
replacement ribbon.

3:32 PM.
Meals arrive in unit.

3:56 PM.
Meals delivered yet microwaved beforehand to reheat.

3:56 PM.
Requested plastic tea spoon in order to consume Weet-
Bix, as mine was removed from cell earlier in the day.
F responsible and states not allowed.
    I said, 'Bullshit, who said so?'
    He replied, 'You have two hours to consume breakfast
once issued, then return spoon.'
    I told him I ate cereal at night during the evening
when I became hungry — which he was well aware of
— and nobody's removed spoon before, yet he leaves
plastic bowl intact!

4:50 PM.
Buzz up via intercom PO C ask for Panadol and plastic
spoon. 'No probs.' Receive soon afterwards.

<u>END OF DAY</u>

DAY 2

BREAKFAST ISSUED.
Requests conducted, consisted of: phone balance check,
typewriter, canteen account printout — never received
previous day!

11:40 AM.
Buzzed up and asked when would we receive newspaper,
which are delivered each morning. Reply: 'not yet
arrived', highly unlikely event as are delivered on a
daily basis with no delays.

11:45 AM.
Meals issued, I then proceed to produce faeces on
newspaper and inform them this is a symbol of the
times. When is all this shit going to stop? Placed
newspaper in centre of dayroom area in unit.

12:30 PM.
SPO G comes to cell and orders me to clean up and
remove newspaper — if not be removed to unit 4 as a
result: LOP, or loss of privileges unit.

2:30 PM.
Gov S speaks to me on what's the problem. I advise him
of certain officers inciting and provoking incidents
— F — and the current atmosphere and attitudes shall
in. It's only fitting to represent a symbol of the times
in the unit as a monument.
  Once again advised to clean up or go to unit 4.
  I refused.

3:10 PM.

EMU [Emergency Management Unit] officers arrived. Handcuffed, hobbles, removed to LOP [Loss of Privileges] section – unit 4.

3:30 PM.

Receive meal and limited writing material and reading items.

<u>END OF DAY</u>

DAY 3

<u>BREAKFAST ISSUED.</u>
Request to SPO G consists of: clothing, food items, legal papers and documents in cell and typewriter, legal call.

Soon afterwards SPO G and PO L deliver meagre rations and clothing, court documents. I noticed missing canteen items as I had packed up the day before anticipating the movement to unit 4.

He said, 'I'll see you later.'

1:20 PM.

Buzz up and enquire into the missing canteen item, being Weet-Bix, advised he would speak to me later about it.

2:20 PM.

Buzzed up and pursued into what's going on with canteen items being denied me? Advised G would see me later about it.

<u>3:05 PM.</u>

Let out of cell for legal call and indicated I wanted to see G about being denied access to canteen items, Weet-Bix and cereals issued to me!

<u>3:30 PM.</u>

Finish phone call, in process of returning to cell, notice G in Chief's office and proceed in this direction. Met by him in doorway where I confront him on why I am not allowed Weet-Bix, as I had previously purchased these items while in unit the week prior and I am not on any regime where it states I'm not allowed such items. I said I starve at night, I have very little in my possession due to the restrictions on items available and limits placed on money spent. These were the only items of canteen in my cell apart from some chocolates.

He said, 'You're issued cereals in the morning.'

I said, 'Yes, but what has that got to do with my canteen purchases?'

He said, 'I let you have your chocolates.'

I said, 'How kind of you. Where does it say you can't?' I then said that the chocolates do not satisfy or quell the hunger at night like the Weet-Bix do.

His reply was that it was his decision due to his belief and it was designed to slow down my bowel movements.

I stated: 'What's next, deny me my meals? I shit every day as it is and this bullshit would not affect it.'

He said, 'Enough's enough. Bad luck.'

I then spat the dummy — 'spit'.

I was then placed back in cell with handcuffs still
intact.

3:44 PM.
Buzzed up to see when or if handcuffs to be removed.
Reply Gov has been advised and will get back to you.

4 PM.
Gov M arrives, informed me that I am no longer able to
make legal calls or use typewriter and I'll be charged
as a result of my actions against SPO G.

END OF DAY

DAY 4

BREAKFAST ISSUED.

9:45 AM.
Gov K arrives to cell. Informs me of the procedures of
handcuffs during exercise and shower periods.
　　I stated: 'You got to be joking.'
　　Gov K said, 'I am not — I am serious.'
　　I then brought up my legal position and I relied
upon access to my solicitor via phone and required
access to typewriter in preparing documents for defence
and a private prosecution against certain parties and
this decision of terminating access to solicitor and
typewriter is unjust and illegal in my circumstances,
interfering in communicating and receiving advice and
instructions on various matters currently at hand.
　　His reply was: 'Bad luck and no calls — nothing.'

10 AM.
Exercising in cuffs — one hour period.

11:02 AM.
Shower in cuffs. Finish shower.

11:10 AM.
Reverse procedure.

11:40 AM.
Meals arrive in unit.

11:42 AM.
Meals issued.

3:14 PM.
Meals arrive in unit.

3:20 PM.
Meals issued.

END OF DAY

EXTRADITION

9 OCTOBER 1996:
TRANSFER TO NSW

CHRIS:

New South Wales is seeking my extradition over outstanding arrest warrants and charges.

Yet, it seems like it's gotten personal down here: head office doesn't want me going anywhere if the conditions I'll face will be less harsh than in Victoria.

For NSW to get their man, they have to agree to keep me under the spartan isolation regime that Victoria has imposed.

I have never heard of this happening before, nor would I hear of it again.

The extradition is approved and I'm told to have my bags packed and be ready to move.

Weeks go by, however, until the night after my 26th birthday when the Barwon security squad arrives at my cell.

Rustled from sleep at a quarter to midnight, I say my goodbyes to those in the unit and ask to wear my civilian clothes for the transfer. Permission denied; I am to remain in red. The squad makes me kneel, fits me with leg-irons, the body belt and cuffs, and takes me to the squad van.

A four-car high-security escort accompanies my transport van through the dead of night to the police hangar at Essendon Airport.

Shackled up and left in the rear of the prison security van, hours go by as we wait for the NSW State Protection Group to fly in. They're to be my hosts and hostesses for the flight north.

I tell the prison officers that I need to have a piss. 'Let me out or I'll piss in the rear of the van – it's simple,' I tell them.

'Hang on.'

They wait while the chartered twin-engine ten-seater taxies in from the runway and State Protection Group officers then secure the area. Now Barwon security officers and dogs walk me to the grass edge of the runway, hands and feet still chained to the body belt.

When I pull down my track pants, red dots light me up like a Christmas tree: I'm covered with the State Protection Group's laser gunsights. They're not fucking taking any chances. Let's just say this is a nervy piss indeed.

In flight to Sydney, the heavily armed police don't really play the host role. No movies, either.

Arriving at Mascot airport the security is even greater than at Essendon. The hordes of State Protection Group officers securing the area seems to alarm the NSW prison security personnel who are picking me up. They've never seen anything like it; the president of America would be jealous.

Surrounded by a six-car security escort, we drive south. Now in NSW custody, I deem the order to remain in red no longer applies and set to work tearing off my clown clothes. The screw watching me via the rear perspex must have thought 'What the fuck?', as I struggled in my chains, cuffs and irons, throwing shreds of the despised garments on the van floor.

It's all drama and fanfare when we reach Goulburn where a section of the prison has been locked down for my reception, four years to the month that I escaped from Parramatta.

And straight into segro [isolation] I go.

INMATE 219 LUCIFER

CHRIS:

My NSW prisoner number is 219666, or 219 LUCIFER as I enjoy telling the more biblically inclined Christians among the prison staff.

One senior officer, later to become a governor of Goulburn, is so offended by my official devil status and by my enjoyment of his discomfort, that he seeks to have the number changed.

My ranking on NSW's list of High Risk Inmates hits number one (later to be bumped by the infamous Ivan Milat).

The isolation of Goulburn's high-security confinement – starting here in the Additional Support Unit (ASU) – is maddening but I decline to buy a TV for the first 22 months. To hell with it. My mind is my freedom.

They want to reduce us to dependent slugs slumped in our cots on meds watching the telly. They tell the outside world that we're the 'worst of the worst' undergoing 'corrections', and they pretend that this isolation is a neutral state, something like a boring dream passing by over many years, but I know that they realise that what they're doing is not keeping us in suspended animation. They know that isolation like this breeds despair, rage and madness. They know that something profoundly bad is occurring beneath all the telly watching, beneath the pill-popping, beneath the vacant ceiling-staring and obsessive case-working. They know that while isolation prisoners often appear pale and slack on the surface, deep inside we're desperate; we're panicking as we slip out of orbit – as we detach from the gravitational pull of day-to-day life with peers. They know that we are coming undone as communal human beings and they know that we are reforming as lost, atomised, insane souls of a stark universe ruled by an all-powerful god who gives no shit whatsoever for anything but absolute control.

And one day we'll be released.

卌

I hear a fellow inmate, a Koori, complaining about being hungry all the time and having no smokes and no TV, so I have $400 sent to his Spend Account. He can't believe it – doesn't know me from a bar of soap.

LATE 1996

Barry visits, but instead of our meeting being held in the usual areas, they have us face each other in the front segregation yards.

I am in leg-irons and the rest, talking to him through grill bars, in caged yards strewn with litter and in wind of stagnating bowls of green shit.

Barry is deeply disturbed and doesn't want to drive eight hours again for this kind of horror.

Goulburn is horrible, man. Horrible. The officers are brutal; they are nasty. Their whole exercise is to break inmates down and crush their will – destroy them. That is the mentality and that's how they operate. When you engage with them that's when the us-and-them thing comes to the fore. They literally turn inmates into their enemies. Hate on hate.

An old associate arrives in the ASU. I know him well, and he is able to sort out a $500 upfront order I've placed for two full-length hacksaws. Word is that I'll have to wait for them to arrive by escort from Long Bay jail.

The courier is a protection-classified inmate who is housed in the cell next to me here in ASU. To the staff this bloke's troublesome and incident plagued. He taps on the wall and calls out to me to pump out the toilet water so we can speak. My order has arrived; it'll be in the gym yard tomorrow for me to collect.

But within days I'm getting a lot of attention, the prison officers taking a keen interest in searching my cell. Again and again they tip it upside down, going well beyond the usual inspections done.

It's okay. I've hidden the blades well.

But it becomes pretty clear that the courier is lagging me, trying to generate brownie points to get himself out of the unit, knowing that it will bury me in the process.

After another week of failing to find the blades, the prison staff come up with a bullshit story, claiming that they have intercepted a key hidden in my vegan meal. So back I go on the most restrictive regime they can offer.

The protection inmate had stolen the key from an officer at Long Bay and it was his way to load me up, the blades having seemingly disappeared. It works for him; he gets moved to greener pastures.

Weeks later, a Long Bay security squad arrives unannounced at my cell. The officers say they are moving me to an unscheduled court matter. They scan everything I want to bring with handheld metal detectors – me included – conduct a strip search, and then dress me in their own overalls.

Now there's half a hacksaw blade hidden in a cardboard box full of legal papers, but if I want to bring it they'll scan it and if I leave it here it will get found when they ramp my cell in my absence.

So I leave it and when we reach the prison's reception, I feign that I forgot the box of legal documents and I need it for the case. An officer goes back for them but now we're running late and the officer isn't subjected to metal detectors as we hurry for the court appearance.

Unfortunately, a search conducted in my absence reveals that someone has been cutting my cell to pieces and I'm rushed back to the prison. Stepping up their thoroughness, they find the balance of the hacksaw order.

Transported for a 1996 court appearance, Chris greets the paparazzi.

‖‖

During my term in NSW there were claims

of another two escape attempts somehow linked to me, and countless finds of plastic cuff keys. Once, during a squad escort, I use a piece of plastic for a bit of a fiddle of the leg-irons but they seize up, yet again causing ALARM to my correctors.

1997–98

Realising I am a man who values liberty and initiative, staff at the high-security unit scatter spies around me, hoping that I'll discuss matters with them.

So, for a laugh, I make matters up, quietly telling the snitches that a 'high risk kamikaze plan is in play'. It's on for the big exercise yard, I say – the area closest to the wall. What's going down is the escape team knows the rubbish truck schedule and after the yard roof bars have been cut, certain parties are going to hijack the truck and plough it through the front gates. It'll be huge, I tell 'em.

Goulburn prison is ringed by barricades within a week.

I'm kept in isolation for years, while over in the mainstream population there's a fucking killing spree. Bosnia, they call it. Seven murders in three years and dozens of people seriously injured.

In my unit I have people getting plucked on the jail murders, coming in here to isolation for two weeks, a month, three weeks, and going back out. I've never killed anybody but I just stay here forever, watching murderers come and go. I don't get to mix with these hardcore elements 'cos we're in solitary, but I get familiar with 'em; we can communicate.

They're saying, 'Why the fuck are you here?'

''Cos I've escaped,' I tell 'em. But it's four years or more since I pulled one off.

They can't understand. They've actually murdered people and they get out of isolation. And there's people here who come in pinched on escapes that maybe get a couple of months in the pokey and then they're back out. The hardcore inmates respect me; I respect them. They can't believe it, and the screws just give me a fucking hard time, a really fucking hard time, man. Trying to break me.

They're concerned that in the last robbery no proceeds have been recovered; there's a lot of money outstanding. They think I can finance another escape and I don't know what the fuck the information was that Victorian intel forwarded on but they know that I was involved in two escape attempts from the high-security unit there, so they're on eggshells. And they know that I'd used a firearm before when escaping from hospital. So they are paranoid to begin with and then Victoria just feeds them a whole heap of shit.

So I am put down. Not even Russell 'Mad Dog' Cox who escaped from Katingal served anywhere close to fucking three and a half years in a management unit, in a high-security unit, for an escape.

Solitary, man. Lock a dog in a laundry. For years. See how well it develops.

ISOLATION COUNTERPRODUCTIVE, SAYS PSYCH REPORT:

Chris stages a hunger strike in 1998 to protest against his long-term isolation in Goulburn's amusingly named Additional Support Unit.

After interviewing Chris, ASU staff, and other mental health professionals who worked there, a senior psychologist writes a July 1998 report advising that Chris be let out of the harsh

conditions of the ASU that he has so far endured for
over a year and a half.

The psychologist notes that Chris has been given
no specific reasons for his placement in the ASU, no
indication of when he might leave it, and no access to
programs running in other sections of the prison.

The psychologist recommends that Chris is moved
to a setting that, while secure, is more conducive to
rehabilitation.

Keeping Chris in isolation is unlikely to teach him
any constructive or desired lesson, the psychologist
reports.

Rather than being a deterrent, Chris' subjection to
prolonged isolation creates a sense of heroism and
is emotionally damaging — compounding feelings of
frustration, helplessness, anger and distress — the
psychologist reports.

Furthermore, the possibility exists that Chris will
become a hero or martyr to others as well.

CHRIS:

Meanwhile out there they're stabbing each other like there's
no tomorrow. Not that there is any fucking tomorrow in this
Groundhog Day world. But really, it's hardcore and the damage
isn't just to the dead and wounded. Hundreds of men live in
a permanent state of fear and trauma, of action and reaction.
This venomous environment takes them over – its rules are
so immediate and so harsh that they displace and replace the
decent ways of being that some prisoners still had when they
arrived.

||||

MAYHEM

The inmates here strut around showing no weakness but that's all it is: a show. I thought I was bad after being wound up tight at Pentridge and then released, but God help the people unlucky enough to be near this lot when they get out. Physically they might then be free, but their minds, their souls, will still long be jerking to the strings of Goulburn and its ugly little killing cages.

LITHGOW ICE PICK

2001:
INCIDENT IN COMPOUND YARD

CHRIS:

I am at Lithgow, a maximum-security facility west of Sydney's Blue Mountains, along with a Koori inmate that I bonded with in difficult times at the Goulburn ASU.

He asks to lend a good pair of runners to wear on a contact visit, because his family are due to come and see him and his shoes have holes.

'No problem,' I say.

Three days later his unit and mine are both in the compound yard and when I ask when he is going to return my runners, he says someone stole them from his cell.

Not believing this at all, I talk to some senior Koori elders that I get along with. They pretty much run the jail, bullying everyone – Lebanese and Chinese included. 'It's not good to steal from me like this,' I say. 'If he wants them, let him fight for them instead of being sneaky – that's the coward's way.'

The inmate's brother is a senior solja in the field – he's killed more than once – but I'm not going to get walked over. For many reasons, one important factor being that if an inmate lets anyone get away with stealing from them or standing over them, then it turns into open season. It might cost you a bashing or worse, but you have to draw a line and retaliate. These are the rules of the jungle.

So I said, 'Let's be fair: you control the jail but why do this to me? He should fight for the runners, one on one, and the best man keeps them.'

I finish up a shift at the tailor shop factory, exit through the metal detectors, get patted down by staff, and thus walk out unarmed into a reception party of the Kooris' group.

One of them blind sides me with a cheap sneak shot and when I return fire the shoe thief's brother rushes up to show me his knife.

Prison staff on patrol intervene and escort us back to our separate pods.

Later, however, when I am in the compound yard that is about 70 per cent Koori, I stand up for myself and fight a mob of them, losing a tooth but holding to my principle.

Months later a group of seasoned murderers attack me in the compound yard, cutting me and worst of all stabbing me in the chest with an icepick, the metal puncturing my left nipple directly over my heart.

Bleeding profusely, I have no illusions about what they intend. I argued about the runners; I won't back down on theft. So I am to die.

In the stand-off after the initial attack, outnumbered 60–1, I put serious pressure on the wound and stem the bleeding. A mate loans me a clean t-shirt to try to keep the incident from the knowledge of the staff, but someone else reports it and it becomes an 'incident' – albeit one I deny ever happened.

This is prison life: a factory of fear and resentment, hatred and dominance, us versus them, me versus you. When society dispatches a convicted criminal – who is already no doubt disturbed or messed up – into a 'correctional' facility, whether they are then sent into the arena or placed in isolation, the real lesson that's taught is that we're all in a war for power and that the weak have it coming.

My fear goes off the charts and I refuse to leave my pod. I just can't do it.

I have read many times in the media how I am one of the 'most dangerous prisoners in the country'; how I am one of the 'worst of the worst'; how whatever prison regime I am subjected to is not harsh enough for scum like me.

But when the staff order me out I won't go. I'm shaking. I'm breathing rapidly. I'm a man in my early thirties who has done wrong but I won't walk out into an arena for a mob to kill me.

'Fuck off!' I roar at the staff, flinging my stuff at everyone, not budging. Guards wearing gas masks and carrying riot shields enter the pod.

They threaten to blast my cell with CS gas and I tell them to do what the fuck they want – I'm not leaving. But the other inmates in my unit implore me to go, go anywhere, go to segregation, just don't get their pod and everything in it stinking of that fucked up chemical weapon.

So I'm placed in isolation and then, as the staff correctly felt that my life was at risk, transferred back to Goulburn.

RACE HATE CAGES

2001:
GOULBURN

CHRIS:

Goulburn is now racially segregated: the authorities hoping this will prevent a relapse into the Bosnia situation.

To stem the kills down, the rabid packs have been separated: there's a cage for Aborigines, a cage for 'Lebanese' (and others that the racial purity geniuses at Corrections NSW deem to be Lebanese), a cage for Pacific Islanders, and a cage for Asians. 'Aussies' like me have the choice of running with the Islanders or running with the Asians. I go with the Asians.

The memories of Bosnia are still vivid to many, and the stench of death and hate is still strong and obnoxious.

The security units are on a knife edge to intervene in the yard and there have been no more killings yet. But the state of mind is the same, and sub-lethal stabbings and bashings are flourishing, indeed. The state of mind is the same.

I'm now in the general population here, which by its approximation of a society – even if a twisted, sick, distorted society – is better than drooling and playing with my poo in solitary.

But to get by here you have to be in a state of constant vigilance. While the yards are segregated you never know when someone or a few people will just fucking show up, and, as the warring groups have issued attack-on-sight orders, things are tense. Combat mode in the red zone.

The Kooris have their own wing and a yard adjacent to a bigger area into which inmates are herded to collect their canteen which is issued on Sundays by a lone officer. The gate between the Koori yard and the canteen-issue yard is secured only by an old Jackson lever padlock.

When we line up for the canteen issue, the Kooris hurl missiles through the yard bars, and to get out again means walking through a storm of spit, sometimes other bodily fluids, and even a hot-watering.

The segregation breeds enmity, if you ask me. There's no incentive to get to know each other and get along. Us and them.

Our yard gets wind from another yard that the Kooris are big-noting that they're going to storm the canteen yard whilst our group is in it and turn it into a bloodbath. Apparently they have prepped for it by manipulating the old lock.

This sparks a crisis council among inmate groups, and I order an emergency call to bear arms and have various inmates report to me about our stockpile of weapons for defence against the impending onslaught.

Our cache of perspex and wooden shivs is wrapped in a plastic bag with porridge poured over it and then placed in a freezer for the oats to form a solid cover. Weapons secured.

In what is almost a religious ritual, on Sunday morning I

remove the bag from the freezer, flip the container upside down, peel out the items from the mould and issue them to those who feel the need to protect themselves.

I make it a point not only to make myself safe, but to provide for the entire yard, and give them a chance to defend themselves, as otherwise many would not have been in a position to at all. It's important to me that, on my watch, everybody is provided for in combat.

I don body armour: a turtle neck jumper tailor-made with double layers, between which I slot books that function as protective plates. I slide on my beanie and fit my sunglasses tight, ready for war.

Yet, like the others, I feel sick in the stomach to see that a bedsheet has been draped over the fence, blocking the staff's view of the yard.

As we draw close, their most seasoned killers gather at the gate, waiting for the staff to secure and leave the yard.

Unsupervised in the arena now, we split into small teams and position ourselves in strategic defensive locations – although a lot of us simply clustered at the far end of the yard and others simply shit themselves and won't leave the cells – that's accepted, too; it's understood that not all are soljas.

I walk up and down the yard, stopping three metres from the gate as they fiddle with the lock. In the horizontal pouch of my jumper, each of my hands holds a perspex shiv. If they want to enter – not a problem at all.

There are headphones over my beanie and I've been feigning grooving to music but they're silent and now near the gate I taunt the killers, walking just short of them and then turning my back.

Rarely have I felt so exposed, so expectant of a savaging, so finely balanced over death. And it excited me: truth.

Every Sunday for five weeks this jaw-clenching drama plays out – all of us suffering from the sheer anxiety of not knowing if the murderers gathered on the other side of the gate would finally simply push it open.

Over the weeks, many inmates known as staunch, tough and solid, bail: not just joining our noncombatants back in the cells but giving the screws reasons they should be sent to the bone yard.

But the solidarity of those of us who stick it out in the yard, our standing firm week in and week out, neither bailing nor telling the screws, outlasts the Koori death squad and they abort.

It's a victory for us but for all the coming generations – maybe not. Many good blokes have been bashed, stabbed, raped and killed by these inmates and no doubt more will suffer in the years to come. If they had done their charge, we could have eradicated them and done so legitimately in a field of war.

One of the Kooris is the multiple killer who tried to stab me in the heart with the icepick at Lithgow. I wanted him to come in. Do enough time in prison and just about everything gets personal.

I am in a state of constant vigilance. My world is guerrilla war.

‖‖‖

Even at the yard delegate meetings at which we discuss inmate issues and grievances in the presence of prison staff, all-in-brawls occur with people getting chairs smashed over their heads and inmates fleeing the circle only to be run down and bashed by their foes. It's a spectator sport, with crowds of other inmates watching from the yards, roaring and cheering at the violence. Yes, this is how it is here.

The prison says I'm to be transferred to Bathurst, an Aboriginal stronghold full of the icepick man's friends and kin.

I'm blasted with the terror of being in the heart of enemy territory.

I'll do it but I must always be tooled up. I must never relax. I must watch every person, every corner, every movement, every shadow, every screw. And even that's doomed when mobs hit deep and fast and move on, leaving a man on the concrete, blood bubbling out of his mouth.

The screws find me with perspex shivs and plastic cuff keys and cancel the transfer. The parole board want to know why I had these items. I write back: 'For defending myself – nothing more.'

A crazy thing about Goulburn's race war segregation is how the prison staff say the hate is too extreme for us to mix but on transfers they pile us unsegregated into the back of meat brawlers where countless assaults occur. I think the staff get off on these handcuffed cage fights. Although when it seems like the transfer officers might get in trouble because someone in their charge is being so seriously bashed by another inmate, or by a group of inmates, they pull to the side of the road and halt the bashing.

2002

Rumour has it that there is a *fatwah* out on me from the Lebanese yard – this coming in a time of plenty of verbal abuse, exchanged at the yard gates, between me and the Lebanese leadership inside NSW prisons.

I hide and remain in C Wing until an entire Lebanese yard-full comes in: convicted killers and hardcore gang members known for extreme acts of violence in and out of jail – including shooting up the Lakemba police station. I'm unarmed and alone but sometimes this is about who is the maddest cunt on the jailhouse floor.

Eight of them mob-attack me and I'm in the storm when the Special Response Group break it up. I'm bleeding from a split above the right eye but I don't want any stitches; I don't want anything but to stare down these fuckheads.

The next morning I go to the leader of the Lebs – right to his cell door. He didn't even come out when I was there yesterday. Just left it up to his group. The bloke's eyeballing me through his peep hole. 'So much for Hezbollah,' I say. 'Hiding from me. Were ya? Was that really the best your yard can do? I didn't even need a bandaid.'

He goes ballistic. But stays behind his door.

‖‖

Not willing to join the White Power group, I become more or less on my own in the Aussie–Asian yard.

I'm fairly tight with the Asian leadership and we do a lot of sparring, mainly when I'm bored and jump up on tables when they're playing cards. The screws are at first alarmed by this, especially when up to eight of them use me as a kick bag. 'Is that it?' I say, laughing at them and trying to increase their passion, the nasty little fucks. I'm having fun, even if I'm bruised and sore for days afterwards. I don't want to get stabbed or any shit like that, but the pain of a good barehanded fight means nothing to me. What little I feel of it feels good.

The Aussies in the yard don't like it at all. They're confused and feel powerless. I tell them to stay out of it as I throw the Asians around like rag dolls and cop a good pounding in return.

┼╫╫

Sometimes it's hard to feel at all.

One occasion in the yard I black out after hitting my head on concrete guttering, opening up a slice that needs ten stitches. The doctor isn't a bad bloke and he's asking if I want pain relief, but I just cut him dead: 'Stitch me up and stop talking,' I say. There's no pain anyway, nor emotions.

┼╫╫

I run solo and everybody knows this. So a lot of the time I'm at odds with the White Power group that run the Aussie side of things here.

When there's a real problem brewing between the yards, however, they want to hear my views and often let me make the call.

┼╫╫

There is an edict in the yard that I enforce passionately and brutally: sex offenders are not welcome.

When a sex offender is escorted into the yard, I give them two choices: leave voluntarily or be stretchered out never to return.

None of these vile animals are exempt, not even if they are well connected in the yard. I don't care who they know: no pass is given, and some hard fucks bleed.

Sometimes there are assassination attempts made against me in the yard, but vigilance-vigilance-vigilance saves me: life in the combat zone.

┼╫╫

Towards the end of my time at Goulburn I change into the Aussie–Islander yards, but the two groupings associate on the same oval together anyway for shared oval times, three times a week, and then we're in yards adjacent to each other. Plus we're living on the same landings. There isn't much difference.

LATE 2003

In 2003 I'm accepted to be paroled in Victoria.

But then the Purana Task Force supposedly receives intelligence that my life is in danger. I'm an associate of the Moran family, they say, causing Carl Williams to worry that I might target him; causing them to worry that Carl has decided on a pre-emptive strike on me. I'd love to hear more about all this and try to stop my parole being rejected but Purana make their presentations in secret and I have no fucking clue what's going on.

The duty parole solicitor tells me that in twenty years he's never seen such conduct. I can't get parole in either Victoria or NSW.

Am I pissed off? You fucking bet, and I refuse to comply with prison routine.

ͰͰͰ

Everything is revolting me so much I go to segregation for a self-imposed exile from the yards.

Studying Buddhism, I swipe a red Christmas tablecloth and bleach it heavily until it is orange. My prison greens get shredded and now I wear the orange cloth, focusing on peace and tranquillity.

The staff try to seize my orange robe; they don't like it and they don't want to tolerate it. But their attempts to strip me of my Buddhist clothing inflame the situation beyond where they want to take it. The staff are worried that my spiritual insubordination will spread to the rest of the jail.

It is agreed that I can have the orange sheet, on the condition I only wear it in my cell. If I go out it must be in normal prison garb.

This is how they reluctantly come to return my robe and leave me in isolation to protest peacefully and practise the teachings of Buddha.

The Buddhist retreat ends when a friend needs help in the yards.

The staff let me know that Gavin Preston – the bloke who got nabbed at the protest with Mum and Barry – is in custody over some foolish caper and that he is having major issues in the mainstream population.

How he winds up in NSW custody starts with his house getting shot up by Victor Brincat – one of Carl Williams' big triggermen – during the Melbourne gangland wars.

Gavin shit himself and fled the state in his car but he ran out of petrol and he ran out of money.

He was doing a petrol drive-off near Port Macquarie. The service station owner realised that he didn't pay, called his sons on the phone and what's happened is they done a scout of the area, spotted the car, followed him down a back road; he got bogged – it was muddy, okay. So he's jumped out of the car, produced a sawn-off shotgun, told them to fuck off.

They said, 'Listen mate, you didn't pay for your petrol. Maybe you forgot – we're giving you the chance before we call the police.'

He didn't have any money on him, but he tried to offer them four pills – eggies – and two grams of pot.

'Nah, we don't want the drugs, we want the money. If you can't pay the money we're calling the police.' They called the police. The police arrived and he's run to hide the gun. They just followed the footsteps in the mud, recovered the gun and got him.

Anyway, he winds up here eventually and the yard is refusing to accept him because of past acts that I won't go into.

But I am in debt to Gavin. He supported me and the other H Division hunger strikers even when he had a warrant out on him and we cost him his liberty. That's solid.

So I abandon my teachings and go down to confront the entire yard. It works, there's no blood spilt, and Gavin now has a place.

But Gavin and me?

Maybe we used to have something in common: our roots, our stomping grounds as kids, and I know Barry gets on okay with him and is good mates with his brother. And like I said about Gavin supporting the HSU-5 even at the cost of his liberty.

But something's shifted, you know, something's rubbing the wrong way, and don't forget everything I've said about how prison is a fucking rage factory where just breathing is to infuse hostility, and when it happens that Gavin's in that bloody yard fighting tooth and nail with somebody, that somebody is me.

We're both sent to isolation and face internal disciplinary charges over the stoush. And we're both later returned to the same yard, annoying the fuck out of each other.

I'm now 35 years old. It's about 22 years since I first entered custody. I've had some time out but mostly it's been in, and years of that have been spent twiddling my thumbs in a shitty little cell by myself. It's about eight years since arriving here via that crazy flight and power convoy, that crazy gunned up, maximum enemy-of-the-state danger-man extradition that had me feeling like Pablo Escobar. Who needs a fucking private narco-army, though. Here, if you can get your hands on a hacksaw blade it's enough to shake civilisation as we know it.

But anyway, I think after all this I'm qualified to say that Goulburn jail is a fucking awful old place. What's starting to really get at me is noticing an alarming rate of inmates being released and then returning, some within days, sadly.

And no wonder when there's little or no work opportunity and a lack of education time allocated to each yard. The inmates and education staff are both frustrated – you can tell – because it's so hard to make any progress.

On top of that, there's no real pre-release program to help prepare inmates for walking out into a fucking very complicated world that lives by a totally different set of rules, and a whole lot more complex rules than this jungle of fuckheads.

If they go out there and continue living the way that gets entrenched in here – for survival's sake – then they are fucked; people are going to get hurt and they are guaranteed to get locked up again.

Inmates getting out need post-release support. They need help to stabilise with housing once they're free from jail. You'd be amazed how many people walk out with nowhere to go, except maybe back to ask a favour of the kind of people that are still getting hectic.

We need some help getting productive and we need some help to transition.

It's playing on my mind so I decide to conduct some unauthorised research into inmates reoffending. Many of the education and prison staff support what I'm doing and they help, enabling me to photocopy and distribute the secret-ballot style questionnaire I make. Part of it is about the shitty conditions of the jail: our exposure to the weather and the lack of basic things like the means to hang up wet clothes, but the guts of it in terms of looking at reoffending is the section looking at what inmates actually get and what they want in terms of education and rehabilitation.

Despite the usual state of war, I manage to get all the different yards and ethnic groups of C Wing onside for this. We're not all fools, not all the time, anyway.

Without the staff's involvement, this exercise would never have got off the ground. Enough of them recognise the damning indictment unfolding for all to see: inmates who may as well have never left, so short was their time before reoffending; the same faces in the yards for years. And each time one of us goes out and reoffends the community is damaged again. Helping to stabilise and educate prisoners, helping them become productive members of the community outside, would be making society safer. Caging them in these rage factories and then dumping them out is not.

The results from the 130-odd completed questionnaires are overwhelming: we want help. We need and want a prison system that takes in fuckheads and unwinds them, that educates them, that calms and stabilises them, that teaches them how regular society works and prepares them for a place in that. And we want help afterwards so that we're not lost and confused and screwing up and regressing.

-HH-

I'm not afraid to say I'm too often Exhibit A. Just days before my release I get in a blue in the yard and the Emergency Response Group has to gas me to bring me down from rage mountain.

So don't get me wrong; yes, part of me can step back and see how fucked up things are and recognise the need for change. But my nerve endings, my adrenal glands, the solja in my soul, have been formed over decades of interlinking brutal contests between me and the police, me and the prisons, me and the inmates, me and the world.

So when the day comes after thirteen straight years in jail, almost nine in NSW, with years of it solitary and years of it race-hate combat zones – when the day comes that they open the gate, giving me half a dole cheque and a train ticket to Sydney: when that day is now I walk free with Charles Manson eyes and the heart of a pitbull.

Into a limousine.

At liberty after thirteen years.

INTO ANOTHER WORLD

2005:
SYDNEY'S STREETS

Looking around at Sydney my head is spinning. I'm walking into a different world. Literally. I've spent so long inside that I've come out and the currency's different; when I went in in 1992 the currency was still paper and now it's all plastic. So much has changed: the cars, the mobile phones, technology, everything.

When I went into custody in 1992 there was the Motorola bricks. They were fucking like $5000 each – not many people had them. Now every cunt's got a little Nokia. And what's this other shit – walking through the city there's all these people talking to themselves. Or talking to me, are they? What the fuck? But no, it's Bluetooth. Weird fucking devices, man. My life has lurched into the future. It's spinning me out.

Everything's doing my head in. Especially 'cos I've been in isolation so much and I'm used to a little yard like about three metres by fucking four and a half or something like that.

I wish I'd been settled before release; inmates need to be acclimatised before being released from those environments and conditions. But I haven't been and inside I just want to run wild. What am I good at now? War. What skills do I have? War. Oh, and I can drop and do 100 push-ups without breaking a sweat. I can do 600 in a few sets.

But what do I do now? How do I contain the BADNE$$? Take the cell away; take the cages away; take the screws away and now I don't have those ego boundaries. I'm feeling silly. I'm a spinning top. I'm deranged; I'm electric; I see all the daily hurly burly of normal civilian life around me and I'm like, 'I don't give a fuck about this; I don't give a fuck about that.'

I'm full of hate. I'm angry. Sure, I enjoy being able to buy food and clothes; of course I like freedom, but after a short period you start to get – well, it's hard to explain: you just don't fit in. You're not settled. You're not comfortable. You feel awkward. You don't feel right. You just feel out of place – you really do.

And it's so fucked up, you know, because you'd think, 'Oh great, I've put that life behind me. I want to forget about it – they're bad memories.'

But it's not the case. It doesn't work like that. Especially with me. I've done so long, I don't know any better – my nerves are fused. I don't know any different. Out here, it's all foreign. It's another world.

MEDIA BLITZ

CHRIS:

Staying in Sydney, I do a four-day media blitz to get this message out. With the help of good-hearted, good-headed comrades like Brett Collins, a rehabilitated former inmate who runs Justice Action, I'm doing interviews with newspapers, with TV – the ABC even interviews me for *Four Corners* – I talk to Peter FitzSimons on air and a legal program on

A freshly released Chris telling the Sydney Morning Herald about prison life

ABC Radio National. I keep explaining what negative time prison is – how it's even worse than a lost opportunity – and what society needs is for inmates to be educated, settled, prepared and helped. Then everybody's safer.

A NSW Greens MP, Lee Rhiannon, holds a press conference with me at which we discuss the unauthorised

Chris and NSW Greens MP (later Senator) Lee Rhiannon front a press conference.

survey I ran at Goulburn and the great desire it shows that inmates have for real education in prison – not Mickey Mouse courses squeezed in (more like squeezed out) here and there but a sincere and serious program of educating us misfits behind bars. And it shows how bad conditions are in that wretched old place. Pentridge was like that and it's been shut for years.

I want to present my survey to the NSW Government but they won't take it. Not interested. I'm a scumbag.

What a bunch of stooges. I guess they're waiting for some mild-mannered choirboy who's never done anything wrong to come out from years in jail and give them the word on what's really happening.

The longer the prison system goes on entrenching its pig-headed us-versus-them mentality in inmates, the more inmates are gonna come out in a brutalised state: a state of anger, a state of trauma, a state that is dangerous to the community.

Why the fuck wouldn't you want to take a crim, someone who is at war with society, and do everything you reasonably can to calm them, to get them educated – I didn't even finish Year 8 – to get them skilled as tradespeople or professionals, to teach them how to be responsible and make it in the regular world, instead of taking all the illegal shortcuts that seem easier at the time.

But if a crim's talking, quick: stick your fingers in your ears.

7 DECEMBER 2004: NSW LEGISLATIVE COUNCIL 13383
GOULBURN CORRECTIONAL CENTRE SURVEY

Ms LEE RHIANNON (10.22 p.m.): Christopher Binse, a long-term inmate of the C-Wing of Goulburn maximum-security gaol, has undertaken a survey of his fellow inmates, and it paints a revealing picture of conditions at the gaol. Mr Binse photocopied his survey on slips of paper and circulated them. He got 134 responses to his questions about conditions in the wing and the availability of rehabilitation programs. The survey results show that Goulburn gaol is violating the United Nations standard minimum rules for the treatment of prisoners. Under rule 6.1 there is supposed to be no discrimination, yet inmates are separated into different yards on the basis of their ethnicity. Under rule 10 prisoners are supposed to be protected from weather extremes, but the yard is exposed to the elements. Inmates are also refused permission to return to their cells when the weather is bad. Under rule 17.1 prisoners are supposed to have adequate clothing, but it is not enough to withstand Goulburn's winter. Under 17.2 that clothing should be kept in proper condition, but there are no facilities for inmates to hang up their wet clothes, jackets and towels. This has caused illness among the inmates. Rules 58, 60.2 and 64 relate to rehabilitation and post-release care, but it is clear from the survey that, although prisoners are very willing to undertake education and rehabilitation programs, and they want to get out of gaol and stay out, they are simply not getting access to adequate programs. I congratulate Mr Binse for undertaking this survey, and I urge the Minister for Justice to seriously consider how to improve conditions and rehabilitation programs at Goulburn gaol and indeed all New South Wales prisons.

3 MARCH 2005: NSW LEGISLATIVE COUNCIL 14573
PRISON SYSTEM REFORM

The Hon. AMANDA FAZIO: My question is directed to the Minister for Justice. What is the New South Wales Government's response to recent calls to reform the prison system?

The Hon. JOHN HATZISTERGOS: Honourable members will be aware that, following the release of Christopher Binse from prison in February this year, a number of requests were made of me—both publicly and with the support of at least one member of this House—that I accord Mr Binse a visit to my office and, according to one media report, that I employ him as a consultant on rehabilitation, which Mr Binse was severely critical of in the context of the New South Wales prison system.

Honourable members will also recall that on 7 December 2004 Ms Lee Rhiannon took the opportunity afforded by the adjournment debate to congratulate Mr

Binse on circulating a prohibited questionnaire among fellow inmates and encouraging more to do the same.

On 11 February, following Mr Binse's release from custody at the end of a 13-year term, Ms Lee Rhiannon accompanied him to the Parliament's media room for the purposes of holding a press conference to expound and support his claims.

Let me make it quite clear that I will not employ Mr Binse in any capacity, let alone to advise on rehabilitation.

Before any member of this House decides to push the agenda of individuals such as Mr Binse they ought to know with whom they are dealing.

The correctional system tries to give all offenders opportunities to address their offending behaviour, but in some instances it is dealing with very difficult material.

I will edify the House about the sort of person Mr Binse was, to confirm the Parole Board's wisdom in denying him parole on four occasions and ensuring that he served the whole 13-year term before he was released.

This is a man who describes himself as 'Badness'. He was described in a publication entitled *Tough: 101 Australian Gangsters* in regard to offences including armed robbery, kidnapping and using a firearm in public. He had previous convictions in Victoria for escape, attempted escape, threatening life, assault police and illegally possessing and using a pistol. After he committed an armed robbery in Melbourne he took out an advertisement in the Melbourne *Herald Sun*, which stated 'Badness is back'. He bought a Queensland property with armed robbery money and named it Badlands.

The reason he gave as to why he enjoyed committing armed robberies was: For the excitement, the rush ... you're in control, your blood starts rushing ... it's an addiction.

In 1993 he was the leader of a plan to free up to 30 of Victoria's most dangerous prisoners, including double murderers, drug traffickers and escape experts, from Pentridge Prison. His plans involved taking hostage prison guards and other selected inmates to be killed as a payback.

That is just one of the reasons that while he was imprisoned in Victoria he was the only prisoner to be shackled in leg-irons and handcuffs for 23 hours a day.

As I said, the Parole Board is to be commended for its wisdom in denying him parole, not only on the basis of that history, but also because his record in custody was frankly appalling, including assault, possession of contraband, fighting and refusing to provide urine samples.

He claims he was denied opportunities to reform his offending behaviour. I can advise the House that he was offered, and refused to complete, a violence prevention program at Long Bay Correctional Complex—a program which, bearing in mind his prison and previous record, one would think was one of the most important programs for him to undertake.

I advise Ms Lee Rhiannon to use her position in this House a little bit more responsibly, and not support the twisted agenda of people such as Mr Binse. I wish him well on his return into the community, but I am certainly not going to provide him with any platform to rehabilitate anyone in the prison system.

ROAD TO FATHERHOOD

AROUND MARCH 2005:
GOLD COAST

CHRIS:

After four days going hard on the media campaign, blitzing the airwaves and papers and going to fucking Parliament House twice, I'm fucking overloaded – drained out.

Once I have achieved what we had to do and the initial straight-from-the-horse's-mouth public awareness mission is complete, it's time to let it settle and let things take their course.

So I say, 'Listen fellas, I've gotta go but I'll come back in a couple of weeks, time to allow the momentum to gain – catching up with academics, professors, this and that, community groups, victims of crime, and all this sort of stuff.'

I'm planning to head to Melbourne to meet a juvenile justice worker from Turana. We've had lengthy discussions about making a pilot program together to scare the young boys straight with firsthand accounts of the perils of crime. He'd even presented his superiors at Turana with a paper on it. I would be unpaid and we'd both supervise it.

But word comes that it's rejected by head office. Apparently, I'm unsuitable for such programs. I'm gutted.

What the fuck. How worthless am I?

#####

Man, I don't know what to do; I'm overwhelmed. I just hide behind a haze of pot, except when I pop up through it with the aid of an eggie. And then come down and keep on smoking.

Society and me are at odds. I don't fit in it. I don't in jail, either. Nowhere.

#####

Time for R&R. I haven't even caught up with a sheila – that's the first thing a bloke wants to do: get out there and have a fuck!

Some mates are staying at the Gold Coast and tell me to get up there so with the campaign finished I decide to head north.

I'm met at the airport and they take me back to all the fucking strippers, you know, especially at Hollywood, because they have friends there, they know people there – these are underworld figures, too, you know, and they have a little bit of influence.

What happens is I haven't seen pussy in thirteen years – except for half an hour with a prostitute in the Cross when the media blitz was winding up. Now I'm seeing that much skin and flesh of naked women, I am overloaded. I am just overloaded. Every sheila, every worker, every girl that was there, me mates make sure: 'Here, we'll just pay you this – take him in for half an hour.'

I've got so much pussy in me face it's like, what the fuck? By the end of it I can't even get a fat I am so overloaded with pussy, you know. Some of them two or three times. They are going out of their way for me, you know: 'You're with us, you're part of our crew. We'll look after you, you haven't seen pussy.' Bang! Overloaded!

My group of mates have a timeshare penthouse apartment. They're heading back to Melbourne but they leave me the pad to stay in for a bit. I can just kick back and relax in the sun and catch up on life. The extended group gives me a large stack of cash donations to help me out and get me on my feet. So from the shithole of Goulburn, now I have free accommodation across from the beach, the weather is great, there's cash in my pocket: life is good.

I ring up a sheila friend of mine. I say, 'Listen, you got any girlfriends?'

She goes, 'Yeah, Kylie. You'd like her. She's a bit of a wild party girl and she'd be up for it – she'd love you.'

I say, 'Yeah, really? I'm not after a relationship.'

She goes, 'Nah, she's sweet for that, you know.'

The sheila takes my mobile number to pass on to her friend.

Kylie calls soon afterwards; it turns out she's living in a penthouse apartment not even 50 metres from where I'm staying. Four of 'em, they rent out a penthouse in Broadbeach for twelve months, spend three months each on the rent or whatever. It is cheaper for them than a motel and they have more privacy. And she's working doing cleaning in a couple of the units.

She knows I've just got out from jail after serving thirteen years but this doesn't scare her off at all. It excites her.

She's rapt because she comes from a criminal dynasty – I'm like a trophy to her. She wants to impress: 'Oh, you've got to meet my mum.' Because her mum was a gangster moll in her day, too. Still is. Kylie's stepdad was Laurie Prendergast, one of the Great Bookie Robbery crew from 1976. He disappeared in 1985, presumed murdered and probably put through meat processing to turn him into pig food. But anyway, Kylie's excited by me.

I take her out to dinner, have a bottle of wine; we return to the apartment and go to my room to smoke some joints. She wants to go to the beach for sex instead of doing it in the room, so we walk down and she's talking about the underworld in Victoria, big-noting herself like it somehow matters in gaining my acceptance.

But then under the stars on that beach I'm fucking her, you know? And that's all it is. I say to her, 'Look, I'm not after relationships or anything like that.'

She says, 'Yeah, I'm fine with that.'

We spend about two weeks, you know, and she's not much to look at – I'll be the first to tell you – but she is warm, woman and wet. And she's willing. I have a joint, a glass of wine or an E or something and I just close my eyes while she's sucking my dick. It's nothing serious, you know?

After two weeks I leave, go back to Victoria and catch up with friends and family and all that sort of stuff and then it's back to Sydney and then back up to Surfers where I catch up with her again.

And where she deliberately falls pregnant.

She deliberately falls pregnant because she wants to be a permanent fixture in my life. That's what she tells me, and that's what her mum tells me.

All the time I say to her, 'I'm not ready for this, I don't know where my life is at this point in time. I've got to get grounded first myself.'

It puts so much pressure on me. I don't want to be a father yet. I'm not ready for it. I'm not even in a relationship with her – what the fuck? If you're going to have a child you're going to have a child with someone you love, someone you're committed to, that you want to be with, that you're living under the same roof together – not just a party moll.

She's clucky; she really wants a kid and for her it's the genes: me. To have a child born from me. She knows that I haven't had any other kids and she wants to be the one that basically has the trophy: 'I have his child.' Because of the criminal fucking underworld fucking ideality that she got brought up in. I have a reputation – I'm crazy – which a lot of people respect!

So: 'I've got his child.' And that's how she parades herself.

I say to her: 'Listen, we're not in a relationship. I'll be the best father I can but I have my own independence. I'm a bachelor, okay? I'll try to be the best, but I don't come with the kid.'

She knows – I never hide it – that I'm seeing five different sheilas at the time. I am fucking them. No word of a lie: when I say I'm catching up, I'm catching up, mate. I'm a playboy, a player, and I never hide them.

One is a lesbian and I get her back on track, then I have the bi ones – whatever craving I have for the day I catch up with that sheila, you know. If some of them just love arse I'll catch up with that one for the day. Or I'll catch up with two or three on the same day. It just depends how I am going.

There's a following, man. If you've got a bit of a reputation they all thrive on it. Tattoos, bald heads, stuff like that – it excites 'em. They like that naughty thing, you know. I don't know why but they're drawn to that.

But I never hide the fact, and they all know that they're not the only ones: 'Listen, we're buddies. If you're not comfortable with that – listen, I see other people and I encourage you, if you want to see other people, mate, please don't let me hold you back. Don't think that I'm exclusively yours or you're exclusively mine; it's not like that – no.'

While Kylie's pregnant she's living in Queensland. She comes back down for a little bit and tries to spend more time with me but she realises I'm not interested.

DEBT COLLECTOR

2005:
MELBOURNE

CHRIS:

Gotta make a living, right – one that doesn't involve jumping counters.

So, having weighed up the lessons learned in prison and what abilities I have, I become a debt collector.

Now I'm working with people who the community might see as not quite so decent: the way this gig operates is that Person A owes a stack to Person B but Person B isn't really in a position to do what has to be done to collect, so they sell that debt at a markdown to Person C who then hires Person D, being me, to collect as close to the full amount as possible, thereby delivering a payday to Persons C and D.

It's not what you'd send your kids to university for, but then again I wouldn't be surprised if the whiz-kids at the banks operate their own version of this.

With a child on the way and all, I'm serious about making a good fist of entrepreneurialism and I print a run of business cards.

My trading name is MAYHEM INCORPORATED, with the company motto: 'Let's Get Hectic'. Cheeky, no doubt, but true to my can-do spirit.

Yet someone's going to be calling in the collectors on me if I keep hitting the drugs this hard. It's not just pot and some eggies, either. I'm pressing the pedal to the metal with the cocaine. It plugs straight into where I'm at: when I shake my jowls after a good snort it's like I'm shaking off all the shit pulling at me, all the black shadows coming in, all the pressure, all that fucking need to sort shit out in the most direct way possible. It calms me up to absurd heights, if that makes any sense.

#

You should see my dog, Runty. He's the fucking best. I tell all the women in my life that.

#

And man do I need a line when a debt recovery comes up that requires dropping in on a bloke who is not the type to get pushed around: Amad 'Jay' Malkoun.

Malkoun spends a fair amount of his time at the Spearmint Rhino strip club on King Street in Melbourne; it's his lair. Sometimes it pays to have the element of surprise and other times it's best if everybody knows what's happening in advance. For this mission, it's best there are no surprises.

Call me old-fashioned but I like chasing that white streak down a mirror. Either that or off a ticklish sheila's backside.

Duly fired up again, I call the Rhino and spell out to some clown how it's going to work.

I tool up with my trusty .32, fire up again for the road, fire up a bit more, and fucking hit the club.

NOVEMBER, 2005

It doesn't go well. No one knows what I'm talking about or will tell me where Jay is, and the fucking massive dumb prick of a bouncer tries to get hostile, tries to engage, so I produce the weapon and point it at both of 'em. 'Wanna die, cunt?' I ask the bouncer. 'Wanna fucking die? I'll fucking shoot ya.' The receptionist is practically peeing her panties, and still no one has a fucking clue. 'Which fuckhead here was I talking to before, hey? What the fuck! Where's Jay?' Placing a bullet on the counter, I say this is for Jay and storm out. Only to fucking realise that in no way did I hide my identity and it's probably all been videoed so I go back in and fucking play it again, Sam, with the poor bastards. Once again I tell the petrified sheila behind the counter that one word to the fucking coppers and I'll find her – I'll fucking find her. I'll shoot her.

Now I'm storming out again. Jesus, what a debacle; what a fucking putrid grub I am. And I'm going to be a father. What the fuck, you know.

What were those fucking songs we used to drive Chopper Read up the wall with a lifetime ago in the yard at Pentridge? Seal's 'Crazy' and Bon Jovi's 'Wanted Dead or Alive'.

Well I'm both, yet again. Triple-A fucking dickhead. Snorting fucking blind rhino I am. De-fuckin'-ranged.

Warrants are soon out for my arrest. I'm indeed hot again.

ꀀ꜔꜔꜔

'Hey, Runty,' I'm saying as I ruffle the fur of my beautiful dog, my Argentine Dogo pup. He's riding shotgun as we cross the city.

Such a good dog. I love my little furry solja.

Fuck we're cut off. Here we fucking go. Fucking SOG.

Mayhem Incorporated: Chris in custody following his debt collecting efforts at the Spearmint Rhino.

One of Chris' surprisingly understated business cards.

THE FATHER

CHRIS:

Shot straight into isolation in the Charlotte punishment unit of Port Phillip Prison. I fucking demand to be placed in mainstream but they're not even fucking listening; they won't explain why I'm in management, why I'm in isolation. It's a bullshit abuse of power. It's persecution. And Kylie's going to have my baby. They won't even let me have a contact visit. Can't even hold her. Just stare through perspex. And she's going to have my baby. My child. Where's fucking dad, hey? And Runty's on a destruction order. I can't take this shit. I can't take it. Can't take it. Pacing the cell. What are they fucking doing? Why are they doing this? Headbutting the fucking door. Why are they doing this? What the fuck, what the fuck, what the fuck. Let me the fuck out. Round and round. Gonna be a daddy. Where's daddy? He's in a tiny room. Where are you? Out there. In Kylie.

Where am I? In a tiny room. The belly of the beast. I'm a beast and I swallow myself. I swallow hope. But the prisons, man. What is this shit? Where's Runty? They're going to kill him. Where's daddy? He's in a tiny room going fucking insane. Why doesn't he come and feel me kicking? 'Cos he's a total fuck up. He's nothing. He's total rubbish. Let me the fuck out. Get me the fuck out. I need to hold my people. I need to hold my dog. I need to protect everybody. I need to stop the destruction. I'm sorry. Fuck you. It's about time everyone else fucking stepped up. It's about time these fucking walls fell down. I need more room. I can't keep pacing here. It's too small. I'm sorry. I want to die but I'm going to be a dad. Dads don't die. Mine did, but only after he handed the instrument of liberation to his eldest son. Blow the fucking trumpets. Knock the fucking walls down.

卌

So I'm medicated. I've taken the weak way out to cope and to blur all this shit out. Last time I accepted their zombie pills was, I think, eighteen years ago in Geelong Prison. That jail's long gone – shut down. But I'm still stumbling around.

They tip me to Barwon. Hello Barwon – I'm even in the fucking Banksia Unit again – remember me? I remember you. I remember having you fucking whipped. I remember sawing my way out and having the ladders that could have been stilts to walk like a giant over your walls and into the fog of a winter's night on Corio Bay. But it was Johnny's call and call it he did.

In April Kylie has my baby. She brings my daughter into the world.

While I'm locked in here.

My daughter is the sun. My heart doubles, triples – in love and pain. I never understood before. I never knew that I hadn't really loved anyone or anything more than myself but now I feel it through everything and in every moment, day or night, light or dark. I love her. I want to protect her, to hold her, to care for her, to play with her. I am her dad. And I'm not there.

‖‖

It's May. She's a month old.

‖‖

An inmate is saying that Gavin Preston is getting transferred here. Merry-go-round, hey. Makes ya dizzy. I feel dizzy.

The inmate is a bit geed up about Gavin, who lands in Acacia alongside his POW gang-leader mate, Matty Johnson.

I didn't know but the inmate had an axe to grind with them both and he's really laying it on about Gavin: 'He's saying all this shit about you. He's saying he bashed ya in NSW.'

I go, 'What the fuck?' Then I explain to him that Preston thinks he's a hard cunt, thinks he's a fucking hitman, 'cos he's running around with Benji – Andrew Veniamin the hitman – that he's saying they're really good mates and they've done this and done that, all these murders. And that it's all bullshit.

I say to the guy, 'Mate, that's a fucking load of shit. He's a fucking liar. He's a fucking shit-talking anus. He couldn't even take petrol. Ask him about that.'

So I unearthed Gavin.

And now they decide to move Matty Johnson and Gavin to Banksia. I don't mention to the screws that I have issues with him. In fact, I say, 'We'll get together in the yard and we'll catch up,' thinking I'll sort this out myself.

And once that bloke starts declaring what I've said in front of all his mates, everyone hears what's going on. He's got all the inmates crouched up the rear of the cells listening and watching through the windows, you know. There's a bit of an audience.

There's a bit of stage play, a bit of performance, and Gavin knows it's come from me 'cos I was the one in Sydney at the time.

He goes to me, 'You think you're a hard cunt, coming out with that?'

He's dirty 'cos he's lost his self-esteem, he's lost his respect; he's lost his standing in front of all the POWs – in front of his boys. He's made to look silly.

That consumes him, but he and Matty are concerned that they aren't prepared for the confrontation, so they gee up two fucking idiots: a fella pinched on murder and a fucking psycho – two gooses. Gavin and Matty put the pressure on them, put the fear in. These gooses are – well, one of them is a deadset spastic. No, I won't say spastic but brain dead.

I'm in the yard, heavily medicated. I've got a lot of issues. I don't know what the fuck's going on. All I can think about are my daughter and my dog.

There's a commotion in the yard adjacent. It's Gavin and Matt Johnson, yelling, 'Go go go! Get him! Get him! Get him!' Get who? What?

I don't know what the fuck's going on until the third time in a row I'm smashed in the head with tins of tuna in a sock. That's how fucked up on medication I am. The third fucking smash to the head and just now I'm thinking, 'What the fuck?'

There's two of them attacking me. And everyone's pressed around the wire yelling, 'Do it, do it, do it! Get him, get him, get him!' I'm in the arena. Two of them are attacking. They're trying to knock me out and my reactions are so dulled.

Now I realise what's going on. I chase them. I hit one, the big fella pinched on murder, and he's going down but he's pulling me down with him and it's like a bear hug on the ground. He's not worried about fighting, he's just wrestling with me, and while we're wrestling the other cunt comes from the side: slash-slash-slash-slash-slash – all within five seconds with a razor. It's this quick, and I'm up and gaining control. I'm recovering my wits, my switch to combat mode. I know there's blood. At first I think it's from around my eye, the side of my face, where they got me with the tuna cans. But I'm starting to realise the extent of my injuries; I'm cut to shreds – my wounds hanging open. And I'm trapped in the yard. I disarm one of them, get his weapon: two plastic knives with razor blades fused in between, like a cut-throat. So now I've got it off him and they run to the corner where I bail them up. I know the law on self-defence and I'm in a crime scene now. If I do anything, my blood trail will show that I challenged them, that I am no longer in defence, that I am attacking them. If I try to slash them, to kill them, whatever, then I'll be charged. I try to lure them back out to fight: 'Come on, give me a chance.'

Then I'm looking at the situation – what the fuck – with my blood still settling, staring at Gavin and Matty thinking: 'What the fuck? Youse behind this? Youse didn't want to get in the yard, and whatever I do to these fools here doesn't get me closer to who controlled it, who organised it.'

The two gooses won't come out. And I have to walk up and down for an hour and a half. I feel nothing but war mode: no pain and no emotion.

The psycho has made a deliberate attempt to severe the main arteries on both my inner thighs, along with other, serious slash points on my torso, head and neck. I also have defensive wounds from fending this off – the fingers of my right hand are damaged.

The murderer got slashed, too, in the frenzy.

ℍℍ

When it's time to front up and get medical help, the first thing they do is ask what happened.

'Nothing happened. Why?'

An officer tells me years later, and I believe this, that I was hated by the staff, especially senior management and the POWs were very close with them. I believe this was organised and orchestrated by staff and inmates, the POWs. The tuna was passed to the fools from Preston by prison staff fifteen minutes before the attack. They launched when I was in the right position in the yard – right down the end, out of the way – where staff could choose not to see. They walked past twice within an hour and a half. I don't yell out asking for intervention or anything like that. That's exactly what they were hoping for. The others were hoping that I would bail out, I'd leave, I'd surrender, fuck off see ya later. But I kept on walking up and down. I nearly bled to death, man. And I made sure that when there was a yard change, a swap over, that they left the yard before I did. That they got back to their cell. I had to clean up the fucking mess – get rid of the evidence. There was bits and pieces in the centre of the yard: tins of tuna, the sock, other things, and blood. They weren't prepared to come out into the centre of the yard and clean that, to get rid of that. I had to mop that, to clean that up, I had to get rid of that. If I'd left it there they would have got charged. None of them got charged. I never said a word. Police come to see me but no one was ever charged in relation to this.

Gavin and Matt were the leaders of the POWs, so they had influence on these other two people who were shitting themselves because one of them was going back out to the mainstream, out back into the general population, and he had issues, problems, and he needed people's support. So he basically found himself in a situation where 'I've got to do something, I need numbers, I need people, I need help. Basically, I'll do something for youse; youse do something for me.' But it wasn't like that. It was forced, and they knew that, too. So they said, 'Listen, we'll look after ya. You go out the back: you're with us. You prove yourself here, then you go out the back and you're with us so you haven't got a problem.'

And then the other one was just psychotic. He had a history of slashing inmates really bad, you know, and slashing prison officers – cutting their throats and everything. An officer nearly died as a result of his wounds. But again, slash and run. He's just a fucking coward. Wouldn't stand toe to toe. Couldn't fight. And they used to root him. Seriously. This is no word of a lie: they literally used to root him.

I looked at 'em. Two fucking gooses. Two fools. I felt sorry for 'em, in a way. But I was still fuming.

JULY 2007

CHRIS:

I'm transferred to Marngoneet, which is a satellite jail of Barwon that offers what passes for rehabilitation courses. I've been slated to participate in programs for people with drug and violence problems.

╫╫

The compound I'm in has a total muster of 110 inmates, all specifically identified for violence, and the astonishing fact is that the kitchen knives are untethered and accessible to all of us.

Meeting No 06/33   Type SENTENCE MANAGEMENT PANEL
Date 08 JUN 06 Meeting Name PORT PHILLIP CHARLOTTE SEPARATION

CRN   43517   BINSE CHRISTOPHER DEAN   Status USOO
Person Id 534090730 PORT PHILLIP CHARLOTTE LOPS   DOB 07 OCT 1968   A2*

Reason   1. DISCUSSION

Decision   1. INTERMEDIATE PLACEMENT PORT PHILLIP CHARLOTTE
           2. CLASSIFIED LOCATION PORT PHILLIP CHARLOTTE
           3. HIGH SECURITY ESCORT REQUIRED
           4. HIGH PROFILE PRISONER
           5. SECURITY RATING A2* (MANAGEMENT
              SECURITY
              NOTORIETY
              SECURITY/PENDING INVESTIGATION)
           6. REFER TO DIRECTOR STATEWIDE SERVICES

Comments   MEETING WITH MOU, SEEN IN ST JOHNS
           HOSPITAL AFTER RECENT INCIDENT IN
           BANKSIA WHERE HE WAS ALLEGEDLY ASSAULTED
           ██████████████████████ WHILST THE 3
           OF THEM WERE IN THE EXERCISE YARD. THE
           EXTENT OF THE INJURIES TO BINSE WERE
           OBVIOUS ON INTERVIEW HE THOUGHT HE WAS
           LUCKY THAT THE INJURIES WERE NOT WORSE.
           ASKED ABOUT THE MOTIVATION FOR THE
           ALLEGED ASSAULT, FIRSTLY, AND
           UNSURPRISINGLY BINSE REFUSED TO COMMENT
           WHICH IS CONSISTENT WITH THE APPROACH TO
           INVESTIGATING POLICE.
           ASKED WHETHER HE KNEW EITHER OF THE
           OTHER TWO IN THE YARD WITH HIM AT THE
           TIME BINSE STATED NO, HE DIDNT KNOW THEM
           PREVIOUSLY TO THE INCIDENT THEREFORE HE
           DIDNT BELIEVE THERE WAS PERSONAL
           MOTIVATION. GIVEN PRESTON & JOHNSON WERE
           DIRECTLY ACROSS IN ANOTHER YARD AND HAD
           FULL VIEW OF THE YARD BINSE WAS IN, AND,
           BINSE ████████ ALLEGEDLY HAD A FIGHT
           AND A FALLING OUT WHILST BOTH WERE
           IMPRISONED IN NSW COULD THIS ALLEGED
           ASSAULT HAVE BEEN ARRANGED BY OTHERS,
           THAT THE ACTUAL ASSAULT TURNED INTO A
           SPECTATOR SPORT FOR OTHERS. BINSE
           INDICATED THAT HE DIDNT ████████████
           THIS VIEW.
           *** PLACEMENT***
           CLEARLY BARWON PRISON IS UNSUITABLE FOR
           THE FORESEEABLE FUTURE.
           BINSE REMAINS A MANAGEMENT PRISONER NOT
           WITH STANDING THE LATEST INCIDENT
           THE LATEST INCIDENT ONLY MAKES ANY
           FURTHER PLACEMENTS VERY DIFFICULT INDEED
           MRC MGT UNIT IS NOT YET OPERATIONAL -
           MAY BE A CONSIDERATION AT A LATER STAGE

There's no need to make a shiv here, although with only about 30 knives available, some inmates would have to share.

Within weeks a convicted murderer with a history of extreme violence in jail confronts me wielding a large kitchen knife. Fearing for my life, I flick to attack mode and he bolts. I chase him across the compound as he runs to prison staff, wanting to be locked away secure in his cell.

I can see the severed tendon in my left index finger.

When the inevitable investigation comes, I tell them I was cutting a grapefruit in my hand instead of on a chopping board. But the staff see it all on CCTV.

Back in Marngoneet after micro-surgery, I'm acting up – I'm going ballistic and threatening staff over visitation screw-ups with Kylie. I'm getting paranoid, assuming the worst all the time. I'm jumping out of my skin. My little girl's out there, and she's one heading towards two, ya know. Time's going by; it's really going by: slow in here and fast out there. It's excruciating. It's driving me nuts. And how is this place, that place, any of these fucking places, going to help me settle. I need help. I need help to get calm. I need help to settle. But this is just twisted shit. This is the opposite of therapeutic. I'm getting troubled and angry. Please help me. Please change this. Psychologists keep writing reports about how bad isolation is and how lacking our prisons are in seriously tackling rehabilitation. I've been in this shit since I was thirteen. What the fuck? That's what – 26 years ago. So what's happened in that time? The bash, the belting by guards, is no longer acceptable but at the drop of a hat they'll stick me in solitary confinement to go crazy. Otherwise it's gladiator time. What is this – some weird experiment? Am I a lab rat? Why was I selected as a child for this? Who selected me? What god does this?

＃

My threatening tirades at staff land me in solitary again, and then I'm tipped back to Barwon where the psycho who sliced me up is still in residence. Officers tell me he's now fixated on me, making threats, yelling and screaming. The guy is a drooling freak that normally I'd dismiss but he's got the blood lust. He's not a rational combatant. He's a glaze-eyed thing from the depths.

When officers catch him with a shiv, they move me.

And then I'm moved again.

It's back to Marngoneet for a six-month 'intensive violence' course – hopefully without knife-wielding killers coming at me. But during a three-day drug seminar I am accused of laughing and sent back to Barwon to be placed in solitary in the supermax wing, Melaleuca. The other inmates include a cast of warring gangland figures. I sit in my isolation unit and listen to the shouts and abuse traded between cells.

My release is coming up and, to my utter horror and dismay, this is how I'm being prepared. Like many times before, I revert to a hunger strike. I won't take part in this world.

＃

They move me to the Melbourne Assessment Prison to make reports on possible parole but when that's complete they say it's back to supermax, back to Melaleuca, back to 22 hours a day in a small room, with the brief times out never in the company of anyone but guards, and all the time living amidst and getting caught up in thunderous hate-fuelled slanging matches.

311

The idea that this is how you prepare a damaged person, an anti-social person, to re-enter society is dogshit insane.

I'd rather be in hospital with a drip hanging out of my arm, so in front of the staff I swallow metal objects. I'm kept overnight at St Vincent's – yes, back to St Augustine's Ward: around and around we go – where they keep me overnight, and then I do it again.

After treatment I'm sent to Port Phillip Prison where they keep me in solitary until my release. Except for a couple of nights in hospital, the last six months of my term are all solitary.

And I'm regressing. Eighteen years ago in the depths of Pentridge, I made the 'Eat Shit & Die' t-shirt for my classification meeting. I make another one now and wear it out the fucking gate.

I am a time bomb.

Released 2 April 2008.

What better paper weight for an outlaw?
Later discovered in Chris' arsenal.

SHEILAS

2005–08

In or out of jail, the mid to late 2000s were a complicated time for Chris in terms of relationships.

CHRIS:

There was a couple of sheilas that I wouldn't rate highly. That were nothing, really. But then there was Rachel. I'm spewing that I left that relationship. I actually abandoned her. I was with her in 2006 at the time that I was with Kylie. I was with a couple of them, but Rachel was my numero uno – my alpha: she was my alpha mistress. I was living with her and when I come to jail I was with her and then I ended the relationship in exchange for Silvia.

And Silvia was just nothing but a headache. Just a drama queen. That's all she's been in my life. Nothing but dramas. It's so fucked up.

And then there was another one, Jess. She was seventeen years my junior. I felt uncomfortable with the age gap, but she didn't. We got along really well. She still writes to me now. But again, what sabotaged that was Silvia.

Some sheilas that I've had stable relationships with in my life, Silvia's come in, poked her head in because she was a mad fuck, really good sex, she'd come in and gatecrash it and just destroy whatever I had going. That's what happens – she keeps coming along and sabotaging things. But she was just a really good fuck, you know, and I always abandoned them and I'm spewing about that.

Especially Jess. I was with Jess when she was twenty. This was in 2005. And I was starting to see her in bits and pieces – off and on, you know. I was seeing five different sheilas at the same time. Didn't hide it either. I'd say, 'Listen, I'm not after relationships.' But Jess and me just started getting things together: slowly, slowly, because I had reservations about women. I wouldn't sacrifice. I wouldn't commit myself to them. I'd just see how they go and how I get along with them. That way every time I spent with them was quality time.

When I come to jail in 2006 I was in a relationship with Jess and a couple of others, Rachel too. I stayed with Rachel for about six months and then I ended the relationship and then Silvia started coming out to see me and I also held on to Jess. All of them wanted to come out and see me. They were all actually coming out to see me.

And then towards the end I just started culling them back. Know what I mean? So I culled them all back and remained with Jess, and let Jess and Kylie only visit me – Kylie only because she was the mother of my child.

I had people outside providing her an allowance: $500 a month, whatever she needed, if she needed anything for the kid – whatever. I bought her two cars during that period. The first one she had for a while and then she just ran it into the ground, damaged it, smashed it, this and that, decided she didn't want me to see the state of the vehicle, okay, so she sabotaged the motor – got a friend to pull something – and complained to me, 'Oh, it's not working.'

So I reach out to a mate again, a mate who is in debt to me, who is obligated to me, and tell him: 'The car is fucked; she needs a new car.'

'Yeah, no problems.'

My mate pays all my legal fees and when I get out he gives me a bit of money. A quarter of what's owing but he says I'll get the rest in six months' time. Never happens.

Anyway, whilst I'm in custody I say to her, 'Listen, I'm not having you come visit me by public transport,' because, at one stage there, she is. So I got her the car, then she's run it into the ground; she's got no licence; she's fucked it up.

So I get her another one, and that was a nice car.

The sheriff actually seizes that car off her leading up to my release, because she has outstanding fines. And she wants me to fucking pay for the car. 'I have to pay again? Come on, man, I already bought you fucking two cars.' No, it doesn't work like that.

And then probably three months before I get out she is living with her mother in Toorak. And she doesn't get along. Living under the same roof as her mother is too much for her because her mother is a control freak. She'll tell you that; she told me that.

They are having so many arguments that she wants her own place. So I say, 'All right, fine. How much?' Another three grand. She is coming out to see me and those are the terms.

At Marngoneet I would have Jess come out to see me on the Saturday and Kylie would come out on the Sunday – it would be the family day. And she knew Jess was coming out to see me – I never hid it. 'I'm in a relationship with her. Me and you have a child. You want me to bond with the child: I'm bonding with the child. I'll do what I can – the best I can as a father, but I'm not in a relationship with you, Kylie. Okay? Let's get that straight. All right, from time to time we might have a little bit of sex, play on the side or whatever, but there's nothing there, Kylie.'

So we got that straight.

When I was released Jess picked me up in a limo. She was in the back of the limo. I was in a relationship with Jess for about six weeks after getting out. But being released straight out of isolation I was not settled. I was all over the place and I hadn't lived with her before. I'm hard to live with by myself, let alone with someone else. It was just too much. I've been used to living by myself and then bang, I'm living with someone else. And she was a little bit younger – a lot younger – and immature. It just didn't work.

I moved in with Rachel's brother, helped him out, and he actually fuckin' robbed me – stole all my stuff. When I got arrested I had some money there, a couple ounces of pot and just under an ounce of eggie, of MDMA. He fuckin' stole that, you know. Just before I got out I said, 'Mate, you owe me a favour: I need a house. I need a place to stay.'

I still write to Rachel's sister. They're twins. I used to take the kids out all the time. I was the adopted uncle. Even when I got out in 2008 I wasn't in a relationship with Rachel but I'd still take them out and actually bought one of them, the boy, a motorbike, a trail bike better than mine. I spent fucking 1600 on mine and his bike cost 1700. Even in 2011, I went around there and caught up with them and said hello and all that.

Out of all of them Jess is probably the one I connected with, that I'm fond of, but I just blew, basically. She was a lot younger than me and just wasn't ready. That's why I said, 'You need to go out.' 'Cos she was a virgin at the time I met her and I kept her that way. I'd just give her a lick and that.

See, I had all sorts of different sheilas so I didn't penetrate her for a number of years. I used to say to myself, 'I'm just licking where no one else has been and keep it like that.' It'd drive her crazy, and if I want to fuck someone I'd just fuck one of the sluts. I kept her intact for years.

Then when I got out in 2008 we spent the night together. That was all right. That was good.

DOG DAYS

2 APRIL 2008:
RELEASED ON PAROLE

Out in Footscray on parole getting welfare payments sorted
I run into *The Footy Show's* Sam Newman and his crew doing
Street Talk interviews.

Sam asks why I was in jail and I mention having gone to
catch up with somebody but they weren't there so I left a bullet
on a counter.

'You didn't shoot anyone, did you?'

'No, I didn't shoot no one.'

'Oh, I thought you said you shot someone.'

'No. I was going to.'

As we're going our separate ways, cameras still rolling, I ask
if I'm going to make the cut.

'We just take all this shit back to the studio and someone else
does it,' says Sam. 'But I'm sure you'll be put on.'

I tell him: 'If you don't put it on I'll shoot ya next time I
see ya.'

'I can assure you, sir, you'll be on,' he says, cracking up at my cheekiness.

The Footy Show airs the footage, but the parole board doesn't laugh. Nearly breach me for it.

卌

Close friends that I have known for twenty-odd years give me a job in their concreting business. They want to keep me occupied and see me stay out of trouble. I'm humbled by their warmth, and they do everything they can to make me feel accepted. But standing around on jobs, I feel like a right gronk – totally awkward. Four decades on this earth and I'm a charity case. I'm just slowing them up. And it's no secret who I am: what I am. Wish I could forget. I'm smoking enough pot to take the edge off the memories. Maybe 'memories' isn't even the right word 'cos the experiences are right here, right now, sharp enough to cut through time. 'Get him, get him, get him!' Slash-slash-slash-slash-slash.

I need to withdraw. I stop working.

卌

One bright spot is that my daughter and I are bonding well, thanks to overnight access. I love her so much. My girlfriend, Silvia, has a daughter of her own and is good with her, too.

Kylie is extremely jealous of Silvia and tries everything she can to get us together in a relationship, but I am not interested at all.

With no warning, Kylie moves to Queensland, taking our girl with her. It's a package deal now, I learn: if I want my daughter, then I have to take Kylie, too.

I was already lost. Now I'm in freefall. I tell Kylie I'm not interested in either of them.

-HH-

It's all too much but I have a newly appointed psychologist who isn't experienced enough. He's too raw. Too much like a bull in a china shop. I have to smoke pot before the sessions just to slow it down, to step back.

Seeing him is part of my parole obligations but I give him the flick and press on with drugs instead – coke and pot, up and down, on and off: all at the same time. I'm stroboscopic.

-HH-

The ranger seizes a fucking beautiful pup of mine, Crystal, from Barry's place. So I ring the Brimbank City Council and order the ranger to free my fucking dog.

'I've had Crystal since she was six weeks old,' I tell him. 'I love her as my own child and I want her back.' Having done my homework, I'm able to refer to the ranger's kids by name. Maybe this will make him come good: 'How would you like it if someone seized them? Do we have to do a swap – one for one?'

There's a bit of tension on the street these days and I don't much like being out and about but I'm not getting anywhere with this fuckhead. So I tell him that I didn't want to have to do this, that these are dangerous times for me, but I'm coming down to get my pup. 'And the police better not fucking be there.'

Runty and I jump in my car with a couple of mates and park across the road from the council works at Keilor. Should a crew try to jump me, I've got a couple bumbags packed with basically non-lethal weapons including a taser, capsicum spray, and a pen-gun.

Whoa, black van swerving in!? Black tactical uniforms shouting and guns all at me and I'm seized: thrown on my face.

BATHED IN LOVE

2008–11:
CHARLOTTE UNIT AND BEYOND

After being arrested by the SOG on 18 December, Chris returns to Port Phillip Prison.

CHRIS:

On reception back into custody I break down in tears in front of the prison staff.

I hate it here. I can't assimilate out there. I hate it here. Can't assimilate out there. Hate myself. Hate them. Hate and despair.

And just to make sure I am even more profoundly screwed up when the time comes for my next release, they make me serve the entire three-year term in management – half of that in solitary confinement.

That'll fix me.

DEPT OF JUSTICE VIC MEMO
FRIDAY, 19 DECEMBER 2008
As you are all aware, Chris is back at PPP.

During interview Chris presented as very flat and stated on numerous occasions that he had 'had enough' and was 'filthy' that the police didn't shoot him yesterday. Claims he doesn't fit in on the outside and says the only life he knows now is being locked in tiny concrete rooms. States he is refusing to eat and wants to fade away and die and his only interest is in how long it takes. Says he is going to remain non compliant with orders and that Sentence Management can go and %na@# themselves.

‖‖‖

While I'm remanded to the void of Port Phillip Prison's Charlotte Unit, Kylie decides to return back to Melbourne to patch things up.

She books a 'relationship visit', using our girl as a bridge. 'You have to bond with your daughter,' she says.

I really look forward to the visits with Charlize. She has grown up so much since I last saw her some six or so months ago – before losing all control of my life – something I often remind Kylie that she contributed to by taking Charlize from me.

She swears that she will never allow it to happen again.

'What? You want to get close and when it doesn't suit you you'll run away again?' I say to her. I'm not going to let it happen. 'I'd rather walk away now than be emotionally destroyed by you doing it again.'

Kylie swears it won't happen again. She says she accepts not taking up the allowed relationship visit.

Silvia often says, 'Why does she have to come in for? I am your girl not her.'

Which is absolutely true, as I say to Kylie on countless occasions: 'It ain't about you – it's about Charlize.'

28 JULY 2009:
TRANSFER TO SCARBOROUGH NORTH UNIT, PORT PHILLIP PRISON

There are thousands of prisoners in Victoria with whom I have no history, no trouble, no issues, but it always seems that if it's not solitary – war of the universe against the lone soul – it's into the arena to face the rotating cast of disturbed clowns that the system's Major Offenders Unit keeps circulating together.

So I'm moved to a management unit controlled by one of Gavin Preston's associates – a man with a great reputation for prison violence.

I don't tell authorities of the threat to my life because I don't do that. Instead, I make improvised body armour, strapping magazines to my upper body to protect against stabbings.

Also equipping myself with an improvised chemical agent to use as mace, I walk alone into the enemy's unit.

Within three minutes it erupts and I'm using that chemical agent as if my life depends upon it. Which it does.

So now I'm tipped to Banksia in Barwon.

TRANSFER TO BANKSIA UNIT, BARWON PRISON

I'm in total machine mode: training, training, training, harder, harder, harder. I hit the boxing bag with such ferocity that it reverberates through the wing, blow after blow, hammering it for 20 or 25 unrelenting minutes of 110 punches per minute. Ditching normal routines I slam it thousands of times in unexpected rhythms, irregular piston combinations, every single strike shattering jaws, all the jaws, all the fucking teeth that have ever come to grind me. I destroy everything.

Drill complete, I now load food into the microwave, set it for five minutes, shower, dress, eat, pluck a flower from the prison officers' garden on the way to the visitors centre, proceed through a two-stage strip-search, advance to my daughter, embrace her and at last feel bathed in love.

During my time at Banksia, I make cards for my daughter, paint them and irritate the staff by cutting up an expensive book about Arabian horses so I can have pictures for her.

I'm transferred back to Charlotte at Port Phillip for harassing Hugo Rich, aka Olaf Dietrich, one of Chopper Read's mutts from all those years ago in Pentridge.

Kylie visits every week now, bringing my daughter; I have established a great bond and relationship with her by this stage. Even the prison officers comment on it.

I don't speak to Kylie, though, unless it is an important matter about my child's welfare or schooling. Otherwise, entire visits are devoted to playing and interacting with my daughter.

I've always plucked flowers from the officers' garden on the way to the visitors centre, hiding them up the sleeve of my overalls to play a magic trick for her, getting empty foam cups and saying abracadabra, waving my hands around, predicting colours of the flowers that will magically appear, and then letting them drop into the cups. It gets complicated when she demands her choice of colours – those days I just disappoint her.

But best of all our time together, she wants us full-on running around together, up and down the kids slide, having races and rolling around wrestling and doing cartwheels, hopscotch and star jumps. She wants to jump up and down on me and she really wants Wizzy Dizzies! When I spin her it draws in all the other kids who are so often ignored by their parents. They line up and plead for a turn.

She always leaves the visits with the flowers hidden in foam cups – or at least she does after staff point out signs warning that damaging the flora can result in 'Termination of visit'.

She loves seeing me and I love it even more.

↕↕↕

As my release date gets closer I don't know what happens.

I do know what happens.

Everything that's unhinged in me but has been held in place by the stark, hard routine of prison starts vibrating so fiercely that now it's not held in place. Not really.

Because I can't cope out there.

In 30 years of jail I have been a laundry billet and a unit billet, done a little kitchen work twenty years ago and that's about it.

As a kid in the early 1980s I was a store packer at Coles and a carpenter's assistant for my dad. Didn't finish Year 8.

No work skills. No social skills.

What I warned about when campaigning in NSW is coming true for me again. I'm gonna to fail again. I'm gonna fail.

And as I inch towards the disaster, I spend most of the day lying in a little room. Tick. Tock. Tick. Tock. Corrections Victoria. Corrections NSW. Tick. Tock. Tick. Tock.

9 MARCH 2011:
MAKESHIFT SWING FROM TIER

With a bedsheet I fashion a makeshift swing, unfurl it from the top landing of my management unit and start swinging back and forth whilst complaining about not being ready for release.

The general manager cuts me down and my plea for help adjusting to the outside world ahead of my release is ignored and they tip me into an anti-suicide solitary confinement observation cell at the Charlotte Unit at Port Phillip Prison.

So I continue my protest at the lack of preparation and help. I am classified as a 'major offender' and as 'high risk', but I receive the opposite of 'major' assistance and a 'high' degree of training and rehabilitation.

I receive the empty room. Tick. Tock. Tick. Tock. Inching towards release.

11 MARCH 2011:
CAT SCAN

I run at the perspex interior door of the cell, crashing my head into it.

And collapse.

Off to St Vincent's.

'BEHAVIOUR APPEARS OPENLY MANIPULATIVE DUE TO INABILITY TO NEGOTIATE A MORE SATISFACTORY PATHWAY TO RELEASE, WHILE HIS NEED FOR SOME SORT OF SUPPORTIVE PRE-RELEASE PROGRAM APPEARS REAL.'

They coax me out of the observation cell for a visit from my daughter – she turns five next month! – and then transfer me to another unit and then back to the punishment unit of Charlotte.

I have twelve weeks before release and I'm going crazy. I start making shit-bombs again. It starts with this fucking putrid grub who stabbed his own 2-year-old daughter to death to get at her mother. I fill a milk carton with faeces and piss and when I'm passing his cell door I place it under the lip and stomp. It sprays everywhere, covering not just him but me in shit, too, but I don't give a fuck.

I shit-bomb anyone with a sordid past, hitting four targets in one day, all down the spine of the Charlotte Unit. The staff go for me but I sidestep 'em and plant another under a door – stomp!

The staff stopped issuing me milk in a carton and instead serve it in foam cups, but this proves no deterrent at all as I relentlessly focus on one particular target. Eventually they move him to a safe area upstairs.

Usually I don't attend my Major Offenders Unit review in protest at the absence of rehabilitation, but now I go to one wearing a t-shirt reading, 'Shit Happens.' It's confiscated.

I'm primed to explode.

Leading up to my release I seek assistance through the prison system to find accommodation around Melbourne – close to my daughter. Unfortunately there is nothing available in Melbourne – just a handful of two-week residencies in a choice of Seaford, Wangaratta and the Ballarat region.

Bitterly disappointed, I discuss them with Kylie. Given my record, I'd hoped for far more post-release help; they know stability in accommodation is a critical element in reducing recidivism.

Kylie and I agree that taking up a fortnight somewhere outside Melbourne is unsuitable. She's going to let me sleep on a couch at her flat until I am able to sort something proper. This will allow me to spend more time with my child.

I find it awkward being alone now, my self-worth and confidence is shot, and I'm totally dependent on the mother of my child to help get me through the transition from jail, sadly.

Released straight from isolation into the community, I walk through the gates wearing another 'Eat Shit & Die' t-shirt.

GETTIN' HECTIC

25 SEPTEMBER 2011:
RELEASED FROM JAIL

I get picked up by Smiles. He takes me to Coffee Addiction in Niddrie, just across the road from La Porchetta where the owner once killed a bloke by shooting him twice in the head with an illegal firearm. Self-defence, it was ruled.

Anyway, it's Sunday morning and we're all catching up; we're having fucking breakfast, coffee, all that sort of stuff, and Smiles goes: 'By the way, you've got issues.'

'What do you mean?'

'I'll let Bill tell ya. He's coming down to catch up with ya.'

Bill arrives. He says, 'Oh Chris, you better fucking tool up. Gavin's trying to find out where you are; he's going to try and fucking take you out. You better tool up; you better strap up. He's looking for ya.' All this sort of shit.

What the fuck? The first day I get out I hear this shit. I'm trying to have breakfast and eggs and I'm focused on going to Luna Park this afternoon with my daughter and people are telling me I've got to watch it; he's going to do this. What the fuck?

It doesn't settle me. Really, I don't want to hear this shit. I want to relax the first day. You know?

It starts getting me paranoid, worried, all that sort of stuff; my life's in danger; same with those around me, too – what the fuck? Probably, maybe, Bill's hoping I'll tool up, that maybe I'll be proactive and neutralise this cunt, because he's got issues – he doesn't tell me he's got issues with Gavin; he just throws me up in the ruck.

I've just got out of isolation, solitary confinement, which makes you very paranoid and very confrontational, and they know what sort of person I am. What do I fucking do? Do I walk away from this or confront it, or engage? Well I engage, okay, so they're hoping for me to tidy things up.

So I take my daughter to Luna Park but I can't conceal from her the worry I've got. Instead of being happy with my child I am overloading with the concern and totally struggling with this foreign world.

My first night free I'm fucking doing countersurveillance. I've got a fucking car parked up the street, across the road from where Kylie is, sitting off, doing fucking countersurveillance in case Gavin knows where Kylie lives and sends someone. It wouldn't be hard to know where Kylie is because she big-notes that she's with me or that she's seeing me – she likes to make it look a lot deeper than it is because she doesn't want to look funny, silly. I keep saying, 'Listen, Kylie, you're the mother of my child – that's it. We're not in a relationship.' But she tries to present it like that to everybody because that's what she's craving: to be a part of this – what the fuck, I don't know what to call it – criminal dynasty. You know what I'm saying?

She was seeing one person while I was in. She told me later, and I knew that person so I was a bit disappointed that he would go near her. Even though we weren't in a relationship I was disappointed he'd fuck her. There's plenty of sheilas to fuck. Really, at the end of the day, you don't have to fuck the mother of my child.

〜 ‖‖

Next day I take my daughter to Highpoint West. I've got some funds on me, probably about eight grand that I've collected. I take her to Toys-R-Us to buy her stuff, do some shopping: a bit of a treat for her, ya know? A bit of a shopping spree with her, ya know?

Fucking you wouldn't believe it: I get pulled over.

The car is not even in fucking my name. These are not normal coppers. They're not in normal uniform. Tactical Response Group coppers in commando gear in a four-wheel drive decide to pull me over.

Random they say. Random. What the fuck random. Please: Tactical Response Group don't pull over randoms. Especially with a kid in the baby seat in the back. You know what I'm saying?

I think, 'What the fuck's going on?' I was happy spending time with my daughter, showering her with gifts, the whole back seat's full of fucking toys, and now I'm saying to myself, 'What the fuck?' I am dirty, man. If she wasn't in the car I might not have pulled over. And the car isn't even registered in my name.

Their first words are, 'You got any weapons in the car?'

And they don't even know who I fucking am. Haven't even asked for my name. 'Got any weapons in the car?'

'No. Why would you say that?'

Now they ask me for my details. I know it's a targeted search: they know exactly who I fucking am. Normal coppers don't pull me over unless it's by chance. Every time they have dealings with me, it's always SOG – they send in the heavy artillery to make an arrest. And these guys are just one level below that. If they had sent in the SOG it would have been too obvious so they send in the Tactical Response Group. And they're still kitted up in their overalls. They're not uniform, man. I just think, 'What the fuck? This is so fucked up.' I've only been out one day and someone's suggested I'm tooled up and then spearing them in, hoping I'll be arrested with a fucking weapon and sent back to jail.

This is how fucked-up it is. This is why I decide to stay away from Smiles. He's prepared to maybe suggest I have issues that are far greater than they really are, hoping that I'll be in possession of a weapon, okay, and get pinched the very next day. Knowing that I had just got fucking four years for a weapon. I get out and

Masks of Mayhem: the many faces of Chris.

within 24 hours I'm pulled over looking for a fucking weapon. Lucky I didn't have a weapon, huh. Otherwise, I would have been back in jail and who would have been looking after my daughter? She was in the car with me at the time.

I was supposed to collect a lot of money yesterday and it didn't arrive. Things just start falling into place. I've gotta back off from Smiles and his gang. Now I'm deadset, 'I can't trust these fellas.'

Who the fuck do I trust?

So I just stay away from them. I've had suspicions about Smiles for many years. Daylesford. Jockey Smith's inquest didn't identify the informants but there were two informants involved. Okay? Two people that lagged me. The coppers weren't after Jockey, they were after me. They were sitting off, they let him go. I've got the transcripts from Jockey Smith's coroner's inquest – all the evidence and stuff. They don't identify who it is but it's not hard to work out because there was less than five fucking people who knew I was there. We had different projects happening, and when I say 'projects', I mean work – robberies – planned. One group would be focused on this one and another group focused on that one. Both weren't aware of the other – they weren't working in tandem. Understand?

So when the police started disclosing certain things about certain things it made it a lot easier working out who the fuck it was.

Smiles knew when I escaped from St Vincent's: he was in touch with Roxy. He used to send her up some money from time to time, so he had her phone number. Within 48 hours of me arriving in Sydney someone rings that number and asks for Erica. When anybody talked to Roxy they call her Roxy, which was her middle name. Erica was her Christian name and only coppers call her Erica. It was a male voice and the other sheila who lived there with her picked up the phone and said, 'No, there's no Erica here.'

'You sure about that?'

'Yeah, no Erica here.' She knew there was something wrong because she never introduces herself as Erica at all. She introduces herself to everybody as Roxy.

She thought it was strange, and that caused me to leave that place because I knew it was compromised. The only person who had that phone number in Melbourne was fucking Smiles. You know? And then from one place I went with her to another: she said I know someone – he's sweet – Bill. He was a fence; he used to buy stolen stuff off her. Shifty cunt, a bit dodgy an' that, so we went to him. He ended up giving me up, too.

Roxy went into witness protection later, ended up testifying against me and just lied for the coppers in Sydney. You know like I'm not saying I didn't do both of the robberies but there was no evidence: there was only evidence of the weapons and some images. They found me in possession of the weapons fucking nine months later. Big fucking deal. So I bought the weapons. 'Yeah, I come into possession of the weapons: 100 per cent. Ballistic experts will tell you that this is weapon is one of its kind identified in New South Wales in thirteen years.' 'Cos it wasn't just a run-of-the-mill weapon; it was a modified semi-automatic assault rifle. So they knew straight away.

But the coppers needed to put that weapon in my possession at the time: come in Roxy.

Her evidence was at odds with the facts. She had to create a role, so they made up that she was a driver in one of the robberies. She was never a driver at all. They made up a role for her to support and corroborate me being in possession of the weapons. She said that she was there when the panel van was stolen and all this sort of stuff; she described the back of the panel van. It was a carpenter's fucking whatever –

Tooled up: more ammo from BADNE$$' weapons cache.

someone that worked in the tool trade. He had cabinets all through the back, built cabinets where he had all his tools. They said to her I had tools in the back and when I cross-examined her about the tools and asked if there was a cabinet she goes: 'No, there was no cabinet, just tools on the floor.'

'You sure about that?'

'100 per cent.'

'You wouldn't lie?'

'No.'

She even got the days and location wrong. She fucked right up. Her evidence was inconsistent but the jury was so tarnished and tainted by the evidence already coming out about me: my name BADNE$$; that I was an escapee; that I was involved in another robbery; robberies all the time; money, guns – all this shit. So polluted, so tainted, so prejudicial, and this was all allowed in. What the fuck was my barrister doing? I go, 'What the fuck are you doing, man?'

Legal Aid – fuck me; you'd expect better.

Everything Roxy said was a lie and she was so bad at lying but the way that trial went after three days I sacked my counsel because I reckoned I could do better on my own. After that I said, 'If I'm going to get sentenced, I'm going to get sentenced by my own hand. Fuck off. See ya later.'

The judge wasn't prepared to give me a retrial. I had to proceed. I was representing myself in shackles. The squad would arrive, all surrounding me, so prejudicial, and you could hear the fucking jiggling. This is how ridiculous it was. I said, 'Your Honour, this is not prejudicial? Of course I'm going to be convicted!'

And he'd go, 'I can't hear a thing.'

Later there were issues with some of the fucking evidence so we had to replay some of the tapes, the transcripts, and what do you hear in the background: ching-ching-ching.

I said, 'Your Honour, what's that? I can hear fucking chains.'

And the jury could fucking hear it and see it themselves. Everything that occurred in those proceedings was designed. It was deliberate. I had no fair hearing whatsoever. I knew I was fucked.

At the end of it I said to him, 'I wasn't sentenced on the evidence 'cos there was no fucking evidence. You know that and I know that. I was sentenced on what was said, what was introduced, all the prejudicial stuff.' He accepted that and in deterring me from appealing against the conviction he ended up giving me six with a [minumum of] four. Now I could have got that just for the weapons. That was a pretty good outcome. As much as I wanted to appeal, I decided against it because it was a fair sentence.

Court is about who lies the best.

Anyway, this is the thing: Smiles and his mates have been running around with coppers for years. I know that because he's introduced me to off-duty coppers, and I said, 'Please leave me alone, mate. I don't want to know this shit – I'm going.' So I was wary of him before, and more so now. I used to catch up with him; I used to get some finances off him, but after this, 'Nah, fuck off. See ya later.'

I'm not even collecting Centrelink benefits. I tried but found it too daunting. I was so confused by the forms and what to lodge and had so much difficulty that I'm just avoiding it.

Kylie suggests I go on a disability pension, and then she can become my carer, and be paid for this role in looking after me, as I was a real case. I find this idea hard to cope with;

I'm insecure and lack confidence within myself. I've become so dependant upon her and I feel as if I can trust no one.

Even though I'm not in a relationship with Kylie at all, I remain vigilant and on sentry duty, sleeping when I get a chance on her couch. I need to be in a position to defend them in the event that my foe finds this location.

Plus, it gives me quality time reading bedtime stories to my daughter and waking her up in the morning with pillow fights – although she's not a morning person at all.

I keep Runty by my side with the balcony door open next to the couch. His breed is bred for security and he barks at the first hint of movement. I take my dog everywhere with me, and some of me mates end up howling because they come too close to me and he nips them right in front of me and I don't even see it. Runty is like a cobra, man – he's that quick. I'm talking to a person and he fucking nips them. He doesn't growl. He's not aggressive. It's a little nip like, 'Just fuck off.' Just a warning sort of thing, you know. And that's enough for them to fucking back off. With a hole in their jeans. I have to laugh.

As I say to everybody, even Kylie, even Silvia, even the other girls I see, all the females in my life, I always say to them, in front of my daughter: 'There's only two things in my heart: number one is my daughter; number two is my dog. Nothing else matters to me.'

I didn't realise but some of the sheilas spew later, like, 'What the fuck? A dog comes before me?'

But that's how I am. I'm inseparable with my dog – my dog's spent time in lock-up – the pound – too: that's how close I am with him. Everybody will tell you: there's me and him. I buy a Peugeot with a sunroof, immaculate condition, beautiful condition inside and out, and you know what? I buy that car for my dog. It's my dog's car. Leather interior, black carpet – he moults and, mate, I don't give a fuck. I love hanging out with my dog.

So, rarely does he leave my side; he's also my protection, no weapons needed.

I start wearing a bulletproof vest that the police returned to my mother back in 1994.

Chris and Runty, his beloved Dogo Argentino.

MID OCTOBER 2011

I'm dipping into the money given to me for a place to live.

My Land Rover has serious mechanical problems costing me over four G's to fix, and I'm finding it hard to get a toe in the door with real estate agents, and I don't think I want to be on my own.

But the main thing is I can't move to another location away from the possible threat posed at Kylie's flat. I can't leave them alone at the mercy of my foes.

One reason I'm so geed up is that it's not an unknown occurrence for people associated with my foe to strike at females and even children in order to get at their enemies. And some of these persons have depraved and sadistic sexual appetites, once infamously chaining a woman to a bed for days of brutal sodomising and years later she still needs heavy medication to numb it out.

So no way am I leaving my post.

─┼┼┼─

Gavin's not the only bloke who's feeling ill-disposed towards me. A totally separate group of men wielding iron bars bash me senseless. I sustain head trauma, black eyes and a broken nose. But I tell the police nothing.

⊬⊬⊬

There's a bloke I have coffee with every week or two named Toby Mitchell. He's a bit of a hard cunt: sargeant-at-arms in the Bandidos and all that, while I fly solo, you know – I've never been one for gangs. But we get on all right and catch up.

Toby knows Gavin and he knows that Gavin's dirty on me; he says he can have a chat with him and see how this might be de-escalated. How everyone might stand down from this fucking tension.

Within a week – before we can catch up on his chat – Toby is shot five times in broad daylight outside Doherty's Gym in Brunswick, his two would-be assassins fucking spraying lead near innocent kids in a shopping centre car park.

Deadset, it feels like open season. Feels fucking very grim, very exposed. Especially at Kylie's flat or when I'm taking my daughter to school or collecting her at the end of the day. I can't just go away and let my daughter grow up thinking I'm not devoted – that I don't care and I'm not here for her. And what if they try and snatch her.

So due to the level of threat, I wear my bulletproof vest when I am going to and from school with her. I'm also carrying a handgun – a silenced pistol I was given for protection which I've now taught my daughter to shoot with. I hope it doesn't come to that but she needs to know for her own safety and to defend others. If I'm down and they're coming for her then it's better she knows what to do.

Gavin gets picked up on firearms charges but there's still evil vibes spreading everywhere about Toby's shooting – who did it and why, and who's lagging about it.

卌

I meet some associates of Toby's including a bloke by the name of Adam Khoury who is almost as paranoid as me. Maybe more so. Whenever I see him or hear from him, he's sweating blood about Gavin and his intentions.

卌

'He got bail, mate,' someone says over the phone.

Gavin's out. Various people are now saying he's actively searching for my whereabouts.

I source a cache of weapons and rent a shipping container under a bodgy name.

Bullet-proof BADNE$$: one of Chris' ballistic vests.

卌

The ice is getting a bit of a grip. One of the women close to me has introduced me to smoking the shit. I wasn't into speed, hadn't been for years. I done it when I was a kid, went crazy when I was a juvenile and basically fried my brains out and never returned to it. I never wanted to go back near it.

But because I had to stay up, stay awake, to do countersurveillance I'd go out and source some and what I sourced was really good, really pure. Quality the woman couldn't believe.

So what's happened is I would snort it. She goes: 'No, no, no, don't snort it – smoke it.'

'What do you mean smoke it?' I'd seen people smoke heroin before in the foil, you know.

'I haven't got a pipe,' she says.

'What do you mean pipe?'

'Ice pipe.'

It's all foreign to me. I'm not into this shit.

So she goes: 'Just use a foil.' She put it in a foil and starts inhaling it through a rolled-up note. So I started having it like that with her. From there I progressed and went to other places where they were smoking the pipe. And then later on I'd be smoking it with her.

Smoking it dulls everything. It doesn't give

Chris' camouflage clothing.

Chris catches some rays at a music festival. Like bandit medals, his various tatts marks violent confrontations that he has survived.

me a rush. Maybe at first the ice does but then it mellows me, relaxes me – the opposite effect of snorting it. I feel like I have ADHD and this is like a medication – mellows me down a little, balances me, settles me.

And I start hitting it a lot.

‖‖

Turns out Gavin has a house in Seaford. I start surveilling it but there's only limited cover, a little yapper dog across the road, and children constantly in the area, so I abort my plans for a confrontation.

But pulling back each time, being so passive at this time of lethal threat to my family, makes me feel sick in the pit of my stomach.

After clearing the inner foliage of a big tree on a corner house opposite Gavin's, I climb up and perch in the branches dressed in army camouflage. It's my observation post.

I also hollow out bushes across from Gavin's house, lying in wait only for the little yapper to compromise my position. I had no beef with this pooch. I admire him for protecting his turf.

Meanwhile, Gavin is closing in on me and on Kylie's address.

I tell Kylie to pack up what they need: 'We're gonna move', and we spend the Christmas holidays down towards the Mornington Peninsula. A friend has floated me ten grand, and we have fun camping, swimming and stuff.

Meanwhile, Silvia's spewing as I took my daughter and Kylie away from the danger, but not her.

卅

Keeping that ice pipe busy. Keeping calm.

EARLY JANUARY 2012

With Gavin living at Seaford, I figure that would be the last place that he'll look for me, so I make arrangements to book a room at the Seaford motel.

I pack guns in my black Land Rover, along with all the camping gear, a rubber four-man zodiac with outboard motor and the dogs. Kylie drives the Peugeot with our child in the back and we head off in a two-car convoy.

One night after spending the day at Frankston Beach and having a barbecue with Kylie, my child and the dogs in the picnic area just off the beach, I'm returning to the motel.

A few mixed alcohol cans from the drive-through bottle-o at the motel gets me a bit drunk and I drive to my foe's place. He's home.

I am pretty pissed and get the urge to confront him on the spot, but there's a big chance it will turn out ugly and I don't want my car seen in the area – which it's likely to be, given that he's in a tiny little court. So I decide to return later this evening.

Back at the motel, I gather car stealing implements and start looking around the local area for a vehicle to steal. Spotting a suitable car, I park a distance away, leave my keys in the ignition – which you can't see because of my illegal limousine-style tinting, and get to work. However, either I'm out of practice or it's harder than it was back in the day and before I crack it the fucking owner disturbs me in the act and I have to leg it.

My Land Rover is up the other end of street so the police have no right to search it, but they go ahead and conduct an improper search – so there goes my pistol, silencer and a laser sight.

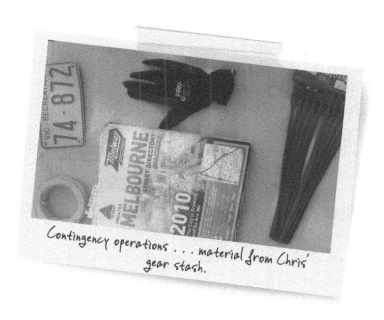

Contingency operations . . . material from Chris' gear stash.

|||||

Word of the drama – including a description of my car – might have made its way to my foe. A few good smokes of the ice are needed to get calm, get clear. Ice is good for that. I need a bit more.

EARLY FEBRUARY 2012

If Gavin enters the zone around Kylie's flat or my daughter's school I need to know so I return to his home and place a GPS tracking device under his blue Holden ute.

|||||

It's evening when I check in and the device reveals Gavin on the grid just a short distance from Kylie's. Extreme panic mode now. His bail conditions include a curfew – he's not even supposed to be out at all.

I have a pipe, tool up, and go to the Ascotvale location to sit off him. He's doing something in an abode there. What's your fucking game, Gav?

He must have a local associate, and I sit off the address on a number of occasions waiting for him.

The tracker is useless now – batteries only last a few days. But it's given me this – this fucking extremely alarming knowledge – that he has an associate, a position, an outpost right here near my little girl and Kylie.

11 FEBRUARY 2012

'Adam's dead, mate. Someone's shot him.'

Twice in the head and once in the body, as it turns out. In his own apartment.

I work through another point of ice and get me head together. Adam's been executed. What did he say first? What did he know to say? I can't stop thinking about how once I met him in the underground car park of Kylie's units. He might have said where she lives. Before getting fucking two bullets through his brain.

‐╫╫‐

I'm white hot now. Not with the cops but with Capable – that being Gavin's street name. Toby, Adam, me. It's no secret he's gunning for me.

‐╫╫‐

Silvia hits the roller doors when I phone and give the word. Then I just drive straight into the garage and she lowers them.

We do some pipes and have a fuck. She's fucking dynamite in the sack. But I can't relax. I keep having visions of us here fucking, fucking or fucking smoking or fucking just sitting and having a fucking chat when the gunmen come – when they move in for the kill. So I work my way around the house, studying every fucking vantage point, every angle from every window and door, every point to be barricaded or used to decamp. I have visions. I know it's coming.

'You gonna teach me Croatian?' I ask Silvia, running a hand over the curves of her arse-cheeks. 'If I get through all this I want to go to the old country.'

'Not going to fucking talk to you in any language if you keep staying with that slut Kylie.'

ǁǀ

What the fuck? Look who's here – the drooling psycho that slashed me to bits on Gavin's command in the Banksia yard.

I'm stunned.

We stare at each other as he drives out of the underground car park. He sees my motorbike or more alarmingly its allotted car space identifying Kylie's unit number.

Turns out the psycho's living in one of the rear units.

He knows I have a baby girl, as he was in on those circles of talking in the yard when Kylie became a mother. Just weeks before he attempted to murder me.

ǁǀ

Lost in panic, I rent a series of cars and vans, parking them with eyes on Kylie's flat, smoking ice to stay alert and keep a close watch.

If he comes anywhere near them, he's dead. But he's already near them. He's in his flat fucking probably running razor blades up and down his old fella waiting for the call from Gavin.

-||||-

'I have to relocate you both,' I tell Kylie. 'You'se are in extreme danger.'

-||||-

But how. I need cash. Fucking cash. I need to get them out of here. His associates are everywhere here. I can't sleep, I can't eat, I can't do anything but focus on the solution, on evacuation, on getting the means to place my family in a safe and secure location.

-||||-

It's been almost twenty years since I robbed a bank. They're totally different now. Modernised. I'd be lucky to get ten grand. And I don't want to put tellers through that anymore. In my trial in NSW I saw how fucking traumatised those women were. I don't want to terrorise soft targets. I'm a different person now. I'm in my 40s. I'm a fucking dad. A dad who has to take whatever measures are necessary for the protection of his child. Even if the thought of them makes me sick. I don't want to do this. And big earning armed hold-ups are very rare these days so I'll be a fucking prime suspect. I want to throw up.

If I do it, no more exposing women behind counters to this conduct; it will only be men, and not civilians, not easy prey, but uniformed armed guards – men trained and equipped with firearms who have chosen to place themselves in the arena.

I'll hit an Armaguard pick-up. Sure to be a large sum which is to be left to my daughter in the event of my death – an event likely to come very soon given all the people hunting me.

Masks from Chris' extensive collection of disguises.

But this is to secure her future, not mine. I have none beyond carrying out the mission.

卌

Every Saturday and Sunday there's a huge outdoor market in Laverton: fourteen acres or some crazy shit like that. Fucking thousands of people go. It's actually not far from Barry's place – Dad's old place – or where Mum's at. In fact, Mum goes sometimes, I think, probably to buy orchids for her collection. Anyway, a stack of punters would stop in afterwards at the pub next to the market for a drink, something to eat, or for a bit of a flutter on the pokies – the Westside Hotel, that's it. It's even a bit of a motel; that place would have to rake it in big time over the weekend.

So if I hit the Monday morning cash pick-up, I'll clear a couple hundred G's easy, I reckon.

Well, not that easy. I really haven't got the stomach for this shit anymore. Fucking nearly twenty years since I last did a hold-up and here I go again. Fuck me.

BACK ON THE JOB
12 MARCH 2012

CHRIS:
Time, man: my old master – everyone's master. My resting heart rate's around 40 bpm but sitting here on a folding chair in a narrow gap between the Westside car-park fence and a giant market shed, waiting for prime-time, it lifts to a good one-per-second – something handy to tune me in to the clockwork of robbery.

I've drilled a series of holes through the fence so I don't have to expose myself until I strike. It's a quiet morning at the pub, as you'd expect, with not a lot of activity in the car park. What a beautiful, sunny autumn day. Be great to be kicking back with my daughter, soaking up the rays as I push her on some swings or we take Runty for a walk at the beach. Be great if I wasn't me and I wasn't once more cloaking my identity and gripping the stock of a 12 gauge, and if that armoured Mercedes Sprinter van now pulling in with two armed men aboard was an ice cream truck instead, but this is happening and my ladder's in position. I observe the pair of Armaguard officers, one looking a bit old – about 60, poor bastard, step out and walk into the hotel to collect my money. The flow is on: they'll do the fucking chitty-chat small talk with the staff and one'll sign for the proceeds while the other supposedly looks out for bandits and this'll all take a few minutes while I crouch here eye-spying through the hole, all coiled and ready to pounce, my old soul knowing exactly what to do at every stage, my outlaw muscle memory all wound up and ready to pounce, even as the new me feels sick, sick, sick and lost, lost, lost, but I override the feeling when they emerge with the old bloke holding the cash consignment bag.

I let 'em take a dozen steps. 'Hey, fuckhead,' I shout, now up a mini ladder, my torso above the six foot fence, the weapon trained squarely on the moneyman. 'Give me the bag!'

But they just stand there. They look at me and each other and at me again – wasting time, the dickheads; someone in the office will be calling the police right now. The younger one gestures to his mate. He's sayin' some shit to him. What the fuck?

'Throw me the fucking bag!' But still the old bastard stands there like a stunned mullet. 'Throw it over here!' Frustration swells like a fucking head injury and if this was a bank I'd be at full monster with the shotgun in his face and my voice drowning every other fucking sound in his life. But this distance, and this yelling from behind a fence, makes it hard to exert absolute control. 'Throw it here! Throw the fuckin' money over the fence!'

Finally the bloke hoiks the bag, but it's half-arsed, my payday flopping down a metre or two from the fence. 'Fuckhead!' I shout. Useless cunt coulda put some grunt into it. 'Get on the fuckin' ground!' I wave the gun and the young bloke's down to the ground while the old fella flaps about, but now he's gone forehead to the bitumen, too. Up and over, I grab the cash bag and stride at them. 'Want to be a fuckin' hero?' I say, looking the pair over. 'I'll have that piece,' I say, unclipping the geezer's holster and removing the .38. Probably hitting half a minute now. 'Fuck it, I'll have both,' I mutter, stepping over to the young fella. 'Give me your fuckin' gun.'

All done. Back over the fence, I jump onto a motorbike and ride to a van parked on the other side of the market.

It's gone well enough: north of 200 grand in a drama-free operation that was over in about 35 seconds. Twenty years ago I would have cracked a fat, like that time as a pumped up young fella when I rode the train out of Noble Park, grinning at all the sheilas while on the seat beside me sat a mere ten per cent of this earn.

But now there's no pleasure – 100 per cent the opposite. Everything's changed from twenty years ago.

I want to get clear of here but I don't want to be stopped in the van with the fucking bike in the back. Panic and a kind of grief hit as I roll and shove and drop the motorbike into a creek on the north side of the market. It barely goes a metre from the creek bank. What the fuck, you know, how can I be doing this shit again? Nausea hits big time and I lean over the water and wait. Here it comes: I spew into the creek. Got to get the fuck outta here. Back in the van and off.

Fuck! Fucking forgot the pump-action is strapped to the bike! What the fuck is wrong with me. How fucking sloppy can anyone get? If they mention finding the bike on the news, I'll know it's too late. If they don't, I'll return tomorrow and retrieve the weapon.

19 MARCH 2012

CHRIS:

There's no pleasure in the robbery – 100 per cent the opposite. Everything's changed from twenty years ago.

I want to get clear of here but I don't want to be stopped in the van with the fucking bike in the back. Panic and a kind of grief hit as I roll and shove and drop the motorbike into a creek on the north side of the market. It barely goes a metre from the creek bank. What the fuck, you know, how can I be doing this shit again. Nausea hits big time and I lean over the water and wait. Here it comes: I spew into the creek. Got to get the fuck outta here.

‐╫╫‐

Fuck! Fucking forgot the pump-action is strapped to the bike! What the fuck is wrong with me. How fucking sloppy can anyone get? If they mention finding the bike on the news, I'll know it's too late. If they don't I'll return tomorrow and retrieve the weapon.

20 MARCH 2012

Kylie flies back in from Sydney. 'It's too dangerous in that flat,' I tell her. 'You two have to move out ASAP.' I'll pay a cash bond and six months rent in advance, I say. She just has to find a place.

We head to Highpoint to shop for Charlize and get me some new runners. I'd disposed of everything worn in yesterday's job.

I try to get back into the Laverton Market to get that shotty but the caretaker stops me. 'You'll have to leave, mate,' he says. 'No one's allowed on-site.'

Next day I grab fifteen grand and ask a mate to come to a car sale, where I buy an unregistered white Ford Transit van and a white Challenger. The Ford is going to be my home; to start with I pick up a bedpan and futon.

‐╫╫‐

Within days we're going to real estate agencies. Because Kylie's a single mother on Centrelink benefits, doesn't have any work history (that's not cash-in-hand), and all that sort of stuff, she goes to the bottom of the barrel.

I attend with her, too, and it's difficult: there is a shortage of rental properties.

We are going to so many places but, mate, at one stage they are bidding for them – there was a dozen or twenty before us and they are all qualified, with partners, and they're professionals. We aren't getting anywhere.

So now what happens is, when I give Kylie the money it's in front of my daughter, and I say to Charlize, 'There's $5000 – that's for you. You find a place, not Mummy. You go and have a look. If you like the place you tell Mummy, okay? Not Mummy pick it: it's you, it's your choice, it's for you.'

During Kylie's hunt for a rental, I stay in the van on the street with the back seats removed. With a camping bed and picnic chair, I sit up late watching the flat: keeping them secure.

Until I feel that it is just too dangerous for anyone to be there. They have to stay with relatives until everything is fixed.

The car-hire place has been raided. They've seized the van I used and all records relating to me. The tip-off must have come from the caretaker.

The police are gonna be all over me. I'm going to avoid staying at Kylie's or going to my daughter's school. Got these vans now and they're not in my name, so they'll give me a little breathing space. And smoking space: gotta stay alert and on top of things.

I'm spending. I'm blowing it. I'm giving it to a lot of people. I don't give a fuck. Within two days I find out the coppers are onto me, so I have a short window. I'm living on borrowed time. I dunno – I'm just going crazy with the money, giving it to people here, there, everywhere. And the ice, too: I am on a binge.

I split the cash, placing 140 G's in a black bag in the bushes of a paddock next to Silvia's place and the remainder in nearby bushland.

My daughter comes to stay with me at Silvia's for the Easter weekend, and we have an egg hunt on Sunday. As well as hiding eggs around the backyard, I've placed bundles of $50 notes.

My daughter and I have a wonderful time squashing six boxes of red grapes in Silvia's bath tub, making wine that will last from today, Easter Sunday 2012, to when she is old enough to drink. We also use boxloads of sultanas. When she comes of age, she will be able to raise a glass and recall her dad, who will no doubt be long dead by then.

Afterwards, I call Kylie's mum, Ursula, and give her a blast. I don't trust her at all.

I should buy my daughter a rural property – maybe a hobby farm – but Kylie says she has a flat to inspect tomorrow, so I give her five grand and tell her to say that she can pay months in advance.

Then I hear she's big-noting to everyone about the money like she's in some kind of underworld family so the next day I demand it back, saying I'll give it to the agent myself.

But it's $200 short. No fucking surprise; I know exactly what that went on.

Days later I go to her flat to check on them, she's cleared out, vanished. What the fuck. And this week I've planned to take my daughter hot air ballooning as a late birthday present.

It's because she's jealous of Silvia. She's made up some lies to get crisis accommodation at a women's shelter.

Crisis? I'm taking care of the situation; I'm taking care of security. I'm tooled up and I've been sitting off the flat and watching; I'm endeavouring to locate secure accommodation. There's no fucking crisis.

Kylie gets other people to tell me that she wants space to sort things out and will see me in a few weeks.

I'm crushed; I'm crazy; I'm lost – dead inside; my heart torn out. Kylie told me I should bond with our daughter and I have and we're real close and yet now Kylie divides us.

Pure evil, this is.

~~||||~~

An associate whose mate is seeing Kylie's mum asks me out for coffee, and tells me that I'll see my daughter in a few weeks.

The one reason I can accept is that if I can't find my daughter then neither can my foes. But I love being a daddy to my child, and her being taken away kills me inside.

In Silvia's garage I cry like a little baby, and I'm so ashamed that I have to turn my back. I don't want her to see me like this.

I can't even look at her and want to be alone with Runty. Me and Runty sleep on the dog bedding in the garage.

Silvia finds us in the foetal position and gets a doona and joins us, remaining in a vigil to support me in this time of extreme despair and heartache.

I am prepared to die for my daughter. I am guilty of being a loving and caring dad to my only child. I am trying the best I know.

I'm not fleeing or going interstate even though I know the police have me as a suspect for the robbery, because I can't abandon my daughter.

Freefalling, I hit the pipe hard, taking the edge off the ice with pot: sharpening up from pot with ice. More and more drugs, more and more drugs. Everything hurts so fucking much.

Life isn't going to last much longer – I know it. There's no future for me but death.

MEYHEM 666

Coked to the fucking gills, I'm high-wiring it at a fight night at Melbourne Pavilion with Will Tomlinson defending his super featherweight title against Mexican Daniel Ruiz.

Jay Malkoun is also here – that gentleman I went to the Spearmint Rhino to catch up with.

Now he's the fucking Comancheros' president. Can you believe this shit?

And there he is fucking sitting ringside with Mick Gatto and a pack of other fucking underworldly associates, and of course no shortage of bikies.

Emergency pack: sixshooter and a beanie from Chris' gear dump.

Fuck him, ya know, and his pack of killers. Gonna go have a bit of a word to him.

卌

Well that didn't go so well. Outta here.

Odd, hey, how not long after I leave, the venue's fucking power fails – and during the title fight. With no lights, the fight's over, night's over – bad luck, huh.

Cunts.

卌

20 MAY 2012

Two nights later plain-clothes police are out cruising north-west Melbourne as part of Operation Mono, a crackdown on motorcycle thieves, when they spot a pair of motorbikes side by side at a red light in Pascoe Vale South. The police report that a bike with a solo male rider has stolen plates, while the other, sporting a man on the handlebars and a woman riding pillion, has plates starting with MEY – black masking tape covering the rest.

When the light turns green the police follow the bikes for a short distance before hitting the lights and sirens. Both riders glance back but instead of stopping they peel off a roundabout in opposite directions, one to the right the other to the left. The police turn after the rider with stolen plates who then really opens up some speed and shifts to the wrong side of the road, prompting the police to let him get away in line with orders not to pursue motorcycles. It's about 8 pm.

A bit over an hour and a half later, another plain-clothes unit with Operation Mono drives through Niddrie and approaches La Porchetta, the Italian restaurant on Keilor Road where the restaurant chain's founder, Rocco Pantaleo, once shot a man dead in self defence. In touch with their comrades who earlier got left for dust, the police see a Honda CBR1000 Fireblade parked outside and decide to take a closer look.

Moving the black tape out of the way, they find the rego reads
MEYHEM, *with the black tin plate beneath displaying 666. The
other team is soon on the scene.*

ǂǂǂ

CHRIS:

Everything's tense. Very fucking tense with Gavin's crew
stalking, hunting, looking to slice and murder, rape and bleed.
Coppers are positioning: last time they got me for spitting the
dummy with that fucking puppy-killer ranger, but any day
they'll connect a-fucking-nother dot to the Laverton job, and
then it'll be open season for the SOG to shoot me on the spot.
And now fucking Jay Malkoun can unleash his bikie hordes on
me. It's not fucking easy flying solo sometimes.

After giving the slip to some clown-arse coppers who hit the
lights and sirens when I was riding, I stop in at La Porchetta.
But soon there's a male acting suspiciously near my motorbike.
The guy's wearing a fucking hoodie; now it looks like a few

A few more plates from Chris' collection.

more, a group of 'em, one with disposable blue gloves. What the fuck? Comancheros up to no good? This is fucking serious.

Here they come. Outta here.

One fella grabs me! I drop my helmet reaching for my weapon. He's dropped something reaching for his. I'm faster. 'Fuck off,' I shout, showing him the business end. He pisses himself and fucking bolts! And it's a radio he's dropped – a police radio! The coppers are gonna fucking knock me for sure. Only minutes before there's a total swarm. Betta fuckin' run.

Sons of God

21 MAY 2012:
KEILOR EAST

Leaving behind his bike, CCTV footage and other evidence, Chris heads to Silvia's house at Sterling Drive, Keilor East. She later tells police that he had gone out to dinner at La Porchetta with some mates, but she wouldn't have a clue who they were because Chris, like most blokes, don't tell their missuses 'jack shit' about boys' nights out.

He came home without his motorbike, Silvia says, telling her that he'd had a bit of trouble at the restaurant – a problem with the police – but he doesn't elaborate, she says.

Special Operations Group gunmen surround BADNE$$.

Letting rip: a section of fence that Chris shot.

By Silvia's account, when she's showering later (which would have been a little before dawn on Monday, going by the police timeline), Runty and her dog, Gucci, start barking right before a loudspeaker booms out with 'Christopher Dean Binse, please go to the front door – go to the driveway.'

Having decided during the night to arrest BADNE$$, the police force has ringed the house with gunmen from his old foe, the Special Operations Group.

At about 6.30 am, before the sun has risen over Melbourne, a SOG armoured vehicle rolls up the driveway with a negotiator inside using a loudspeaker to tell Chris to surrender.

CHRIS:

No more man to man; here comes the beast: the bullet-proof storm-trooper battlewagon. They're gonna obliterate me. No pretence of civilian policing anymore. They've come for the solja.

Sirens going, stopping at the front door; imminent assault; about to be shot; terrified; flashbacks of previous traumatic arrests; hospitalisation; bedside hearings.

Only boxers on, I go to jump the side fence and flee but there's a SOG member fully exposed in the paddock; I could shoot him but I don't, and now that I haven't the initiative is his and the cordon will close in seconds.

Never going to get past them now, so I panic my way back inside. Finger on the table. Boot in the face. Where's the money, fuckhead. Do you know James Edward Smith, fuckhead. About to die, fuckhead.

After blacking out all the windows, I grab a four-litre tin of olive oil and pour it around the rear and front doors and barricade them.

My life's in danger. On with the bulletproof jacket. Don't come anywhere near me, you goons. Take aim at the advancing threat. Gotta keep 'em at bay. I'm not interested in the demands you're blaring from your loudspeaker.

'Chris, leave the firearm inside the house. Come out the front door with nothing in your hands. Keep your hands where we can see them. You will be met by police; follow their instructions.'

Scattered: police picked over every inch of the site after the siege, cataloguing the mad hours in forensic detail.

Yeah? Fuck youse. Wanna play? Come and get me. No? Just gonna sit out there, are ya? Stop wasting my time.

-HH-

The SOG reinforce the point with sirens and flashing lights but there is no response.

Not until about an hour later when Chris aims a revolver through a window and shoots the armoured vehicle. The bullet doesn't penetrate, but after a couple such shots the police reverse out of the driveway and park on the road.

-HH-

CHRIS:

Fuck off, ya dropkicks. Coming back to the sofa in the lounge room, I heat a pipe and watch the ice melt and become smoke, vapour, fucking Satanic mist. The shit drifts in the glass until I whip it into me and all the phones start ringing and the black killers are circling and the engines are revving and loudspeaker booming with my name, my name, Chris, Chris, Chris, what the fuck is a name, it's all a game, and the crystal is boiling and I have a gun, a gun, a fucking .38, mate, ready to hand, ready to spin and see where it fucking lands; where it places me; classo for heaven or hell, it fucking makes no difference to me, to this, to what's coming. Gotta get the message out or in, I'm filled with sin. There's nothing to come after this. Why can't I blow fucking every molecule of ice out of me into this pipe: kilos of the shit solidifying back into all the crystal bags with time folding back, reversing everything, man, getting me down from this emergency, this fucking ladder, this fucking escalator I'm on, that I've fucking always been on.

Gotta get down. I get down – down on the mattress with Silvia, who comforts me, and my boy Runty.

A plain-clothed policeman is escorted near the siege.

Runty, Runty, Runty – I love you, man. We understand each other. You know how this shit plays out. Twice you've seen them throw me on my face and cuff me and both times you've been pining and crying – even yourself getting locked away and put on death row – you know how it is for us. We've got something in common, you poor fuck.

But it won't go down that way today. Fucking not today 'cos if they take me alive I'll end up cemented forever: isolation forever; batshit insane in a tiny concrete room with them doing fucking every sick, twisted medical measure to keep me breathing so they can torture me for fucking years and years and years. So I'd rather die. I'm tired, though, too tired to run outside all-guns-blazing to get shot down in a blaze of glory. Blaze of bullshit.

The police keep blaring out their demands and instructions but I'm not interested. Anyway I'm tired. Lying here in the arms of my sheila – me dog by me side – I fall asleep.

The coppers do their best to engage me but Silvia's mostly dealing with them while I sleep. I'm sleeping a lot during this siege – who would have thought you could do that? Not me. But now I know – this shit's tiring – and if all the ice can't keep me awake then they don't have much chance. Who gives a fuck. All coming down anyway.

My only request of them, really, is a simple phone call to my daughter – a last dying wish to say goodbye; a last dying warning to her that I cannot save her from the evils around her: I want to tell her I just can't save her. Can't even protect her from the evil perils and dangers around her, from the criminal dynasty she was born into. I need to tell her that I am a failure of a father, because I can't save her from the lies and deceit, or from the dangers lurking close at hand.

But the phone call's not happening so I tuck secret notes into cosmetics scattered around the house. That might work.

Silvia is cooking but she can't hold down food. Neither can I. We're vomiting. It's the fear. Fear of maiming, torture, death. She gives me hydrolytes. Still vomiting.

It's night again. She keeps cowering in the shower with a doona over her. I keep bringing her back to the lounge room to cuddle and comfort her as she is extremely stressed by the ordeal too. Whenever I wake she's back in the shower. Come back, baby.

Blasted: inside the house where Chris held out for 44 hours.

Lightning strikes and we are rigid, screaming with terror, blind, ear drums poleaxed, the world ending – they're shooting flash-bang grenades into the house. On fire? I don't know. I can barely see. But I'm going to fire some shots as a fuck-youse, though.

I snap a pair of shots back and evict Silvia. Too dangerous now. I can't run – nowhere to run to – nowhere, nothing to be – but she has to get out.

-|||-

Just me and Runty now. Curled on the mattress with Runty, time going by: nothing but despair.

Better to be shot down in the field.

Honourable end for a solja.

Ya know, to blast them all to hell all I need do is leave the gas lines open in the house and then when they lob in more grenades, maybe the CS ones they're sure to be readying, it will ignite. It would be bigger than Ned Kelly – wiping out the cream of Victoria's SOG.

But I have no desire to kill or maim anyone, really.

I just want to disappear, to relocate – that's all the robbery was for: to relocate my daughter. To be able to take my child somewhere safe, somewhere stable, somewhere where she can be a kid without crazy shit circling her, endangering her, poisoning her childhood.

I can't save her now. Can't even speak with her.

But there's a special clock radio in the house. It has a secret camera in it. I face the clock and record last messages to Charlize and Silvia.

-|||-

It can't be long now, so I rub heads with Runty. He's safer if he can't defend me, if he's out of the way when they launch their final assault, so I say goodbye and shut him in a room.

-HH-

Night is blinding white again, stroboscopic, splitting open, insane, as more flash-bang grenades come in and explode, and now a barrage of gas grenades come smashing through all the windows – glass and debris fill the air ahead of the brutal and rapidly spreading CS fumes.

It penetrates the wet towels I've wrapped around my head and I lock my lungs for as long as I can but I'm heaving and thrashing and there's no holding forever – so it's over.

-HH-

I've held out for 44 hours with one handgun against far superior armed forces with armoured vehicles and automatic weapons.

Chris in custody after the siege.

Renovator's delight.

Gassed to fuck, I walk out to the front lawn where I fuck around with the pistol: everything in a dead spin. About to die. Chris put the gun down; Chris put the gun down. Shoot him. I put it down. I pick it up. Chris, Chris, Chris, Chris, this is the last second I will exist. Here it goes – thwack, thwack, thwack. They're axing my last second to pieces, splintering it, jerking me, smashing me with some shit fired from a shotgun. Thwack, thwack, thwack. Down the hole I go, down to the ground. Black shadow figures swoop in on me: the cuffs they fix are the seals of hell. Someone cuts off my ballistic vest. The fire brigade decontaminates me. I'm a HAZMAT incident.

卌

Chris' vital signs were tested as he lay there gassed and hammered by bean bag rounds, sky high on methamphetamine, stressed beyond comprehension. His pulse was reportedly under 80 bpm.

Silvia tells the police that her mum was against her relationship with Chris, but that Chris has always been good to her, always being flirtatious and making her laugh and being a loveable larrikin. You can't help who you love, she says, and, at the end of the day, he's not a killer, just an old-time bank robber.

While I find her statement moving, Chris – who blurted out a proposal to Silvia in a court appearance after the siege – dismisses it as manipulative claptrap. 'She'd say anything – she's devious,' he says. 'But I did love her. And she was a mad fuck.'

-ɪɪɪɪ-

CRYING. PINING.

I broke down during the police submission. I was really fucking spewing – I couldn't control it. This isn't faking. Do you think I want the media to see me fucking crying and shit? You know, sobbing uncontrollably because they played the CCTV footage of the fucking siege, the flash-bangs, and its re-triggering putting me back into that state – the house is all fucked up inside, it's blown to fucking pieces. And then I hear my dog in the background, crying, pining. That killed me – not being

The siege house at Keilor East.

there for my dog. I know I'll never see him alive again. He's the child I could hold and play with even when my daughter was taken away from me.

Oh my god, Charlize, please know I love you beyond anything. They're burying me again where no matter how much I shout and scream and punch the walls you can't hear. They won't bring you to my grave and I can't go looking for you.

Charlize, I'm your dad. Whatever they tell you about me please know that my love for you grows stronger and stronger always.

TOTALITY

May 2014:
Supreme Court of Victoria
Melbourne criminal division

THE QUEEN

V

CHRISTOPHER BINSE

Judge: T Forrest J

Where held: Melbourne

Dates of hearing: 28, 29 and 30 April 2014

Date of sentence: 23 May 2014

Case may be cited as: R v Binse

CRIMINAL LAW — Sentence — Prohibited person possess firearm — Theft — Armed Robbery — Prohibited person use a firearm — Reckless conduct endangering serious injury — Long history of substantially similar criminal offending — Discount for owner's conditions of incarceration — No rule of law whereby offender who is responsible for the onerousness of the conditions is not entitled to sentencing discount — Pleas of guilty — Evidence of some remorse — Specific deterrence of significant weight — Highly desirable

that prior to release the offender be subject to the
support and strict supervision of the parole board for
a considerable period.

APPEARANCES: COUNSEL SOLICITORS

FOR THE CROWN: MR P CHADWICK QC
OFFICE OF PUBLIC PROSECUTIONS
WITH MS J WARREN

FOR THE ACCUSED MR S HOLT SC
VICTORIA LEGAL AID

...

It is necessary to say something of your background
so that the context of your offending may be properly
understood. You have spent 28 of the last 32 years
in some form of custody. Your father taught you to
steal. You were a ward of the state at 13, accommodated
at Baltara Boys Home. By 14, you were detained at
Turana Youth Training Centre and by 17 you were
transferred to Pentridge while undergoing a Children's
Court sentence. By 18, you had been classified as a
management unit prisoner and were imprisoned in
the notorious H Division of that prison. You were
transferred out to Beechworth after the suicide of
another young prisoner held in that Division.

Since that time you have spent a comparatively little
time in the community. In the 1980s, once you were
eligible for adult court, you committed essentially
street offences that escalated in seriousness. In 1993,
you were convicted of four counts of armed robbery,
receiving in total an aggregate sentence of seven

years six months with a minimum of five years. These armed robberies were committed on banks and, with one exception, during trading hours. The learned sentencing judge noted that by then you had accumulated 96 previous convictions over 27 court appearances. You were then just 24 years old. Judge Lazarus expressed the hope that you were ready to retire from your career choice as an armed robber. Even then 21 years ago his Honour considered you to be institutionalised. He characterised your offending as 'about as bad as bank robberies can be' although he noted a certain politeness and decency in your approach.

Shortly after that conviction you were convicted of being a felon in possession of a pistol and other offences including making a threat to kill.

You had been remanded in custody on the armed robbery charges. In August 1992, whilst on remand, you were stabbed by a fellow prisoner and taken to St Vincent's Hospital. After emergency surgery you escaped and fled to New South Wales. You there committed more armed robberies, were arrested and remanded to Parramatta gaol. Again, you escaped and returned to Victoria where you were arrested by a SOG team near Daylesford. You sustained injuries in that arrest. After commencing a hunger strike you were brought before Judge Lazarus and sentenced to the term I mentioned a few moments ago.

During this sentence, you attempted to escape from the Acacia Unit. In 1996, you were extradited to New South Wales to face the 1992 armed robbery charges that I have referred to. In December 1998, you were sentenced for these armed robberies, kidnapping and other offences. The full details of your sentence are not clear to me but you were released from prison in February 2005. You apparently served your full-term and thus were not subject to parole supervision when you were released. You had served 13 years straight in various prisons by the time you were released.

Your time in custody in the New South Wales prison system was not easy and you made several public statements about prison conditions at the Goulburn gaol.

You remained in the community for about 13 months before being arrested in January 2006. You ultimately were convicted of been a prohibited person possessing a firearm, two counts of common-law assault and possession of a drug of dependence. You were sentenced to an effective four year maximum with a minimum of two years. I am told you served your complete sentence after an unsuccessful period on parole and so once again you were released into the community with no authoritative supervision.

Whilst on remand for the 2006 offences you were seriously assaulted. You believed your attackers were procured by a particular prisoner to carry out this attack. I shall call this man 'Prisoner X'. This has some relevance to your current offending.

After serving a good deal of this sentence in management units you were released on parole in April 2008. During the time that you are on parole you became increasingly concerned that your safety was threatened by associates of Prisoner X. Your parole was revoked in September 2008 and you were apprehended in December of that year. You are in possession at

that time of cocaine, for prohibited weapons, an
unregistered handgun (a pen gun) and various false
identity documents. You returned to prison and after
further threats passing from you and to you, you again
were detained in a management unit. In October 2010,
the possession charges I have just referred to were
finally dealt with and you received a further 12-month
prison sentence. You were released from custody on 28
September 2011.

...

I accept that from the time you were released in
September 2011 you are genuinely fearful for your
life and the lives of your loved ones. Whilst this
may explain some of your antisocial conduct during
your eight months at large it cannot justify or excuse
it. You accumulated an arsenal at the Atack [storage]
facility. For a prohibited person to possess one
firearm is serious enough. For a prohibited person to
possess a loaded pistol, a loaded cut down rifle, a
loaded cut down pump-action shotgun and a Thompson
submachine gun makes this ... charge a grave example
of its kind.

Mr Holt SC, in helpful submissions on your behalf,
put his instructions from the bar table that you
acquired a bag of guns to protect yourself and your
daughter from those you believed responsible for
shooting two of your associates. There is no evidence as
to how or why you came into possession of these guns.
I have indicated that I accept that throughout your time
at large in 2011 and 2012 you feared for your loved
ones' safety. I accept this as a likely explanation for
your possession of three of the four impugned firearms.

It does little to reduce your moral culpability in my view. The offence is aimed at public safety and designed to discourage criminals convicted of serious offences from carrying or possessing a weapon.

I regard the armed robbery as a very serious example of this sort of offence. It was planned and executed with precision. Your Council observed that, with the proliferation of modern investigative tools (including CCTV), this type of armed robbery is not common these days. Whilst that may be so when such crimes are committed they cause terror to those immediately involved and apprehension amongst the wider community. I consider that a purpose of this sentencing exercise is to protect that wider community from you Mr Binse.

...

ONEROUS NATURE OF YOUR IMPRISONMENT

You have been remanded since your arrest. You have been assessed as a high security risk.

An affidavit from Brendan Money, Asst Commissioner of Corrections Victoria, was tendered in evidence. Since your arrest you have been accommodated mainly in the Acacia Management Unit at Barwon Prison. You have been temporarily accommodated in other units. Once this sentence is passed you will be returned to Acacia Unit.

Acacia Unit provides you with a single bed cell. You are permitted access to an exercise yard for between one and three hours a day. Beyond that, you are secured in your cell. I am told, and accept, that it has been determined that you are a long-term management prisoner. There is a real prospect that you will be required to serve all or a large proportion of what must be a lengthy prison sentence in isolation cell confinement for up to 23 hours a day. Mr Holt, on your behalf, argued that this factor must weigh heavily in favour of reducing the overall sentence I must impose. Mr Chadwick, who prosecuted, intended that whilst you are entitled to some benefit arising from this factor that benefit ought be qualified or are limited to reflect that, in many ways, you are the architect of your own misfortune. I have been referred to a number of cases in which responsibility for a prisoner's placement in a management unit has been considered in the context of whether a sentencing benefit for same ought be allowed. In my view, there is no rule which says that where a prisoner's conduct results in them being placed in a restrictive prison environment that fact disentitled them to a sentencing benefit arising from that owner's custodial environment.

It is clear that your current prison status is the product of a combination of factors. Mr Money's affidavit sets them out. You are assessed as a high security risk as a result of the following combination of factors:

- the circumstances of the events leading to your arrest;
- you have a significant prior prison history, including placement in management units;
- you have made several well-planned escapes and escape attempts in Victoria and New South Wales;
- there are placement concerns relating to your interaction with other prisoners. In short, it is considered that you are at risk of harm and at risk

of causing harm if allowed to interact with other prisoners. I quote "his volatile and threatening behaviour presents real risks to prison security';

- whilst Mr Money does not refer to it as a factor relevant to your management unit status it is clear from his affidavit that there have been significant concerns about your mental health during your time in management. You have been placed in a Muirhead cell as a result of psychiatric concerns, have been transferred twice to the Acute Assessment Unit at MAP due to those concerns and are considered at risk of self harm.

I am satisfied that your current prison accommodation is largely the product of your conduct over your time in the prison system. For reasons that I shall refer to shortly, I consider that you are thoroughly institutionalised and suffering from a range of psychological consequences that impact on your capacity to deal with unrestricted prison life, or for that matter the outside world.

A report from Dr Danny Sullivan was tendered on your behalf. Ms Pamela Matthews, Forensic Psychologist, gave evidence on your behalf. Two reports from her were tendered — one from 2010 and one recent. Both Dr Sullivan and Ms Matthews diagnose a form of mixed personality disorder with antisocial and narcissistic traits. Both also commented on the impact upon you of your past and future incarceration:

'Mr Binse has been so long incarcerated that his emotional world is markedly altered.' (Dr Sullivan)

'He reports that innocuous events trigger emotional responses including anxiety or distress ... He is preoccupied with threat to him with those close to him and that he has repeated recollections of traumatic events that have happened to him.' (Dr Sullivan)

'Although he might meet the diagnostic criteria for post traumatic stress disorder, it is perhaps more appropriate to regard his condition as an adaptation to prolonged incarceration in austere circumstances, as well as a number of attacks on him associated with prison life and his lifestyle outside prison.' (Dr Sullivan)

'Mr Binse had on occasion experienced brief episodes of behavioural disturbance, disordered thinking, persecutory and grandiose beliefs, reports of special powers and auditory hallucinations. Most recently these have occurred in 2012 and 2013. On these occasions the symptoms have resolved spontaneously without antipsychotic medication and the opinion of reviewing psychiatrists has been that these did not reflect psychotic episodes ... It is likely that these reflected decompensation in the face of stressors.' (Dr Sullivan)

'In the writer's view, Mr Binse's personality, his coping skills or lack thereof, his mental state fluctuations, chronic post trauma symptomology and and behaviours are all a product of long periods in restrictive custody, which over the course of a potentially lengthy sentence can only be further exacerbated by more custodial time in similar, very onerous environments.' (Ms Matthews)

Although I consider you are largely the architect of your current prisoner status, as I have said there is no rule which necessarily denies a prisoner a sentencing benefit arising from being placed in a restrictive custody or environment. Each case will turn on its facts. In my view, your likely future accommodation will be so restrictive and of such a length that it would be inhumane to deny some sentencing benefit arising from these factors.

I accept the opinions from Dr Sullivan and Ms Matthews that I have recently referred to. I am positively satisfied that there is a serious risk that future imprisonment in the restricted custodial environment that I have explained will have a significant adverse effect on your mental health.

I have considered together the fact of your current and likely future custodial circumstances and the risk that these circumstances will impact upon your mental health. I have concluded that the combination of these two factors ought mitigate the punishment that I will impose.

...

DETERRENCE

There is obviously a powerful need to deter you from reoffending. There is an equally powerful need to deter others from similar outrageously unlawful conduct. These factors must be given significant weight in the sentencing exercise.

PROTECTION OF THE COMMUNITY

Your prior record and the gravity of your current offending necessarily leads me to conclude that the community needs to be protected from you. The community's interests will be protected by your incapacitation for a lengthy period.

...

There is another aspect to community protection. It is open to me not to impose a minimum sentence before parole eligibility. Your last three sentences have been served in full. Despite this, I consider that it would be incompatible with the community's interests to impose a straight term of imprisonment with no minimum. It is highly desirable that, upon your eventual release, you be subject to the support and strict supervision of the parole board for a considerable period. In my view, community protection requires this. If you are simply released after serving your full term with no controls or supervision then the public interest suffers.

REHABILITATION

For the reasons that I have expressed I consider your prospects for rehabilitation are poor. My sincere hope is that you will rehabilitate yourself to finally become a functioning member of the wider community. For that to occur you will need support and self-discipline. To date, you have not demonstrated much of this latter quality.

TOTALITY

I have endeavoured to apply the principle of totality in setting the head sentence and the minimum term. I have endeavoured to avoid a crushing aggregate sentence whilst still reflecting the gravity of your offending conduct in your prior criminal history. I have moderated both the individual sentences and the impact of cumulation in applying this totality principle.

...

Stand up please.

Balancing all these competing factors as best I can, I sentence you as follows:

... a total effective head sentence of 18 years and two months imprisonment. I direct that you serve a minimum of 14 years and two months before you are eligible for parole.

I declare that 715 days up to and including 7 May 2014 be reckoned as served by way of presentence detention.

I declare that but for your pleas of guilty I would have sentenced you to an effective head sentence of 22 years with a minimum sentence before parole eligibility of 18 years.

FROM FORENSIC PSYCHOLOGIST PAMELA MATTHEWS' REPORT, WHICH WAS QUOTED BY JUSTICE FORREST:

From a rehabilitative perspective, moving Mr Binse from restrictive custody to the community without transitional care and support raises questions of duty of care, further that this pattern of unsupported release has been repeated on his last three releases into the community raises the seriousness of those questions. It is the writer's recommendation from a rehabilitative perspective that Mr Binse, in order to manage his next custody to community transition, will require longer term interventions and support rather than short term interventions ... It would be best if such interventions are initiated at the beginning of whatever sentence the Court imposes focusing on the longer term development of: practical, mental state, and interp(ersonal coping skills; and closer to exit practical, concrete, support systems pre and post release.

...

Naturally rehabilitation is only one aspect of sentencing and sentencing is the role of the Court.

Time warp: the old-fashioned Thompson submachine gun found in Chris' storage container.

CLEANSING

AUGUST 2015:
HM PRISON BARWON

After Chris writes to police out of the blue about his unsolved crimes of a quarter century ago, detectives come to see him.

Knowing that this unsolicited confession will lead to charges (for which he has since pleaded guilty and awaits sentencing), Chris explains to the detectives how important it is that he gets everything off his chest:

Chris: I've just got to – I've got to make it right. For me to
– to fucking – I've got to be a hundred per cent pure
inside, not 95 per cent, not 90 per cent, because if I'm
only 99 per cent clean inside, that means I'm still dirty.
Understand?

I want to cleanse myself purely, properly, everything,
expunge everything. I don't want to have any shit
inside of me. I want to be accounted, atoned for all the
stuff, the bad stuff I've done, not leave shit out, not be
selective, not leave this one or that one out or whatever,
you know. It's all or nothing, seriously. For me to make
it right, it's got to be a hundred per cent.

Detective: No worries.

2016:
SUNSHINE NORTH

Annette looks down as I leaf through her son's confessions.

'All this talk of cleansing – I hate it,' she says. 'And these confessions to robberies from the 1980s! Why did he open his big mouth? Who does it help? The police didn't even know about some of them.'

She shakes her head and looks away.

'I know what he's doing,' she says. 'Chris is going to top himself. He will do it. And I can understand. What does he have to look forward to? He has no job skills. His daughter has been taken out of his life. He has no money. We pay his phone account and give him money for the things he can buy in prison. The robbery money? He doesn't have any. All the people around him steal that the moment he gets arrested – and he used to just give it away, anyway. Not to family, mind you, but to anyone he felt sorry for. He'd see someone in a wheelchair and slip 'em a hundred. Never us.'

Annette puts down her washcloth after cleaning the dishes from the dinner she made of Croatian-style fish.

'I'll be dead before his time's up,' says Annette. 'What's he going to do then? He calls me every day – two or three times. I tell him to hold on, to find something to look forward to. But what is there? They just leave him to rot in isolation. They know it's driving him mad. Everybody knows isolation does that. And you can't tell me that out of the thousands of prisoners in Victoria they can't find a few for Chris to mix with under supervision. They're scum. I know Chris has done wrong but so does everybody else – in fact, that's all they know about him. And he's paying for it. But these men running the prisons, the justice system, they're doing wrong every day – they're destroying people, making them worse before they get released – and they get held up as good people.'

AND NOW?

MID 2016:
HM PRISON BARWON

Four years (including time on remand) into what Justice Forrest called the 'onerous conditions' of what he didn't name as solitary but which is, Chris is back out of the anti-suicide observation cell and his usual 'studio apartment' by himself, a continuum that he faces for another ten to fourteen years. Long term isolation runs counter to State, Commonwealth and international standards, but few people care in the 'supermax' era.

So there he sits, sometimes obsessing with appeals or the past, other times painting, or working on a series of kids' books aimed at keeping troubled children off the Mayhem Highway – or joining in the vicious shouting matches that frequently rage between cells.

Chris, the bandit and jailbreaker, is at the time of writing, in a section of Barwon that holds four solitary cells, the other three being occupied by murderers. One of them is a thrill killer with schizophrenia and a taste for rape. Another is a gang leader and killer who helped Gavin Preston orchestrate the arena-style razor attack on Chris. The third murdered someone over a traffic altercation.

While the propaganda on current affairs shows might have you believe that 'supermax' prisoners like these live in near clinical isolation and don't know who is in the surrounding cells, in reality the inmates can and do yell at each other. Some days the abuse, death threats, mockery, paranoid delusions, and so on rage from early in the morning until late at night. Working and mixing with suitable prisoners selected from the thousands in custody might be a little more rehabilitating, but that would be common sense and you know what they say about that: it's not common.

The logic that prevails in jail is more of the Catch 22 kind: if a prisoner in solitary has a predictable response to solitary and gets weirder, more hostile or more suicidal, then the authorities use such responses as justification for keeping them in isolation.

CHANGE

In Chris' only known act of 'lagging' a fellow prisoner, he warns Barwon authorities that an inmate is plotting to take Barwon's governor hostage and behead him unless Australia withdraws its forces from wars in the Middle East. To Chris, that sort of violence is simply unacceptable.

His warning is taken seriously and the inmate is moved, but the incident adds to anger towards Chris from extremist Muslims in prison.

Chris, who has replaced Buddhism with Islam at the time of writing, has been seen as a traitor since making it known he didn't buy into the jihadist ideology of jailed Melbourne terror cell leader Nacer Benbrika (another person Chris has argued with in solitary's cabin-fever slanging matches).

Fellow Muslim convert and serial killer Gregory Brazel wrote at length to Chris, angry at his previous shit-bombing of a child killer who happened to be Muslim (even if Chris has been inclusive of all faiths and persuasions in his shit-bombing phases), telling Chris to:

Chris warned authorities of a beheading plot.

```
Turn from this betrayal of your Brothers ... if
you are a truly committed Muslim, and never ever
backbite a Brother Muslim again ... for if you do
so, and ... continue in your backbiting, [it] will
only bring doom and gloom upon your head ... it
will blacken your heart and soul, and, thereafter,
you will be lost forevermore.
```

Sounds like any other day in isolation for Chris, who tried to kill himself again a couple of weeks ago.

When we started the MAYHEM project Chris told me that he would give the book a tragic ending and he's doing his best to be true to his word. Annette knew something was up when she hadn't heard from him; he normally rings his mum every day. Her repeated calls to the prison kept getting fobbed off until she learnt that there'd been an 'incident'.

When Chris was eventually allowed to use a phone, he told her that very late one night about a week and a half earlier he'd sliced open a vein in his arm and lay down to die but that the next morning guards found him drenched in blood but alive.

This isn't life, he told her.

Maybe you despise crims. Maybe you hate them telling their stories and you cheer on the silencing machine that keeps jails such secret worlds unto themselves (for a BBC article I asked Corrections Victoria a stack of questions about the use of solitary and they refused to answer even one) and that brings in Proceeds of Crimes Acts to stop the few who have the drive and talent to write from earning a quid from books instead of from the dole (or crime!). Maybe you think they deserve to rot in cages.

Well, don't forget that crims, this subhuman breed, were the founding population of the modern nation of Australia. When British forces invaded and set up shop in this vast old land, who did they bring by the boatload?

Crims.

And for decades the crims outnumbered the screws and free settlers.

So if you think you're an Aussie complete with a larrikin streak; a healthy scepticism towards authority and bullshit disguised by politeness; a code of standing by your mates through thick and thin; a taste for risks, gambles, and getting well and truly hectic after a good payday; a dislike for wimps and whingers, and a belief in toughness as a virtue, then spare a thought for the down-and-outers that made Australia.

It's rotten that Britain's losers, its unwanted, helped to dispossess the First Nations of this great southern land, but they did not come by choice. These were expendable people shipped across the world against their will and subjected to however much force or deprivation the State felt was necessary to control them.

In the colonies, some ran free to become bushrangers, men including John Caesar AKA Black Caesar, Martin Cash, and Jack Donahue AKA the Wild Colonial Boy.

Most did not break out and go bush.

When we look back on bushrangers, including famous free-born outlaws like Ned Kelly and Fred Ward AKA Captain Thunderbolt, we can argue all day about where they sit on scales of villainy and heroism, but it's all from a great distance.

Because it is so damn hard to know what it was like to be them.

Had more of the convicts, bushrangers or otherwise, given detailed and vivid accounts of their lives, then we would understand our strange and murky history so much better. Too often instead we rely on official reports and journalists' superficial accounts.

Just as we do now.

And so many potentially hugely insightful stories of, from, and within our criminal underclass are never told in the first place due to the secrecy of prisons and laws like the Proceeds of Crimes Acts which keep the minority of jailbirds capable of writing a coherent and insightful book from becoming authors.

Chris would be in that minority. This is amazing in itself given that he didn't even finish Year 8 and that, in the decades Chris has spent in custody since first being locked up at the age of 13, he has received bugger all education.

That's unless you count lessons in displaying one's anus when instructed, crafting makeshift knives and clubs, racial segregation, hand-to-hand combat, filling out forms, the use of poo as a weapon, the necessity of never giving a fuckin' inch, rolling up one's bedsheets, and how to spot gaps in security systems. And this is during the Clever Country's Innovation Age. Who are we kidding.

As I wrote at the start, Chris is not getting any money from this book. He has, however, now had the opportunity to bypass the media's cardboard cut-out crime writers and show you – and maybe one day the young girl he has lost the opportunity to father – what happened to a little boy with a curse upon him.

Don't believe in curses?

Of course you don't. Neither did I. But I do now. And I know that curses aren't just made of evil spells and blighted stars. They're also built out of people like us – out of the indifference or worse of people who don't want to look at the dirty bastards below in case we see a bit of ourselves down there.

‖‖

A LAST QUESTION TO CHRIS:

Q. If you were pardoned tomorrow and could go anywhere, where would you want to go?

CHRIS:

I'm not telling.

ACKNOWLEDGEMENTS

Thank you to Annette Binse for her trust and courage. You're a hell of a woman: tough, sharp, and good company. Thanks to Barry Binse for, among other things, putting up with yet another round of attention due to your misbegotten brother. Thanks to Angus Fontaine for being an unnaturally calm and understanding publisher full of great ideas. Thanks to Brett Collins. Thanks also to Danielle Walker, Josh Durham, Victoria Chance and Rebecca Hamilton. Thanks to Claude Robinson. Thanks to Richy Cooke. Thanks to Matty Bramall. Thanks to all the media students at the University of New South Wales who endured lectures peppered with references to 'bronzing up'. Thank you to the author of the Gospel of Luke for having Jesus Christ tell the thief crucified beside Him that this day they will be together in paradise. Thanks, of course, to Lord BADNE$$ himself, Chris Pecotic, AKA Chris Binse, for trusting me with his epic tale. I don't know what star fell the night you were conceived but it was a doozy.

Heartfelt thanks, finally, to Renae and Avalon. If writing's hard going at times then close proximity to writers is worse. Much worse. Good on you for still liking books.

Matthew Thompson is a writer and adventurer with a University Medal in English and a broken nose. Areas of his reportage include rebel domains of the southern Philippines, mind-shredding shamanic rituals in Colombia, X-rated underground gameshows in Portland, Oregon, and mixed-sex boxing in Australia. Matt has written for the BBC, the *Sydney Review of Books*, the *Australian*, *Inside Sport*, the *Sydney Morning Herald*, *Dazed & Confused* and many others. Matt is the author of the bestselling *My Colombian Death*, and its acclaimed sequel, *Running with the Blood God*. He has a doctorate in literary journalism and has made documentaries broadcast in Australia by the ABC's Radio National and in the United States by National Public Radio. Born in the USA but living in Dungog, NSW, Matt is a firefighter and rescue operator with Fire & Rescue NSW, as well as being a Conjoint Fellow with the University of Newcastle's Centre for the History of Violence. He has taught journalism at universities in Australia and Fiji, telling his students that if they well and truly get stuck into writing then there will be casualties.

Read more about Matthew at:
www.matthewthompsonwriting.com